DEATH BY COP

DEATH BY COP

A CALL FOR UNITY!

WAYNE REID
JUDGE CHARLES GILL

LIONCREST
PUBLISHING

DEATH BY COP
A Call for Unity!

ISBN   978-1-5445-0596-1 *Hardcover*
       978-1-5445-0597-8 *Paperback*
       978-1-5445-0595-4 *Ebook*
       978-1-5445-0598-5 *Audiobook*

To innocent victims of crimes and brave police officers,
we dedicate our book
in your honor.

CONTENTS

ACKNOWLEDGMENTS

Writing a book about a dramatic incident that touched many lives is an emotional process. I'm grateful for my parents, for their continuous support and for entrusting me with their private memories, shared throughout this book. I'm grateful for our editor, Tracy Hart, for her meticulous work assisting with the development and clarity of our manuscript. Thank you to Derwin Morales and 33 Towns Entertainment for creating amazing book trailers. Thank you to Reverend Cornell Lewis, Josh Blanchfield, Professor Roderick Anderson, the NAACP Chapter in Connecticut, and all supporters throughout the case. Thank you to Connecticut's media for remarkable coverage of the case over a five-year span. And thank you, Judge Gill, for sharing the journey. —W.R.

Thank you to Lisa Meneguzzo of the Oddo Print Shop; Scott Peterson, photographer; John Frawley; Kelly Ward; Attorney Michael Kinney; and my loving and supporting wife, Joan, and our three wonderful children, Charlie Jr., Jimmy, and Kasey! —C.G.

PROLOGUE

It was nearly noon when two twenty-seven-year-old men met for the first time on the main road through New Milford, Connecticut. One held a loaded gun; the other wound up dead with a bullet in his back...in full view of many passersby.

Fate had set a white police officer in plain clothes and a black male, who was more than sufficiently acquainted with the criminal justice system, on a collision course long before their paths intersected. The *41 seconds* they knew each other tells us a lot about the challenges of modern-day police work and, in reality, tells us even more about ourselves in contemporary America.

This is the story of those two young men, which became our story too. Their tale is told through eyewitnesses, photographs, trial transcripts, and official statements. We will take you behind the scenes. The private, contemporaneous mental notes of the trial judge will be revealed, as will the personal reflections of several jurors. Due to the presentation of this unique inside information (previously undisclosed to the general public as well as to participants involved), it is most likely the first time that the truth of this type of occurrence has been exposed to this extent.

Serious criminal trials do not begin when a jury is sworn in. By that time, they are full-fledged dramas. The lives of defendants and their families, the victims and their families, the jurors, witnesses, prosecutors, defense attorneys, and judges are inextricably intertwined forever. This, in turn, ripples through our vast, multicultural society. We hope that through a balanced portrayal of this instance of a white police officer shooting a black man, an event capable of igniting emotions to explosive proportions, readers of all races will feel encouraged to rediscover a path toward unity and support of one another.

So, welcome to the inner sanctum of a controversial murder trial. Join us on the bench as a spectator; judge the case alongside us. Vicariously experience the drama that we lived. Steady yourself through the dizzying "twists and turns." Grab a box of tissues, and let us know your verdict.

By the way, the dead, black male...my brother, Franklyn.

ACT I SCENE I

———

THE SHOT

Franklyn Reid
Twenty-seven years old, slim black male
Wanted
Breach of peace
Failure to appear in court
Has been spotted...
December 29, 1998

"Cramer is in foot pursuit of Franklyn Reid. Maybe you should give him a hand," Dispatcher Cindy Hanford says to Detective David Shortt.

The predominantly white, rural community police department in New Milford, Connecticut, doesn't usually deal with action that could make it into a crime drama. Today is a departure from routine.

Returning from morning investigations, Shortt asks, "Where are they?"

The inclement weather from earlier had subsided, leaving a wet and crappy day to be chasing someone outside.

"Around Heacock-Crossbrook Road," Hanford says.

No time to waste, Shortt dashes to get his partner, Investigator Scott Smith, and retrieve handcuffs from his desk. He finds Smith with Detective Steven Jordan in the Investigative Service Bureau.

"Scotty," Shortt hollers to the rookie, "let's go, we need to provide backup to Cramer. He's in pursuit of a suspect."

Standing up from his desk, Jordan inquires, "Where abouts? I can head out, too."

Shortt tells him, and all three plainclothes officers rush through the door.

"Scott, do you have the keys? You're driving," barks Shortt.

Seconds before exiting the bureau, Jordan informs his colleagues he's going to grab an extra clip for his Heckler & Koch service weapon from his desk. Smith and Shortt scurry toward a black surveillance vehicle.

* * *

Walking briskly alongside Route 202, unaware of police activities, Franklyn realizes he needs to call his girlfriend, Pamela. He stops at Jolly Roger Firearms store. While hastening toward her house, close to the store, Mrs. Roger notices a black man she doesn't know standing in her backyard. Franklyn approaches Mrs. Roger.

"Can I borrow your telephone to call my girlfriend? My car has a flat tire," he says.

Quickly surveying her surroundings, she grants the young man's request and escorts him into her home. Standing next to him, she observes his appearance while listening in on his quick phone call.

"Yo, I have a flat tire; pick me up at Sunoco," Franklyn says to Pam at 11:19 a.m.

Franklyn turns to Mrs. Roger. "Thanks. How far is it to that Sunoco gas station?"

"Um. Just about five minutes, I think."

Watching the young man leave, Mrs. Roger finds it peculiar that he continues walking through other residents' backyards but not alarming.

Thirteen minutes prior, at 11:06, Sergeant Cramer was patrolling in a marked police cruiser, down a side road located on the outskirts of town. Driving northbound, he suddenly saw a white Toyota Celica appear out of nowhere, heading southbound, in the middle of the road. The quick-thinking lawman maneuvered his car over to the curb, providing ample space for the motorist to pass.

The car is still drifting toward me, thought Cramer.

The driver must have realized the close proximity, because he straightened out before passing Cramer.

Cramer didn't get a good look at the distracted driver, but he registered the license plate number. Evaluating the situation, he thought, *Huh, is the driver just being inattentive or should I go after the vehicle in case the driver's drunk?* Choosing the latter, Cramer turned around and followed the vehicle. Momentarily losing sight of the car, the sergeant radioed dispatch, knowing communication is essential in law enforcement. He had to make dispatch aware that he was investigating unusual activities.

"HQ, I'm out with 840-Frank-Charlie-Robert," Cramer said.

He arrived at Dawn's Road, a side street branching off Heacock-Crossbrook Road, and found the Toyota weirdly angled in the intersection with the driver's door open. Pulling behind the two-door Celica, Cramer looked through the back window but didn't see the driver. He exited his police cruiser, removed his service revolver, and cautiously approached the abandoned car in case someone was lying in wait for him. Cramer's adrenaline pumped as he crept closer and peeked through the windows. But something he heard raised his apprehension. A tone, a rhythmic sound in a different dialect. Edging closer, he realized it was music— reggae music.

* * *

When I was born in Montego Bay, Jamaica, in 1977, my family was expanding rapidly and life was challenging. My father's mother, Carmen Reid (who had nine children of her own), embraced the grandmother role and raised her grandkids with pride and joy during work hours. Daycare was not an option; culturally, it did not exist. My grandmother was a petite woman with thick, oversized glasses. When she spoke, everyone listened, especially to her captivating life stories. I was fortunate to spend my first few years with her before she passed in 1980. Her love embodied the human spirit, fostering everlasting bonds. The following year, my parents applied for permanent resident status in the United States. Countless numbers of people hoped to set foot on beautiful American soil. With similar aspirations, we stood in line and waited our turn.

While life continued in Jamaica for the better part of the 1980s, Franklyn became a leader of the pack amongst his friends. Also known as Mark—most Jamaican parents nicknamed their children without rhyme or reason, simply to call them by another name—he constructed go-carts, a popular mode of traveling around town and used in competitions between friends. Franklyn's four-wheel, wooden speedster consistently won those races. There weren't trophies at the finish line, just community bragging rights. Despite the competition, he also assisted others in building better go-carts. His mild-mannered approach rubbed off on those around him, including me.

Going to school in Jamaica kept us in shape. Without buses, we had to walk a few miles each day to get our education. The schools had a strict dress code policy of khaki-colored uniforms that had to be neatly ironed. The only thing not required were shoes as most families, including mine, couldn't afford footwear. It was a remarkable sight: nicely dressed kids going to school, barefoot. Finding innovative ways to get there was quite a fun challenge. One of Franklyn's bright ideas was hopping moving trucks. It worked at times, but I was the youngest, slowest, and always the last to be pulled onboard—if I made it at all.

Growing up was fun and occasionally, well...pursuing silly ideas could be detrimental to one's health.

One day, Franklyn and I were home alone while Mom, Dad, and Dwight Jr. went shopping in Montego Bay. Aunt Joyce, our next-door neighbor, was in her kitchen, occasionally looking through the window at Franklyn and me. A gleaming sun in a clear sky provided the ideal opportunity for Franklyn to explore one of his hypotheses.

"If I leave four D-sized batteries on the roof for a few hours, the sun will recharge them to full strength," Franklyn said.

"Do you think it will really work?" I, at the tender age of five, said, questioning his theory.

"Yeah, I'm sure it will," Franklyn replied. He was eleven.

It sounded feasible; I believed in him. Okay, maybe I was a little skeptical, but also excited to watch my older brother defy logic and gravity.

Verandas are common on island houses, and we had one on ours in Maroon Town. It was conceivable that a brave soul could climb one of the smooth pillars and utilize upper body strength to pull themselves up and over the six-inch ledge to access the roof. The adrenaline experienced after accomplishing a daredevil task would be intense (worth it for Franklyn), but a slight mishap and air and space are the only things separating you from the ground.

Courageously, my brother pocketed the batteries, wrapped his inner arms around the pillar, and used the soles of his feet to stabilize himself as he climbed. He looked like a slow-moving caterpillar scaling a post. Reaching the ceiling, Franklyn extended his right hand and gripped the edge of the roof. He quickly maneuvered his left hand and grabbed another part. He simultaneously released his legs from the pillar and hanging, mustered his strength and, with a loud heave, pulled himself onto the roof.

Excited and cheering, I clapped my hands, pleased at his accomplishment. He placed the batteries at the roof's edge, so when it was time to retrieve them, he could climb the pillar and just extend his arms to reach them.

Taking a two-minute break to gather his strength, Franklyn prepared for his descent. He stooped down, chest grinding against the ledge, feet swinging loosely, and grabbed the pillar while his palms gripped the edge of the roof.

Pleased, I looked on. Then the unthinkable happened— he lost his grip! His feet dangled. His hands flailed wildly. He desperately tried to avoid greeting the ground. In the flurry of activity, his hands swatted the batteries. The first, second, third, and fourth batteries flew. The inevitable overcame his attempt to remain airborne. Gravity won and Franklyn smacked onto the concrete from twenty feet high. He tried using his hands to soften his landing, but to no avail.

I rushed to the edge of the veranda. My brother was lying face down with both hands extended slightly above his shoulders. Not moving. Unsure what to do, I chuckled! But after a minute or so, I dashed toward the back steps of Aunt Joyce's house. It took forever to climb those steps. Well, that's what it seemed like to a five-year-old. Finally reaching the top, I ran into the kitchen.

"Aunt Joyce! Aunt Joyce! Mark fall offa di roof!"

She looked out the window. "Jesus God, a wah hunni do now?"

Scooping me up, she rushed to Franklyn's aid. He was bumped and bruised, but at least he was moving. She took him to the local clinic where the doctors determined both arms were broken. Ironically, Mom and Dad knew we needed batteries, and brought some home from shopping.

* * *

The Toyota was empty. With a sigh of relief, Sergeant Cramer reached inside to lower the music volume. Then he noticed another odd, eyebrow-raising head scratcher: the keys were still in the ignition. Stepping back, he circled the car, surveying the surrounding area before determining it was safe to holster his revolver. Then he checked-in with dispatch.

"What have you got on plate, 840 Frank, Charlie, and Robert?" he asked.

"The operator dumped the car and ran when I turned around to come after him. I think the driver might be a white male."

Frantically searching the database, fingers pounded the keyboard until dispatch received a hit.

"The vehicle is registered to Dwight and Pearlylyn Reid of New Milford," Dispatcher Alex Correa stated.

"Thanks. The car is running with the keys in it, so I'm not going anywhere. Could you send me a hook?" Cramer said.

Dispatcher Correa called A1 Automotive, a local towing company. Fellow officers aware of the situation chimed in with questions and clarification.

"Which way did he run? I'm on 202 near Midway," Officer Mark Blanchette radioed.

"I don't know which direction he headed," Cramer said.

Officer William Kaminski, out patrolling, joined the conversation to clarify the race of Dwight Reid. "Dispatch, let them know, I believe the owner Dwight Reid is a black male."

Listening, Cramer wanted absolute confirmation of the vehicle's owner.

Dispatcher Correa validated the information he disseminated and discovered another connection. "We have warrants outstanding for Franklyn Reid, also at the same address. We have FTA's [failure to appear], breach of peace, threatening, and a bond of $13,500," he added.

"That was probably him who bailed and ran," Cramer said to Correa. "After the hook arrives, I'll start hunting for him. He's got to be on foot in the area."

While waiting for the tow truck, Cramer devised an action plan. At 11:13 a.m., he radioed, "Units, respond to the Cross-Brook area. It's probably Franklyn Reid. We've got a bunch of warrants for him. He was probably tired of driving, dumped the car rather than run with it."

At 11:18 a.m., Cramer instructed an officer to check the area around a local school.

* * *

Investigator Scott Smith is at the helm of a customized Ford Escort with dark, tinted windows as it speeds down the long police station driveway. Previously owned by a drug dealer, the Escort's dark windows prevented outsiders from viewing inside when the detectives were on stakeout. Likewise, however, its occupants have difficulty viewing the world beyond the dark glass.

Smith and Shortt talk over which direction to turn on Route 202. They turn left.

"You know who this guy is, right?" Shortt says.

Smith acknowledges familiarity with Franklyn, a young man who has had numerous run-ins with the department and is considered the most dangerous person in New Milford. He feels a bit worried for Sergeant Cramer, a seventeen-year veteran. How events transpired and developed remains a mystery to the officers. The radio silence is eerie.

Approximately fifteen seconds later, Detective Jordan whisks out from the police department in an undercover Chevy Lumina. Confronted with choices, he formulates a quick action plan. Assessing Sergeant Cramer's reported location with proximity to Reid's residence and possible surveillance areas, he turns left onto Route 202.

After a few minutes, Detective Shortt spots a black male walking northbound in the vicinity of Sandra's Cleaners.

Passing the unidentified male on his right side, Shortt asks, "Is that Reid?"

"I don't know. I only glimpsed him," Smith says. "But this is far from where Cramer was supposed to be pursuing him."

"I didn't get a good look either, can't really see through the tinted windows," Shortt admits.

Curious to identify the walking male, they agree it's worth a second look. Smith makes a U-turn at Park Lane West, the first available road, but the heavy flow of traffic prevents him from pulling onto Route 202. Finally, an opening appears and Smith creeps the Escort toward the Sunoco station.

* * *

Following through on his plan, Detective Jordan positions his car near a parking lot close to Park Lane West. He feels his position is ideal if the driver of the Toyota is Franklyn Reid. The Reid residence is located only fourteen hundred feet further up the road from Route 202. In this position, Jordan might be able to obtain positive identification. The location is also well suited for a foot pursuit. Needless to say, Jordan is also familiar with Franklyn, whose priors include domestic disputes, threatening, traffic violations, unemployment fraud, sexual assault, and failure to appear in court.

* * *

Edging closer, Shortt and Smith spot the black male they saw earlier, this time crossing Howland Road, a dead-end street separating the gas station and dry cleaner.

"Yes, that's Franklyn Reid," Smith confirms.

Shortt concurs. Smith rolls his window down for positive identification while turning left into the Sunoco station.

"Get as close as possible, 'cause he's going to run," Shortt says.

Anticipating Reid will gallop, Smith follows his partner's advice. He stops the surveillance vehicle between the station building and first bay of pumps. Franklyn is about ten feet from the driver's side front bumper. Carrying a jacket, he looks over his left shoulder while continuing to walk toward Park Lane West.

Smith and Reid lock eyes on each other. Immediately reacting, the plainclothes officer flings open his door and jumps out of the driver's seat, leaving Shortt without a word. Reid bolts and a foot chase ensues.

"Police! Police! Stop, Franklyn!" Smith yells.

Detective Shortt initially joins the chase then doubles back to retrieve the car, leaving both twenty-seven-year-old men on their own. Smith is in an all-out sprint about fifteen feet behind Reid.

* * *

Decision time, Franklyn thinks, as he crosses busy Route 202 without becoming roadkill.

Motorists, caught off guard, swerve to avoid him. Traffic begins to slow.

Seconds later, it's Smith's decision time. He eases up his pursuit to avoid being mowed down. *Damn, I thought Reid was surely going to get hit.* Realizing Shortt is not with him, he guesses the veteran is close behind or retrieving the car. Boots meet pavement as Smith resumes the pursuit.

"Police! Stop! Police! Franklyn! Stop!" Smith yells, darting to the middle of the road.

Traffic virtually halts as onlookers and motorists alike witness an uncommon late morning scene in their normally quiet, suburban town. Suddenly, Franklyn veers up on a small embankment. Smith leaves the road and follows him.

Seconds later both men occupy the slope. Franklyn confuses Smith by swerving right into the middle of the road and stops. In football jargon, the move is described as a button hook: an offensive player runs a few yards, immediately cuts right or left, turns around and stops to receive the ball. Except Franklyn doesn't turn around, he only looks back over his right shoulder at his pursuer. Smith is alarmed by Reid's action. Is Franklyn giving up or is he preparing for a confrontation?

Stopping, Smith's thumb snaps his holster's retention strap open, and he draws his weapon. He aims it at Reid's back while squeezing the handgrip and indexing the trigger.

"Show me your hands! Show me your hands!" Smith yells. But Reid appears frozen in time, looking over his shoulder and staring down the barrel of a gun. Cautiously approaching, Smith repeats his deafening command as twelve feet of separation evaporates. *He's staring through me, giving me the thousand-yard stare*, Smith thinks, edging closer toward Reid.

* * *

Darting back to the car, Shortt climbs into the driver's seat and races out of the gas station.

* * *

Still yelling commands to a silent Franklyn, Smith comes within an arm's length of the suspect. Smith stands six foot two; Reid five foot four. Using his left, gun-free hand, Smith grabs Reid's right shoulder, then walks backward, pulling an unresisting Reid toward the curb while still indexing his revolver's trigger.

I need to get us to a safe position to avoid getting hit, and cuff him, thinks Smith. Finally to the side of the road, he repositions Franklyn in front of him, switching to grab the suspect's left shoulder while forcing him toward the embankment. Traffic crawls as curiosity rivets strangers' eyes.

"Get on the ground! Get on the ground!" Smith bellows. Observation checks in; he realizes Reid is not resisting or attempting to flee. He powers his suspect to the ground.

Suddenly, the Ford Escort whips out from the Sunoco station. Smith's head pivots for a split second. Shortt slams the brakes but slides past both men before stopping, spiking anxiety.

Shortt alerts dispatch with a status update at 11:23:21. "We're in foot pursuit of Reid on Route 202, northbound near Sunoco. We got him."

"Get on the ground! Get on the ground!" Smith continues yelling, although Franklyn is already on his knees.

Smith demands to see Franklyn's hands as he spreads Reid's legs and pushes down on his upper body to flatten him out. Franklyn plants both hands on the ground to avoid slamming his face into the choppy ground. At that crucial moment, a second between life and death, Smith glimpses those exposed hands and realizes they are empty.

"You have him in custody?" an exuberant dispatcher asks, requiring confirmation of the previous transmission.

"Yeah, standby," Shortt replies at 11:23:43.

Jordan, the closest officer to their location, hears Shortt's radio communication. Rubber greets pavement; he aggressively speeds from the Bit of Country Furniture parking lot toward Sunoco.

After bracing himself, Reid bounces back to his knees. Smith pushes his right shoulder down, forcing him to the ground once more while still indexing the pistol's trigger. This time, Franklyn's face hits the leafy embankment hard. Again, Franklyn springs back to the kneeling position. His hands disappear toward his midsection and he begins turning toward the officer.

Life flashes before Smith's eyes, and he thinks, *OH SHIT, I'M DEAD.*

* * *

Focused on engaging the vehicle's emergency brake, Detective Shortt hears a pop and instantly recognizes the sound of a gunshot. Eighteen seconds later at 11:24:01, an out-of-breath Shortt radios, "Dispatch an ambulance."

A baffled dispatcher immediately responds, "What type of injuries? For who?"

ACT I SCENE II

———

EPIC JOURNEY

Born seven months apart in 1971, perhaps fate set up Officer Scott Smith and Franklyn Reid to have a catastrophic contact. In a spiritual realm, some believe life is preordained, and choices made by individuals will fulfill their destiny.

Though both came from hardworking, loving families, they sprouted on vastly differently soil. Scott grew up in Newtown, Connecticut, with his parents and sister. In 1986, the blond-haired, blue-eyed boy began high school and enjoyed playing two of America's favorite sports. Wearing number 24, he routinely put up double digits on the basketball court. Likewise, as a baseball pitcher, he accumulated numerous strikeouts; achievements his local newspaper hailed on a routine basis. Summers, he painted houses with his father. The temporary employment provided quality family time but he knew his career was best suited to serving a community. After high school, his path took him to

Quinnipiac College in Connecticut, where he earned a bachelor of science in social services in 1994.

A career in law enforcement appeared inevitable to fulfill Smith's passion. He applied at local police departments and with the Border Patrol, and worked as a store detective for Macy's in Danbury, Connecticut. The tall, young man also joined the Newtown Volunteer Ambulance Corps and became a certified Emergency Medical Technician (EMT) in 1995. In the summer of 1996, his aspirations led him to put in an application to join the police force in New Milford, Connecticut. He was hired in December of that year.

By that time, Franklyn's history with the department dated back to their "in tandem" high school years. Scott and Franklyn's lives coursed through time on divergent tracks giving credence to the adage, "Everything happens for a reason."

Likewise, life intended the paths of Dwight Reid, Sr. and Pearlylyn Grey to intertwine within their first twenty years in Maroon Town, Jamaica. Eager to start a family, the young couple had Franklyn out of wedlock in 1971. However, being avid members at the local church, securing their bond was without question. They tied the marriage knot in 1973. That same year, Dwight Jr. was welcomed as the second child. Often called Doc or Doctor (a nickname from birth), Dwight Sr. worked at a pump house that provided clean water for the community. He also farmed land owned by his father, Mortimer Reid. In order to get milk, Dwight had to catch one of the many cows that freely roamed the property. He would tie the back legs to a nearby post and place a five-gallon bucket (or as Jamaicans say, a five-gallon drum) under the cow's udders. The milk would be boiled, placed in containers, and ready for consumption at home.

Doc eventually picked up tailoring, the trade his father greatly enjoyed. You could see Mortimer sitting on his veranda, legs crossed, stitching away before moving to the sewing machine. As a result, he was branded with the name Tailor Reid. But that was only one of his nicknames. A well-respected member of the Parish Council (the local government), many referred to him as Councilor Reid. You could easily single him out in a crowd with his bright blue eyes, straight nose, Spock-like ears, and signature hat. His tenacity for working hard trickled through the family as the cornerstone for simple living by ordinary people. He was fond of saying, "A family that works together, stays together."

Pearlylyn's education propelled her to become a government employee, working for The National Housing Trust in Montego Bay. A quick thinker, she was dedicated to her profession, giving more than 100 percent before going home to cook, clean, and raise her family. (Her appropriate nickname: Precious.) Jamaicans have a strong work ethic. It was expected that after school and on weekends, kids would assist adults by working the land. Everyone had to contribute in some form or another.

Every family has unruly kids. Mom would say, "Stay away from there," or, "Walk away from trouble," but at times, talking lacked receptive ears. She spoke once, and either you listened or suffered the consequences—a whooping. If we disobeyed, she didn't chase us down; she picked the perfect time to deliver punishment, usually early in the morning when everyone was asleep. Franklyn and Dwight Jr. figured out her strategy. In our two-bedroom house, Mom and Dad had their room; the kids shared a bed in the other room. Being the youngest, I was always placed in the middle, so when Mom came in, I received the brunt of the strap. That was normal life, parents disciplining their kids. We didn't fight back or argue; we took our beating, learned lessons, and moved on.

In 1984, my parents received a response from the immigration service stating they were accepted, but their kids had to stay in Jamaica. My mother said, "Either you approve all of us or none of us." Her request was graciously denied! We waited another two years, and thanks to Uncle Windell, who filed the required documents, my family was granted permanent resident status in the United States. It took a total of five years but it provided life-changing opportunities.

The exciting journey culminated with landing at John F. Kennedy Airport on a rainy April 20 evening in 1986. We couldn't contain our grins while walking the long hallway toward customs. When called to the counter, the officer asked for our Jamaican passports and permanent resident cards.

"Oh, your first time traveling!" he said, smiling.

We waited and waited until the verification process was complete, then he placed the first stamps in our passports. We weren't sure where to go, but the friendly officer said to follow the signs toward baggage claim where my grandfather, Mr. Shaw, greeted us. We embraced my mother's father, as he said in his deep gravitas voice, "Welcome to America."

For a few minutes, we hugged and shook hands. Suddenly, a thunderous sound I can only describe as the awakening of a machine in desperate need of grease, echoed around us. Oddly, passengers gravitated toward it. A perplexed family member asked, "Why are those people standing around that oddly shaped contraption?"

My grandfather explained with a smirk. "It's called a carousel, and that's where luggage is retrieved."

Joining the crowd, we watched the machine rumble slowly, circling with luggage until we saw one of ours, then two, three, four, and five. Each of us had one piece of luggage, essentially holding everything we wanted from Jamaica.

By the time we exited the airport, night had fallen with patchy periods of heavy rain showers. That didn't dampen our eagerness to see this new country. We took turns pressing our faces against the windows, gawking at the bright lights of New York City in the distance, while traveling over a gigantic overpass called the Whitestone Bridge. I felt tired and wanted to sleep, but the excitement of being in America kept me, along with everyone else, wide awake. Strangely, the closer we got to Connecticut, the darker it became. I couldn't see anything except darkness and infrequent headlights from vehicles traveling behind us. I felt scared when the lights veered left or right to pass us. We didn't have highways in Jamaica—or drivers in Jamaica were never in such a hurry that they'd want to pass a car in front of them. But that didn't seem to bother my grandfather. His attention was focused on getting us safely through torrential rain to our destination: 20 Housatonic Avenue in New Milford, the home of our grandfather and his wife, my step-grandmother, nicknamed Aunt Orinth.

The next morning, we went outside and saw trees, lots of trees—but without leaves. We were duped into believing we had landed in America which only had dead trees!

"They are not dead," my grandfather said. "They're just beginning to grow since it's a new season."

"What does that mean?" I asked.

"Well, in America, there are four seasons: summer, fall, winter, and currently we're in spring. Living in the Northeast, you'll experience changes in nature with each season, and you will adjust accordingly," he said.

That's strange, thought my nine-year-old mind. I didn't understand what he meant. Jamaica was hot all the time, and I never saw leafless trees. I guessed in time I would understand.

So, our new American lives started in New Milford. My parents hit the ground running, and it didn't take them long to find jobs. They saved as much money as they could and, in 1987, we were fortunate enough to rent our own place, an apartment at 15 Fordyce Court in New Milford.

One of the ways we were exposed to life in America was through the church. My Aunt Orinth introduced us to the New Milford Baptist Church (currently Northville Baptist

Church) and Pastor George Britt. It felt like a ray of light, like Divine providence had brought us here. The powerful, eloquent sermons the pastor delivered felt like they were meant specifically for us. Being the youngest and in middle school, I became involved with church activities. Mr. Roger Parkhouse, a tall, bearded man, taught Sunday school and ran the teen club for youths who wanted to learn the Bible, go to summer camp, sporting events, or youth revivals. It was through his guidance, becoming best friends with his son, Matt, and spending time with his family, that my everlasting love for the Lord developed. Those important teenage years kick-started my compassionate thought process. Connecting with the church, along with getting involved in sports, was pivotal in molding my developing mind into alignment with my actions. I accepted everyone, no matter their background, skin color, or personal choices.

While my path in life was evolving, Dwight Jr. and Franklyn were going through their adolescent years. Our parents always said learning was important. Their words of encouragement, along with our desires to fulfill their wishes, guided us through the progression of education. But schooling is not for everyone; some may leave the structured setting of a classroom to pursue visionary dreams or alternative methods of learning. That was the case for Franklyn, who turned away from high school in the eleventh grade. Dad demanded he seek employment anywhere that would hire him. Franklyn became a handyman while his interest in music grew exponentially.

In order to explore those avenues, Franklyn had to

obtain a driver's license. After work, Mom took him to one of the many side roads in town and taught him how to drive. Sometimes I tagged along for an entertaining adventure. I don't know if nervousness gripped Franklyn or my mother more.

"You're driving like you're pulling a cow. Stay in your lane; the road doesn't belong to you," my mother would holler.

I could see my brother squeezing the steering wheel as Mom pressed the imaginary brake on the passenger side, cringing at approaching motorists, relieved after they passed. I found it amusing and occasionally giggled and smiled. It wasn't the first time Franklyn had been behind a wheel. Being in charge of steering our homemade go-carts in Jamaica, he'd maneuvered down some wicked, winding roads. He was calm under pressure, knowing the safety of the kids on the cart (including his youngest brother), rested in his hands. He approached driving a car in a similar manner, responsibly. After passing the written exam on his third attempt, big brother finally obtained his driver's license in 1988. He began working on cars and at fast food restaurants, well on his way to becoming a jack-of-all-trades.

Our family felt comfortable in New Milford, though it was a predominantly white town with very few minorities residing in that part of Connecticut. A large segment of the community treated everyone equally; the color of your skin was a nonissue. The racial separation of generations ago didn't seem to be divisive in nature, as demonstrated by the numerous diverse friends Franklyn, Dwight Jr., and

I gained. Over the years, our combined circle of friends included Spanish, Cuban, Italian, Iranian, Mexican, Jamaican, Chinese, and, of course, American, to name a few.

My older brothers would hang out at Young's Field, the local recreational park. It had become the main area of attraction for older kids to congregate since there weren't a lot of places in town for social gatherings. Policing became a daily routine. The force proudly carried the mantle of protecting and serving the community with dignity and compassion. Sure, they had to break up occasional wrangling among kids, but that's life; we didn't live in a utopian society where no one argued or fought, especially high school kids. For the most part, everyone seemed to coexist peacefully. As a result, my older brothers found friendship with members of the police department, such as Officer Ron Young and Officer Guy Samuelson. Law enforcement's special role in community policing is knowing the neighborhood members in order to build trusting relationships for the sake of peace.

There was, however, an issue that raised tensions. Attraction is natural in adolescent years, and many teens are receptive to feeling this connection with whomever—regardless of race. But acceptance of an interracial relationship is not always condoned by the parents, and battles may ensue, pitting people against people. When disputes are unresolvable, the "authority" may be called on to mediate. Unfortunately, some in law enforcement are influenced to take coercive action, blurring the line of impartiality. Why? The idea of interracial relationships often disgusts a small fraction of a predominantly white community. Those feel it's like an insult, a slap in the face, to see a white girl dating a black boy. It unearths a deep-seated resentment in those who do not see all races as equal, those who believe non-whites should not be treated the same as whites. It's hard to acknowledge and outwardly admit this stance. Some people don't want to be seen as prejudiced; yet, in private, the muzzle that filters disparaging remarks is removed.

And then those sentiments can go public. "Why did you come here? Go back to where you came from!" Such are familiar statements minority ears are accustomed to hearing. Sometimes a couple's love is strong enough to weather the storm of hatred. Their relationship doesn't separate like clouds but endures divisive forces aimed to drive a wedge between them. For other couples, the disapproval kills romance.

Those types of objections to mixed relationships had no bearing on the actions of the Jamaican boy. But it did put Franklyn (who had the looks and charm of a ladies' man) on the radar in a visibly homogeneous environment. His first run-in with the police happened in October 1989. The vice principal of New Milford High School, John Lee, wrote Franklyn a letter stating that he was not allowed on school grounds during school hours. Like countless others at that time, he was characterized as a high school dropout. The letter said Franklyn had been seen leaving school property with a female student. If he returned, the letter said, a complaint would be filed with the police department for criminal trespassing.

Soon after, Franklyn picked up Dwight Jr. from school, and as threatened, Vice Principal Lee logged a formal complaint and a warrant was issued for Franklyn's arrest. The egregious act of a brother was considered a criminal offense (and later *dismissed)*.

Coincidently, approximately a year earlier, in 1988, Detective Jordan stated that while conversing freely in "police talk," members of the department speculated that Franklyn would be the first to shoot one of them. Whether the comments were said jokingly or as an act of profiling, being in law enforcement you would remember those words—and that could have a bearing on future interactions with an adolescent turning into a young adult.

Maybe once the town police know who you are, they develop expectations that you don't care about following the law and wait for your next infraction. Maybe that's how fate placed Franklyn on a path to collide with Smith many years later.

ACT I SCENE III

—————

PANDEMONIUM

Confused by the ambulance request, a perplexed dispatcher repeats, "Shortt, what type of injuries? For who?" Within a split second, the lives of two families are connected in a tragic, unusual circumstance.

Dwight and Pearlylyn Reid's morning starts typically: they go to work. My mother is employed as a cashier at Home Depot; my father works as a presser at Colonial Cleaners in Danbury and Ridgefield, Connecticut, respectively. Life suggests a normal day but at approximately 8:30 a.m., almost three hours before the incident, my dad feels depressed and disoriented. He momentarily pauses to analyze these powerful emotions, but unable to determine their root cause, resumes work.

The sun rises on my own day in Fort Lauderdale, Florida, with the University of Scranton wrestling team. About twelve Division III teams from across the country congregate in the sunshine state to participate in the annual Citrus

Holiday Tournament. I have no idea how fast internal clouds would move in.

"For suspect. Dispatch supervisors also," an anxious Shortt replies. The bravery of law enforcement, first responders, and ordinary citizens, will be tested as a crisis of this magnitude unfolds in New Milford for the first time. Shortt's dire request triggers a flurry of alerts.

* * *

Emergency medical technician Michael Gabriel's pager sounds for an unknown emergency in the vicinity of Sunoco, less than two minutes from the EMT's residence. Without knowing the circumstances or what to expect, the New Milford Community Ambulance volunteer dashes to his truck and speeds the short distance to the call.

* * *

Detective Jordan arrives on the scene and quickly pulls into a residential driveway on the same side of the street as Smith and the suspect. Promptly surveying the area, he notices Smith with a gun in his hand hovering over a motionless Franklyn, who is lying face down on the leafy embankment. No time to waste, he rushes to aid fellow officers, believing a car hit Franklyn as he ran across Route 202.

Shortt intercepts him halfway for an impromptu meeting.

"What happened?" Jordan asks.

"Smith shot him," Shortt says.

A surprised Jordan looks at Smith again. The reality of shooting a man must not have set in yet. He appears emotionally blank. Jordan redirects his attention to Franklyn. Concerned for the safety of others, including himself, and thinking that Franklyn's injuries may be superficial, Jordan grabs his handcuffs with the intent of securing the suspect's hands.

* * *

Gabriel arrives, parks a short distance behind a Ford Escort and looks around before quickly retrieving a medical kit and oxygen from his trunk.

* * *

Meanwhile, Jordan reaches Franklyn. *Shit, he's seriously injured.* He sees a wound in the young man's upper back that's slowly seeping blood through pierced clothing. *Man, is that where the bullet entered or exited?* He exchanges his cuffs for heavy-duty work gloves from his pocket and immediately administers first aid by placing pressure on the area.

Smith has since holstered his firearm as he stands around with Shortt, awaiting directives from Jordan. Smith is eager to help, still seeming to be emotionally unshaken at having just discharged a round into someone.

Franklyn is still breathing, though faintly. Life has a grip on the young man, not ready to relinquish him to Death, in the hope he can be saved. The uncommon scene draws curious onlookers, eager to see what's happening. Traffic continues to slowly crawl.

Detective Shortt recognizes the momentous task is overwhelming for his colleagues to manage. "We're going to need more personnel up here, ASAP," he radios at 11:25:18.

Someone needs to step forward, assert command to lead the initial coordination and response. Sergeant Cramer, who initially alerted headquarters about the Toyota Celica, is prepared to carry that mantle. Still stationed with the car at Dawn's Road, he instructs Officer Blanchette, who had rendezvoused with him after searching for Franklyn, to remain there while he rushes toward Sunoco.

Back at the scene of the shooting, Jordan hollers to Smith and Shortt, "Grab the rubber gloves from my car." Jordan fears blood might soak through his work gloves and expose him to something as he continues to apply pressure to Franklyn's wound.

The officers attempt to fulfill Jordan's directive, but confusion arises.

"I can't find the gloves!" says Smith to Shortt. "Do you see them anywhere?"

Shortt paws around papers on the front seat, bends to look under the seats, too. "Nothing," he says.

"We don't see them in the car!" Smith yells to Jordan.

"Look in the trunk!" Jordan answers.

Precious seconds are ticking away. Multiple heart-pounding things are occurring simultaneously; it's hard to stay focused on the simplest task.

"Finally!" says Smith.

The chaotic episode ends as the trunk release is located. The rubber gloves are retrieved and hurried back to Jordan.

While confusion steals valuable time, EMT Michael Gabriel alerts dispatch via his two-way portable radio of a possible accident. The volunteer dashes across the street and provides Jordan with some much-needed assistance.

"He's not breathing!" Jordan says.

He rolls Franklyn onto his back and begins chest compressions.

Gabriel prepares his bag-valve-mask resuscitator to give oxygen, but the contraption malfunctions.

"Let's get it going here," Jordan yells.

Keeping calm, Gabriel places a CPR pocket mask over Franklyn's mouth and breathes air into the young man's lungs while Jordan continues chest compressions.

Knowing an investigation is most certain, Jordan multitasks by scanning the area for specific items of evidence.

* * *

A blue Neon, driving north toward the scene, pulls into Sunoco. Unaware of what's happening a short distance away, Franklyn's girlfriend, Pamela, leaves her car to wait for him. She got his call to pick him up less than seven minutes before. She dressed quickly and rushed from the Reid's residence, taking an alternate road to retrieve her beau.

Where is he? She notices people on the street and in their cars staring at vehicles on the roadside. A few people are frantically doing something. She decides to join the curious and moseys closer toward the tumult to get a better view.

* * *

At headquarters, what started as a routine morning is turning into a tragedy with minimal information. Although Cramer is barreling toward the scene, dispatchers Alex Correa and Cindy Hanford are essential to the lawmen's coordination efforts and, most importantly, to keep the public calm. Communication is pivotal. First, Correa follows through on Shortt's initial request.

"We need a medic at Sunoco station, the corner of 202 and Holland Road," Correa says to the Litchfield dispatcher, operators of the ambulance services.

"Holland Road? For what?"

"It's a male! It's a suspect!" Correa answers. "I'm not sure what the injuries are, but they're calling for the medic right away. I don't know, maybe a car hit him. I have no idea what happened at this point."

Hysteria, coupled with scant information rambled in one breath somehow gets the dispatcher to understand, and he dispatches additional medical personnel.

Calls flood into the station's switchboard; concerned citizens notifying the authorities.

"911, what's your emergency?" echoes throughout the dispatching unit.

"Route 202 in New Milford, there's a person lying on

the side of the road, right by Park Lane Sunoco," reports an unidentified caller.

"Our superintendent just called in and wanted to let you know that on Route 202 by Sunoco, there's an accident, and there is an injured person," reports another unidentified caller seconds later.

Hanford reassures the callers that help is currently at the scene. "Those are our officers out there," she says.

* * *

Pam sees personnel frantically working on someone lying on the ground. Her eyes widen as she realizes the person is her boyfriend, Franklyn. Pam's loud wail pivots the officers' heads in her direction.

"Franklyn!" she cries out, hoping he will hear her trembling voice. No signs of movement respond to her plea. *Maybe if I hold him, comfort him, he'll wake up!* Pam attempts to cross the street, not paying attention to crawling traffic.

Detective Shortt sees that Officer Smith recognizes Pam and is about to approach her. Pam has no idea that Smith shot Franklyn, but a face-to-face confrontation could be catastrophic. Shortt cuts Smith off and intercepts a bawling Pam before she crosses the street.

"I'm Detective Shortt. Can I help you?"

"What happened to Franklyn?" Pam asks.

Deflecting the question, Shortt asks who she is and where she's coming from.

"I'm...Franklyn's girlfriend. I...I'm coming from his parents' house," Pam says in a choked voiced.

Shortt knows not to divulge any information to civilians. Instead, he gives her a directive. "Please do not cross the street. The paramedics are on their way, and we're doing everything we can."

Jordan also saw Smith's bonehead move. "Scotty!" he calls out. "Get in my car."

Sergeant Cramer arrives on the scene. He surveys the area. He sees Smith in Jordan's unmarked vehicle plainclothed personnel around Franklyn, and the slow flow of traffic. He locks eyes with Shortt, who heads over to give him a quick briefing.

Cramer asks the obvious question. "What happened?"

"I guess Smitty AD'ed (accidentally discharged) but I really don't know," Shortt says. "I was across the street."

Cramer approaches Smith, who now looks distraught. The gravity of what he's done is sinking in.

"Are you okay?" Cramer asks.

"Yes, I'm fine," Smith says.

Cramer leaves Smith at the car and shifts his focus to deal with traffic. The scene needs to be contained and preserved. He knows with absolute certainty an investigation is imminent. The most efficient method is to restrict traffic access to certain roads.

"I need units to block Park Lane West and 202 to reroute, and to block Elkington Farm," he radios dispatch at 11:27:58.

While other officers urgently respond, Kim Silvernail, an EMT with more trauma experience than Gabriel, arrives and briefly meets with Shortt, who's tasked himself to provide initial updates.

"What type of injury has Mr. Reid sustained?"

"A single gunshot wound," Shortt says.

Silvernail momentarily stops Gabriel and Jordan from CPR duties to cut away layers of clothing from Franklyn's upper body in order to pinpoint the location of the gunshot wound and check for signs of life. He delicately rolls Franklyn over and finds a single penetrating wound in the neck region, just right of the spinal column, which he covers with a pressure dressing. Franklyn's prognosis looks bleak to Silvernail. His life signs are fading away as Death creeps closer.

"I can't find a carotid or radial pulse, or any sign of respiration," Silvernail yells.

Franklyn has no pulse in the major arteries leading to the brain or in the arteries at his wrists. CPR starts again, using Silvernail's BVM resuscitator to pump oxygen into Franklyn.

Paramedics Burch and Jennings arrive on scene and find Franklyn in cardiac arrest. They hastily start IV lines and hook him up to an electronic vitals monitor. Silvernail continues pumping oxygen into the lungs.

Pam attempts to get closer again. She's screaming and in tears. Jordan sees her and thinks, *Oh, jeez, she's going to cross the street and get hit.* He moves quickly, stopping traffic so he can approach Pam and try to calm her down.

"Um, I demand to know what happened! Um, why can't I comfort him? He's not moving!" a red-faced Pam pleads while pointing at Franklyn.

"The medical people are doing everything they can, and the ambulance is coming, and I do not fully know what happened. Please calm down, get away from the road. We don't need you hurt, too," Jordan says.

As if in a waking nightmare, Pam follows his instructions. A friend happens to drive by, and comes over to console her.

Jordan approaches Cramer. "We need the whole area sealed off," he says.

"I have my officers working on it as we speak," Cramer assures him.

"I'm taking Scott (Smith) back to the station," Jordan says.

Cramer agrees. "Good idea! Dave (Shortt) should stay behind!"

They both know that separating the men is standard protocol.

Jordan calls to Shortt. "Hey Dave, I'm taking Scott back to the station."

Shortt nods in agreement.

* * *

Pam realizes the complexity and magnitude of the situation. The brief consoling period ends when reality can no longer be ignored: Franklyn has not moved, additional emergency personnel are surrounding him, and they are hooking him up to machines. Frantically rushing back to Sunoco, she dashes inside the station.

"They did something to him, and I need to use the phone!" she hysterically shouts.

Ms. Swanson, an employee, recognizes Pam as a regular patron and allows her to use the office phone. She stays close to the broken woman. Pam makes the most difficult call—to Doc, Franklyn's father.

The presser is working on a dress pant when his oversized cellular phone (a gift from Franklyn), rings. He answers and hears someone crying, trying to put words together.

Calming her shaky voice, Pam musters a few words. "Doc, the New Milford cops did something to Franklyn, and he's not breathing. Rush home quickly!"

Instantly, the unexplained emotion Doc felt hours ago overpowers again. His stomach feels like it's falling into a pit. The shocking words, coupled with an emotional realization makes his body feel like it's overheating. "I need to call my wife," the father says in a trembling voice.

Peter Hayles, his boss, is walking by when he notices the look on Doc's face.

"Doc, is something wrong?"

"Yeah...yes...I don't know...my son's girlfriend called and said the cops did something to him, and he's not breathing, and I'm to rush home quickly."

"Oh God!" Peter says. His palm grabs his forehead. "Can I take you home?"

"I'm okay...I just need to speak with my wife."

"Okay, Doc! If there is anything I can do, please don't hesitate to ask."

Doc reassures Peter he is fine but a concerned boss knows his employee will need support in New Milford.

The father's eyes water as he tries to keep his hand steady enough to dial the correct numbers. His wife's phone rings without an answer. *Maybe she found out. I'll try again in a few minutes.*

Mrs. Reid hears her mobile phone ringing while checking a customer out at her cash register. Believing it is most likely her husband, she'll return the call after completing the transaction.

Less than a minute later, she dials her husband. "Hello, babe, you called?"

No words come across the line, only the sound of her husband crying.

"What's wrong?" Mrs. Reid asks, alarmed.

"Pam called and said the cops did something to Mark," he says, using Franklyn's nickname. "He's not breathing, and I'm to rush home quickly."

An emotional woman to begin with, the mother feels flooded by a tidal wave of suffering. Heat rises in her body and, overcome with fear, she weeps uncontrollably. Customers and fellow employees hear and witness the depth of her anguish. The head cashier quickly rushes to Mrs. Reid's aid. Searching for words, Mrs. Reid reiterates the awful phone call.

Promptly reacting to calm the situation, the head cashier redirects waiting customers to other cash registers. The unbearable news overwhelms the distraught mother. Her anguished moaning grows louder. Onlookers stare. The manager hears the commotion and rushes to her side. He instructs her to go home after hearing the news.

The father tries to think optimistically, but the words, "he's not breathing," overshadow his thoughts. Driving as fast as road conditions permit, he stays mindful of the safety of other motorists and himself.

The bond between a husband and wife sometimes produces similar thought patterns. Praying to the Lord and asking for her son to be okay, Pearlylyn, too, is hoping for a positive outcome. Though a careful driver, she sporadically speeds to reach her eldest son.

* * *

First responders cannot slow down Franklyn's deteriorating condition at the scene. They need to immediately transport him to the nearby hospital, less than two miles away.

Silvernail relays the status to dispatch. "Notify 96-A (hospital), male, black, about twenty-five years old, single gunshot wound. We're trauma code."

Forewarning the emergency room, dispatcher Hanford informs the front desk to be on alert for a gunshot victim in bad shape.

* * *

Returning to the shooting scene, Pam feels suspended in time as she looks at the surreal sight of Franklyn, surrounded by EMTs, lying peacefully on the ground. She wants to get close to comfort her boyfriend. Lost in a state of shock, she presses closer, but Jordan approaches her again.

"Why don't you go to the hospital and wait, Pam?" Jordan advises. "The ambulance will be transporting him soon,"

Knowing Doc is rushing home, she returns to Sunoco and places a second phone call.

* * *

Hoping for the best, Doc recalls the loving words on a beautifully written Father's Day card he received from Franklyn. "Dad, you are the one who taught me what life is really about; I should follow your footsteps to the end. Thank you for never disappointing me; thank you for sharing the hard times in my life even when yours may have been harder and responsibilities greater. Thank you for loving me." With a nervous heart, speeding toward New Milford, his mind races, clouded with numerous thoughts. Is he alive? Is he dead? What kind of shape is he in? How did this happen? His cell phone rings again. A sobbing Pam is on the other end of the line.

"Doc, they are transporting Franklyn to New Milford Hospital, and you should go there instead."

* * *

Cruising toward New Milford, Franklyn's mother is fighting

tears but can't stop the breaking of her heart. Her cell phone rings. *I hope this is good news,* she thinks, knowing it's her husband. "Hello, is everything all right?"

Doc relays Pam's message.

Mrs. Reid's heart gives a nervous jolt when she hears the words "Franklyn" and "hospital" in the same sentence. "Okay," she says.

* * *

Assessing the situation, Cramer believes requesting and pre-positioning officers will aid logistical efforts. He recognizes that the unexpected situation requires all hands on deck, but personnel availability is a significant issue. He briefs Dispatcher Correa.

"We've got a gunshot wound. Apparently, Smith AD'ed on takedown. Reid's been shot. Send me the major. Send me all the DB (detective bureau) boys you got. Get me two more units ASAP."

Before the sergeant can finish those words, Captain Lillis (who has heard about a disturbance) happens to check in with dispatch. The words "gunshot" "Franklyn Reid," and "one of our guys shot him," sums up Hanford's reply. The captain knows his department will be thrown into the spotlight as his response, "Oh, boy," suggests.

* * *

Police Chief Sweeney is notified of the shooting and rushes

to the scene. What unfolds now and in the foreseeable future will require his leadership as the department's top cop. He wonders what awaits him. Will the coming events highlight unbiased public integrity—or will they advance the notion that only some lives are worth saving? His officers' actions could further an unbiased investigation or fuel a cover-up.

Sweeney knows Connecticut General Statutes dictate the office of the State's Attorney is responsible for investigating any police-involved shooting. It wouldn't be off-base for him to be thinking: *There's a lot I'm not going to be able to control.*

ACT I SCENE IV

———

LIGHTS OUT

As events unfold, Franklyn and Smith wait to be transported to their intended destinations. Smith has no choice but to sit in Jordan's car, contemplate his actions, and watch. Franklyn has no choice but to fight for his next breath, hoping it won't be his last.

I did what I could for Mr. Reid, thinks Detective Jordan. Now it's time to focus on Smith. He walks over to his car. Oh man, he's in a troubled state.

"Are you okay?" he asks in a gentle, concerned voice. Realization has set in and Smith appears to be in shock. One bullet could haunt him forever and may place his rookie career in peril. But the rule of law must be followed.

Jordan explains the protocol. "Don't talk to me about the case, about what happened. If you need something emotionally, fine, but you shouldn't talk to anybody about this. We're going to do this investigation straight out and separate you from Shortt. You have the right to an attorney, talk to him if you want. Other than that, talk only to the investigators about it, because I don't want this to be the type of thing they think we're trying to cover up."

Smith nods and says that he understands.

Chief Sweeney arrives just as Jordan is backing out from the driveway he's parked in. The chief hurries toward Jordan's vehicle.

"Chill out and stay here," the chief demands, virtually putting the brakes on the car. Sweeney, unaware of Jordan and Cramer's decision to remove Smith from the scene, sees Smith in the front seat.

The top cop wants to know what happened; he approaches Cramer for answers.

"I chased Reid, he dumped his car, a foot pursuit ensued between Franklyn and Smith, and this could be an accidental discharge," Cramer surmises.

He essentially recounts what Shortt said earlier, but Chief Sweeney wants additional answers. He reapproaches Jordan's vehicle. He, too, recognizes Smith may be in a state of shock which prevents an inquisition into what transpired. He defers to asking about his well-being.

Sweeney looks across Jordan at Smith in the passenger seat. "Hey, you doing okay?" he asks the pale man.

"I'm fine," Smith says with a nod.

"Chief, I'm going to bring him down to the station," Jordan says.

Sweeney's reply of, "good idea," rubber-stamps that decision with an order. "Jordan, stay with Smith in the detective bureau, lock the door, and no one enters until

I get there." Then, quickly realizing he needs to be pro-active and that immediate protocols must be followed to preserve potential evidence, he adds, "And Jordan, take Smith's weapon."

* * *

The few minutes' drive back to the station affords alone time for the officers. Jordan reiterates the chief's directives, ensuring no confusion at headquarters. Smith is escorted to the bureau, but Officers Bradford and Pecha are in the room. They heard about the incident within the small department but are unclear of its severity. Their eyes follow Smith as he walks sluggishly toward his desk.

"Chief's orders," Jordan says. "You gotta leave the room."

Once they've gone, he locks the door.

"Secure your firearm on that empty desk," Jordan instructs Smith. The flurry of unexpected and rapid activities within the last fifteen minutes would be overwhelming for anyone to process. Keenly aware of Smith's visible appearance, Jordan asks, "Are you okay?" He takes time to recollect his own mindset but reminds Smith, "Don't tell me anything about what you did and why you did it."

"Okay, Steve. Do I need to speak with a lawyer?"

"You certainly have that right," Jordan says.

* * *

Simultaneous events occur while Smith returns to the bureau. The chief meets with Cramer for another briefing and is satisfied with the lawman's control of the scene. Returning to headquarters, the responsibility of notifying the state's Division of Criminal Justice, the mayor, the town's lawyer, and meeting with Smith, rests solely upon Chief Sweeney's shoulders.

Although he had already made contact at the scene under investigation, Sweeney briefly meets with Smith.

"Do you need anything, Scott?" he asks, before beginning the notification process.

Smith says, "No, I'm okay," and Sweeney repeats his orders to remain isolated.

"I'm contacting the state to come in and investigate. Keep the door locked."

* * *

Also as Smith is returned to the station, the ambulance arrives at Sunoco. By this time, police cars have restricted Route 202 access for at least a quarter mile from the scene. Only residents living within the cordoned-off zone are allowed through. Detours shuffle motorists around the shooting scene.

Paramedics work feverishly to slow Franklyn's deteriorating condition. Approximately eighteen minutes after being shot, the long-awaited transport to the hospital, less than two miles from the scene, is underway. The medics use a defibrillator three times to shock the young man's heart back into action with negligible results.

As the ambulance takes Franklyn to the hospital, Chief Sweeney telephones Guy Wolf, the assistant state attorney in Litchfield, Connecticut.

"There has been a police shooting in New Milford involving one of my officers and Franklyn Reid. I'm advising you of the incident and requesting services," the chief tells Wolf, as required by law.

As the life of a human being hangs in the balance, Wolf says, "It couldn't have happened to a better guy." Perplexed by the attorney's response, the chief tries to distance himself through disagreement.

Life suggests that in a universe where adversaries exist, one side sometimes reacts with gleeful jubilation, lacking empathy for the "other's" human life. The chief knows the severity of the situation, having witnessed the aftermath. He knows that if Franklyn dies, there may be great ramifications, coupled with a long difficult journey.

* * *

Franklyn is rushed into the emergency room. Doctors, nurses, and paramedics do everything they can to hold death at bay. They use intelligence, machines, tools, and speed to keep Franklyn alive but death is closing in on a victory. Franklyn's pupils are fixedly dilated and he remains unresponsive, pulseless, and without spontaneous respirations.

The attending physician inserts two 14-gauge catheters attached to intravenous lines into the young man's jugular veins for a blood transfusion. An endotracheal tube is inserted into his trachea to maintain a stable airway. The tube is attached to a mechanical ventilator that breathes for Franklyn. The line scrolling across the heart monitor only occasionally shows a sign of life.

* * *

While that battle rages on, Officer Marino, president of the police officers' union, barrels toward headquarters after anxiously speaking with dispatch. He is fully aware of what's at stake. Scott Smith's fate and future path rests in the hands of the medical personnel desperately trying to save Reid's life. Officer Marino's focus is already directed toward the future.

"I'm coming in for Scott! I don't want anyone talking to Scott Smith. He gives no statements," Marino barks in Dispatcher Hanford's ear.

Marino wants his message delivered to Smith but dispatch doesn't know his whereabouts. They are fielding multiple requests while trying to find off-duty officers to assist with Cramer's coordination efforts. Fortunately, dispatchers are successful in locating additional personnel in time for another update with Sergeant Cramer at 11:47 a.m.

Protecting the greater community in case of any retaliatory measures is critically important in Cramer's planning process. The department's worst fear is that anger over the shooting could fuel the violence that creates uncontrollable chaos and mayhem in suburban New Milford. The message to his fellow officers needs to be silent and clear—be vigilant and aware of your surroundings. Cramer knows that the scene and hospital are two locations requiring additional resources and protection.

Cramer runs down his list of directives. He orders Officer Ron Young, the department's only black policeman, to replace Officer James Duda at the hospital. Duda is redirected to the shooting scene. Young joins Officer Michael Ward; together they will be the first line of defense for problems that might arise at the hospital where the Reid family is expected to be. Cramer orders Officers Larry Lynch and James Antonelli to road patrol. Officer Kaminski is already stationed at Park Lane West.

Finishing up with Cramer, Dispatcher Hanford fields Marino's follow-up call. The union president firmly enunciates his prior order. "I haven't gotten hold of anybody up there yet. Someone get to Scott Smith. He cannot talk to anyone. You got it?"

Unaware the officer is down the hall, Hanford calls Cramer to deliver Marino's urgent message.

"He's in the detective bureau. Page Jordan and tell him," Cramer says.

Surprised to know Smith is steps away, Hanford dials the room. Smith himself picks up the incoming call.

"I just talked to Henry! He does not want you to speak to anybody or give any statements until he gets here," Hanford relays.

The repercussions of possible future developments impact the present as Smith acknowledges Marino's message.

* * *

While driving toward headquarters, Marino begins his search for a law firm. A family connection and prior union representative suggests the firm of Moots Pellegrini Spillane & Mannion. The chief's "no one in until I get there" quickly lifts when Marino meets with Smith.

"I was able to get legal counsel for you," Marino tells Smith. "I don't know what to do as union president. This is above and beyond my expertise. If you want to speak to counsel, you can."

Smith takes Marino's suggestion and requests legal counsel. But that decision has to flow through proper channels. Chief Sweeney is the gatekeeper who gives final approval, and that requires verbal confirmation. Marino hurries to Sweeney's office to inform him of Smith's request. Moments later, both men return to the bureau. Sweeney grants approval and Smith gets a green light to leave headquarters to seek counsel.

Resuming notifications, Sweeney briefs the mayor and town lawyer on the developments. Soon after, another decision is handed down: Smith is immediately placed on administrative duties. The timing of that edict may have coincided with Franklyn's final breath.

* * *

Hospitals are associated with the continuance of life, but for many they become ground zero. The traumatic experience, coupled with raw emotion can be unbearable. Whatever causes the finality of life, many believe fate decides when it's time to go home. We may not embrace such decisions or abrupt departures, but many times that is the reality one must face. Franklyn drifts into a "permanent sleep" and his passing is recorded at 12:02 p.m.

Franklyn's life may have ended with this battle, but the days and months ahead will bring new struggles, unexpected alliances, divided communities, and an outcry for justice. The truth of "How did this happen?" may reveal itself in time, but will "Why did this happen?" forever elude us?

A MOTHER'S DARKEST HOUR

Police caution tape surrounds the scene. Medical equipment, supplies, and other items cover the trampled ground where a body once laid. Sergeant Cramer and his men effectively have the area contained and are in a holding pattern, waiting for the arrival of the Connecticut State Police to assume jurisdiction.

Connecticut General Statutes, Section 51-277a says, "Whenever a peace officer, during performance of his duties, uses deadly physical force upon another person and such person dies as a result thereof, the Division of Criminal Justice shall commence an investigation and shall have the responsibility of determining whether the use of deadly physical force was appropriate..."

Chief Sweeney initiated the first step by alerting Assistant State Attorney Wolf, who then notified Inspector John Pudlinski from the Criminal Justice Division. The inspector's sole purpose is to preserve the integrity of the scene, and he hurries toward New Milford. News of the incident is spreading, reaching the ears of dignitaries holding high positions in Connecticut. Chief State's Attorney John Bailey quickly assigns the Western Major Crime Squad to conduct the investigation. This division of the state police, stationed at the Litchfield Barracks, has jurisdiction over New Milford.

Franklyn's grandfather, Mr. Shaw, arrives in the emergency room after learning about the shooting. Tall in stature, he can command a room with his deep voice and eloquent speeches, spoken with a touch of his native Jamaican accent. A respected member of the community, he wants to see his grandson. He is confronted by police. Words to the effect of "active investigation" and "we cannot allow you in the room" from officers standing guard, sound foreign to Mr. Shaw.

Adamantly needing to see Franklyn, he steps past the officers. The sight of his grandson lying still as stone is devastating. He begins to sob. While in his moment of pain, the officers attempt to remove the elder gentleman from the room. With tears flowing, he holds the bed rails, unwilling to let go.

The commotion sends doctors rushing toward the room. Quickly diffusing an unnecessary situation, the attending physician speaks.

"Mr. Shaw has every right to be in the room." The officers release their grip on him. "But I'm going to have to ask you, sir, for right now, please do not touch the body." Emotions are running high but cooler heads prevail; the officers stand down based on that directive.

Mrs. Reid arrives at the hospital. Gathering her strength, the shaky mother enters the emergency room. The sliding door opens, offering a silent invitation. A ghastly sense of uncertainty cripples her feeling of optimism as facial expressions tell of a dreadful reality. Beyond the large doors labeled "Authorized Only," the body of her son awaits his mother's presence.

Mr. Shaw has the grim job of revealing the horrific news. Shaking his head like a child saying no, coupled with the words, "Mark didn't make it," sets off an enormous outpouring of emotion in Franklyn's mother. It's a slow-motion collapse as her body gives way and falls to the ground. The wailing is deafening, contagious, and heartbreaking for the strangers witnessing her agony. A mother rolling on the hospital floor, moaning in distress while trying to process dreadful news, means a heart shattering into a thousand pieces. She has lost her first-born child. Caring individuals move to comfort Mrs. Reid. The body resting beyond the double doors has to wait a little longer for his mother; she needs to compose herself and be courageous, and that may take some time.

Fortunately, Franklyn's father arrives. Thoughts of the unimaginable, clouded with Pam's words, "He's not breathing," are confirmed on seeing his sobbing wife and father-in-law. He finally understands the dread and depression he has been feeling, as he absorbs the terrible reality of losing a son. He approaches his wife as she is assisted to a chair. Their eyes meet as despair casts a dark, chilling shadow. This is the worst day of their lives. Words cannot interrupt crying, only arms wrapped around each other can bring relief. A three-way hug engulfs the couple and grandfather.

Life's pattern suggests parents should never outlive their children, but on this day, the pattern is reversed. The doctors approach Franklyn's mother and father, offering condolences with humbling words.

"We did everything we could to save your son's life."

It must be heart-wrenching for them to utter those words, knowing they are the terms of surrender in life's battle with death. Franklyn's parents are grateful that attempts were made to save their son. That is all anyone can ask from medical personnel.

The doctor adds, "If Franklyn's life was spared, he would be in a vegetative state based on the type of injury."

Curious to know why, the parents' memories are seared with the answer: "He was shot in the back."

ACT I SCENE VI

——

INVESTIGATION

New Milford police patiently wait to relinquish control of the scene. The immediate hours following an incident like a shooting are considered crucial to gathering evidence, avoid contamination, and to speak with people of interest. Eighteen minutes after Franklyn is pronounced dead, Inspector John Pudlinski, of the state Criminal Justice Division, arrives at the Sunoco station. He looks around and sees medical equipment scattered on an embankment, surrounded by leaves, and presumes that's where the incident occurred. *How can I protect that area and keep it dry?*

Coincidently, a blue tarpaulin brought to the scene by the New Milford department is exactly what he needs.

"I'm going to use your tarp," he tells the officers standing nearby. Pudlinski covers the items and exposed area from imminent rain.

An hour later, the Western Major Crime Squad, led by Sergeant Warren Hyatt, arrives at Sunoco. His team assumes authority. Officer Cramer meets Hyatt and advises him that the wounded suspect, Franklyn Reid, has died but it's still unclear what led to the suspect being shot.

"The involved officer, Scott Smith, was taken to headquarters."

"Okay. Process the scene," Hyatt instructs his men.

Hyatt relocates to Sweeney's department at 2:15 p.m. with squad member Trooper James Lynch (no relation to New Milford's Officer Lynch), and a contingent of investigators.

Chief Sweeney informs Sergeant Hyatt that Smith requested counsel and was taken to Moots Pellegrini Spillane & Mannion. Hyatt's request to use a phone to contact the law firm is interrupted by Captain Norbert Lillis.

"Can you swing by my office?" Captain Lillis asks Hyatt and Lynch. "I would like to transfer Smith's weapon." He had previously retrieved it from the detective bureau.

"Very well," Hyatt says.

Chief Sweeney follows the men to Captain Lillis's office.

"I understand the functionality of the 9mm Heckler & Koch semi-automatic," Lillis says. "If you prefer, I can unload it."

"Sure," Lynch replies, welcoming the gesture.

Due to its unique operation, very few police departments nationwide permit their officers to use this type of pistol.

"The pistol's safety mechanism is incorporated within the handgrip and must be squeezed to fire the pistol," Lillis explains. "The magazine contains eight cartridges of ammunition," he notes while carefully removing the clip.

Captain Lillis pulls back the slide of the pistol; the eighth cartridge in the chamber ejects out, landing on his desk.

"I'll perform a final check," Lillis states before handing it over to Lynch who also reexamines the weapon.

"I have a shell, brought in earlier from the scene which requires verification. Let's take a look at it," Lillis says.

Eyeing the shell, Lillis can't believe what he sees. Hyatt and Sweeney stare, too. The rear portion of the shell face is covered with a heavy smear of black powdery residue, preventing him from reading the engraved writing.

"In all the years of observing hundreds of spent cartridges from these pistols, I have never seen this black residue before," Lillis states.

He sweeps his right index finger across the rear face of the cartridge, revealing FC (Federal Cartridge) 9mm, which confirms it is officially issued by the department.

Lynch takes the items and places them in secure bags. He also requests the Dictaphone tape used by dispatch. He is directed toward the apparatus that records police channels and select telephone lines while Hyatt calls the law firm.

Attorney Thomas Allingham gets on the line. "I will be representing Scott Smith."

"Very well. May I interview your client?" Hyatt asks.

"No! Smith is very upset. So distraught, he got sick to his stomach in my office," Allingham says.

Hyatt is keenly aware of the forty-eight hours allotted to officers before they have to give a statement after an incident. He defers his request.

"Okay. May I perform a gunshot residue test to confirm Smith did, in fact, fire his weapon?" Hyatt asks.

Allingham balks. "My client admits he pulled the trigger. But I will not consent to Officer Smith being interviewed or submitting to a gunshot residue test, and I don't want any contact between my client and state police."

Allingham's hardball stance blocks Hyatt's voluntary approach. The lack of cooperation puts Hyatt in a predicament as he mulls over a difficult decision.

* * *

Back at the hospital, the state police assume leadership and restrict access to Franklyn's body.

Franklyn's parents now share a common bond with others also struck by overwhelming grief in a hospital, distress the body can barely endure: crying, stress, puffy eyes, and shaky knees, and an overwhelming feeling of powerlessness that cripples control. The ER is famous for unleashing this weakness, even to those who consider themselves invincible in the face of intense emotions.

As part of the investigation, the parents have the daunting task of identifying their son. The door once guarded by New Milford police and now in control of investigators, swings open, inviting the living to view the dead. Franklyn's parents see their son for the first time. There is beloved but troubled Franklyn. Their bare-chested son seems to be resting peacefully, though tubes still stick out of him. His mother feels the urge to yell, "Mark, wake up," as loud as she can, hoping her voice will force him to turn around from his one-way journey.

Instead, someone asks, "Is that your son, Franklyn Reid?"

"That's our son, Franklyn Reid," she whispers.

A second bout of emotional collapse grips the parents. They falter and cannot leave the room under their own accord. The day's shocking events have taken their toll. State police assist the Jamaican immigrants toward the waiting room. Keenly aware that the couple is in no condition to drive, compassion warrants graciousness.

"Can we offer you a ride home, Mr. and Mrs. Reid?"

Fortunately, Dwight's boss, Peter, arrives just in time and hears the question.

"I'll take them home, sir," he says.

Dwight nods his head.

Goodness dwells within the human spirit. Here is an example of its power to unite us—sharing our burdens, lifting us up through presence, kind words, and gestures. Other friends step up and drive Dwight's and Pearlylyn's vehicles to their home. Pam had decided to avoid the hospital and spends time with her kids at a friend's place. She will make her way back to the Reids' residence shortly.

* * *

The events that brought forth death and raw emotions have passed, replaced now with questions seeking answers. Police keep the peace while reporters scatter around town.

Sergeant Hyatt and Trooper Lynch meet State Police Sergeant Wagner at the hospital.

"Mr. and Mrs. Reid positively identified their son at 2:30 p.m.," Wagner says.

The three officers enter Franklyn's room at 3:18 p.m. He greets them the same way he greeted his parents, lying face up without a visible entry or exit wound from a bullet. Hyatt lifts Franklyn's right shoulder and observes what appears to be an entry bullet wound located in the upper back area of the spine. Five minutes later at 3:23, the officers exit.

Some people have journeyed into death and returned to share their experiences. They claim to have seen loved ones that have passed, bright lights, and an unconditionally loving figure of a higher power. If welcomed with open arms, their journey continues; if not, they are sent back to their bodies and the living. In those instances, Life holds temporary victories over Death. But in most cases, the human spirit departs Earth and the body withers away.

Trooper Lynch returns to Franklyn's room with fellow officers around 4:00 p.m., this time to collect evidence. He removes upper garments (three layers of shirts), lower garments (boxers, sweatpants, and blue jeans), and boots, then performs a gunshot residue test. Investigators have a small window to perform such a test for effective results. At this point, other evidence recovered from the scene includes a Pennsylvania driver's license; a red, white, and blue nylon jacket, and medical equipment. All will be sent to the State Police Forensic Laboratory in Farmington for analysis.

The investigators' focus on Smith has not diminished.

After spending a few hours with his lawyer, the officer goes to his home in New Milford, changes clothes, and eventually goes to his parents' house in Newtown, Connecticut. A day of reflection seems to occupy the rookie while the investigation continues.

Hyatt has an additional conversation with Attorney Allingham, but no breakthrough in cooperation is forthcoming. Hyatt is forced to make a difficult decision. He requests a warrant be issued for the seizure of certain items belonging to Smith and to perform a gunshot residue test on the officer's hands. The legal process takes time; by law, a judge's signature is required for the warrant to be issued.

Meanwhile, the police department's fear of violent protests in the greater community does not materialize. No businesses are looted or ransacked. Property is not damaged. Defacing of public buildings is not reported. Small business owners, the backbone of the local economy, don't close their doors early or take it upon themselves to stand guard as night descends. The fact that the gun of a white police officer has killed a young black man does not produce an uncontrollable public outrage. Instead, the freedom to congregate and express feelings in a peaceful manner controls emotions.

Though the worst fears of the police department do not manifest, the streets are crowded with satellite news trucks, and reporters vie with each other for interviews and reactions. The breaking news becomes the lead story, placing New Milford squarely in the spotlight. News travels fast, especially in a small town. As night falls, parents must figure out how to explain to their kids what happened that morning.

News Channel 8's Leon Collins scores an interview with Pamela which, along with some words from Mrs. Reid, will be broadcast later that night. After the police department informs the media that Franklyn had outstanding warrants, reporters start combing through the young man's history.

A flood of people flows through the Reid house while reporters wait outside. Loving friends offer condolences. Support surrounds both families. Though Scott Smith chooses not to share what happened, his family learns of his encounter with Franklyn from the television. One can only wonder about Mrs. Smith's emotions at that moment.

And among the Reid family, there is one blissfully ignorant member who has yet to be told.

ACT I SCENE VII

——————

A HOLLOW TUNNEL

"Where should we go for dinner?" I ask my teammates after a long day of wrestling. By majority rule, the Roadhouse Restaurant is selected. Dinner is all smiles and laughs, reminiscing about the day's activities and planning for the rest of the night. We arrive back at the hotel around 9:00 p.m. As if we hadn't competed enough during the day, we start to wrestle, professional style. It starts as a free-for-all between Matt, Lynch, Owen, Nate, and Ben, but ends with everyone against me.

"All right, let's take a break before dinner makes an early exit," I say.

Suddenly, the room empties and becomes eerily quiet. I turn around. A female cousin of mine who lives in the Fort Lauderdale area stands in the doorway. My teammates have relocated to the balcony.

"Hi, Wayne, how are you doing?" she asks.

"I'm fine. Just a long day of wrestling,"

Looking bewildered, she asks, "Have you spoken with your parents today?"

"No, not today. Why?"

"Well..." She takes three deep breaths as if trying to steel herself to continue. "I don't want to say anything, but the Lord is guiding me to tell you."

A sudden sense of dread rushes through my body.

"Something happened in New Milford." Her eyes tear up. "Something happened to Mark. He's...he's dead."

"Huh, come on, that's not funny, ha-ha-ha, a funny joke," I reply with a chuckle.

"Lord, give me the strength." She bellows out, "Mark was killed this morning."

"I don't believe you. I'm going to call home."

Reaching for the hotel phone, my hand trembles. I clench my right fist a few seconds to ease the shaking in order to dial my number. The phone rings. No one picks up. I try again, growing anxious as time ticks by. I try a third time, and my mother answers in a faint, tired voice.

"Hi Mom, is everything okay?"

"Ahhhhh, ahhhhh, here is your father," she struggles to say.

"Hi, Dad, is Mark okay?"

"Everything is fine." His voice is shaky. "You are in Florida wrestling, and we don't want to worry you."

I sense something is drastically wrong by his tone and demand answers.

"Worry me with what? Where is Mark?"

"Oh, God, oh, God Almighty...they killed him...dem kill him dead today," his broken words reveal.

I suddenly feel as if I'm asleep in a hollow tunnel, having a terrible nightmare. But I am awake, frozen in time, with the phone at my ear. I can't decipher the numerous thoughts flooding my mind. My grip loosens around the handset, the ground breaks its fall. I hear, "Wayne, Wayne, Wayne," from the phone. Instantly, the room appears small as if I'm trapped in a confined space with the walls merging together. Needing air and space to breathe, I dash away from reality.

* * *

In a flash, I'm sitting alone on the beach, staring beyond the horizon atop a dark ocean. Racing through memories, my mind is in overdrive, seeing glimpses of times Franklyn and I were together. "Hold on tight, Wayne, and don't let go," Franklyn yelled, as he steered our homemade go-cart, going wicked fast downhill in Jamaica. Without a care in the world, fearless. There I was, five years old, holding the wooden seat, knowing my safety rested in my brother's hands. Fast forward to the summer of 1998, the countless hours we spent at Nautilus Gym. We each had the competitive spirit. Franklyn tried to outperform me, but I was always a step ahead. Pamela smiled from the elliptical, knowing Franklyn was struggling to keep up with his little brother.

"You may be stronger than me but I bet I can out-wrestle the wrestler," Franklyn said.

"You're on!" I said. "Wait until we get back to the house."

An hour later, we were grappling in the basement. Most of the action started on a small couch, but ended on the ceramic tile floor. Clothesline, body slams, front headlock, a tight waist to a half nelson proved big brother was no match for little brother.

"Okay, okay, you win! Until we meet again," Franklyn said.

Lost in space and mind, a familiar voice interrupts the flashbacks. "Are you okay, Wayno? We're here for you."

The images of the past fade as the present reemerges. My teammates—Nate, Matt, and Joe—are sitting beside me. Recanting the memories aloud, the emotional toll becomes unbearable and tears flow. I am not the type to show emotion in public, but surrounded by close friends, I can't help it.

"Why did this happen to Franklyn?" I say, searching for answers that reside in New Milford. "I can't imagine what my parents are going through, and I'm too far away to offer comfort!"

A brief period of emotional weakness clouds my mind as questions mount with no available answers. The thought of throwing myself into the ocean quickly passes, but in the heat of the moment, I rip the cross and chain from around my neck and throw it as far as I can into the dark abyss. Symbolically, I'm looking for someone to blame; but instantly, I realize my impulsive action is wrong and unworthy in the eyes of the Lord. *Forgive me, Father, for I know not what I am doing.* That quick moment of reflection adjusts my thoughts to focus on a reality without my brother. If only I could dive into the ocean and retrieve my belongings, but darkness rules the night, wielding its power to shroud the sea.

While my coach is busy looking for a last-minute flight, Connecticut news stations report available information late into the night.

"A police arrest in New Milford turns deadly," says Channel 8 Kristen Cusato with their lead story.

News junkies or anyone watching the program in hopes of learning what transpired are greeted with: "Police aren't saying too much about why a motorist was shot and killed during an arrest attempt. Franklyn Reid was shot during a struggle with police today in New Milford, just after eleven this morning. Police say Reid tried to escape from officers."

Leon Collins reports the most up-to-date information from the entrance of the police department, holding a large blue and white News 8 umbrella.

"New Milford police would not go on camera tonight. They did say in a news release earlier today that twenty-seven-year-old Franklyn Reid did have outstanding warrants. However, New Milford police would not go into the details of Reid's fatal shooting."

A portion of the interview conducted earlier with Pamela airs with the caption: Victim's Girlfriend. She looks like a broken woman, standing with two friends.

"I tried to go to him and, umm, wanted him to get a hold of me...comfort him...and they wouldn't let me," she said, beginning to cry.

A second interview clip airs, conducted with State Police

Lt. Ralph Carpenter, dressed in his uniform, and wearing his traditional state police hat covered with a rain cap.

"There was a brief struggle that occurred. During that struggle, one round was discharged from the officer's weapon. It struck the subject, and the subject was transported to New Milford Hospital where he was pronounced deceased."

Mr. Collins adds commentary. "Franklyn Reid's mother said that a doctor here at New Milford Hospital seemed to have information that conflicted with the police account of the incident. She said the doctor told her that her son had been shot in the back."

Those tuning in for additional information are left wondering what really happened on the streets of New Milford.

"You know, this investigation is not over, Kristin," Collins concludes. "And it will be really interesting to see exactly what the facts are—the finer points, the details—to see if it was justified."

The day that changed so many lives approaches its end. Silence settles throughout the community, as most people sleep peacefully. But investigators are on the move. They have issued a public bulletin for anyone who witnessed the incident to step forward. The hunt for Scott Smith continues, this time with a signed warrant in hand. Sergeant Hyatt calls the department inquiring about his whereabouts, but gets little information. He calls Attorney Allingham who doesn't know where his client is. The next viable option is to surrender the night to printing presses and wait until the sun rises on a new day. Who knows what the mood of the community may be?

ACT I SCENE VIII

AUTOPSY

Newspapers' headlines scream in large and bold type. While the officer's identity remains unknown, some print media have crowded their pages with Franklyn's criminal history. Logic suggests the department's timely release of that information is to paint a negative image of the dead man, to demonize him so a public media crucifixion will precede the sainthood of one of their own. Too often, it's the method of swaying public perception to catapult support for the officer. Accuracy of such information is inconsequential; people will be hearing about Franklyn for the first time. A *News-Times* article headline reads "Dead Man Had Long Arrest Record." The story describes a "struggle with police" and adds, "Reid has been charged with second-degree sexual assault, first-degree assault, unemployment fraud, interfering and resisting, and possessing weapons in a motor vehicle."

Others in print media focus on the incident itself. Some

pick up on Leon Collin's reporting that a doctor told Mrs. Reid her son was shot in the back. Reporters seek corroboration, but those holding answers are mum since it's an ongoing investigation. The public's curious appetite may demand satiation, but time is needed to sort through details. It's the steadier side of releasing information: verify and ensure facts can be supported with evidence and documents. Although people tend to believe initial reports, some reserve their judgment until additional details are disclosed.

As awareness reaches a greater audience and reactions pour in, Dr. Wayne Carver II, Connecticut's chief medical examiner, receives Franklyn's naked body. The postmortem examination of the five-foot-four, unclothed body, weighing 129 pounds, begins at 10:18 a.m. on December 30, in the presence of Detective Nicholas Sabetta and Trooper James Lynch from the State Police.

Carver describes the body as "a well-developed, well-nourished, black male whose overall appearance is consistent with the reported age of twenty-seven years." He identifies three white-metal, pierced, stud-style earrings with clear stones—one in the right ear, two in the left earlobe—and a black, plastic watch on the dead man's left wrist. His head is covered with short, tightly curled black hair, eyes are brown, and corneas are clear with pupils in mid-position and equal. Good teeth, the stubble of a short, goatee-style beard and mustache. "An unremarkable nose," according to the doctor, completes the facial description.

Franklyn arrived unclothed and instruments used by the

hospital team remain attached. The endotracheal tube sits in the right corner of the mouth, and the vascular catheters remain in both jugular veins. "The neck is otherwise unremarkable," Dr. Carver states. The intravascular catheters attached to small cavities in the elbow joints were inserted into three main veins that provided easy access through the skin. No other needle puncture marks or needle track marks are noted. Fingernails are of moderate length, clean and show no evidence of acute injury or foreign material. The back of the body shows a moderately intense dependent pattern of purple discoloration of the skin known as liver mortis, which occurs as the blood settles after death. There is a linear abrasion on the right side of the forehead extending relatively straight toward the right temple, a total of two-and-a-half inches in length.

Dr. Carver notes a gunshot wound in the center of the back gapes through the thick skin and tissue. He describes it as a round hole, seven-sixteenths inches in diameter, surrounded by interrupted and irregular abrasion. Soot is easily visualized on the walls of the wound cavity. He removes the wound for additional examination. The effect of a bullet entering a body ravages the inside, causing extensive organ damage.

Subsequent dissection of Franklyn suggests the bullet passed from back to front, slightly left to right and slightly downwards. It traversed through the body at the first vertebra, causing complete separation of the spinal cord, and entered the right chest cavity where it caused a contusion of the left lung and a gouging laceration of the right lung. The wound tract passes between the two carotid arteries and posterior to the esophagus. There is fracture of the tracheal cartilages at this level, but no perforation of mucosa of the airway. The wound tract caused transection of a portion of the right subclavian vein, but did not do demonstrable injury to any of the major arteries in this area. The wound tract ends in the superior portion of the right pectoral muscle at a point fourteen inches from the top of the head. Within this muscle area, a partially copper-jacketed projectile and a single fragment of projectile is recovered. The base of the main portion of the bullet is inscribed "W-532."

Dr. Carver opens the torso for further examination with a Y-shaped incision. He consistently uses the term "grossly remarkable" in describing Franklyn's interior system. Additional specimens are sent for toxicology analysis. More than three hours later, the postmortem examination concludes at 1:29 p.m.

As the autopsy concludes, Scott Smith surrenders to the Western Major Crime Squad Division in Litchfield. State Police Sergeant Lucien St. Germaine meets the officer and Attorney Allingham in the Western District Intelligence Office to execute the search warrant and perform a gunshot residue test. Hopes of finding gunshot residue are bleak based on the time-lapse of approximately twenty-six hours since the shooting, but the test is required. The warrant specifies Smith's gun holster, brown jacket, and blue jeans are to be seized, but they are not readily available. The three men, along with State Troopers DeCesare and Carr, travel to Smith's residence in New Milford. The warrant is executed and Smith also voluntarily turns over a brown knit sweater, brown belt, and a pair of brown Timberland boots, all worn at the time of shooting.

"The boots, sweater, and belt are not in the search warrant, and they cannot be seized without consent," says Sergeant Germaine, advising Attorney Allingham.

"I have no problem turning these items over," Allingham replies.

Smith offers to turn over a pair of green wool socks he was wearing, but they are at a residence in Newtown, and the men travel to get them. All evidence collected will be turned over to the State Police Forensic Laboratory. Fulfilling his legal obligations, Smith returns to Allingham's law firm as they huddle up with other lawyers to craft the officer's affidavit of what transpired.

Connecticut is one of a few states that do not have an independent grand jury to investigate police-related shootings; oftentimes that review falls within the state attorney's office. This lack of impartiality could compromise the process. Litchfield County State's Attorney Frank Maco knows the spotlight will be bright, and in order to avoid what could appear as a conflict of interest, he recuses himself and his office. This action paves the way for an outsider and "eliminates any attack upon the investigation at its inception." Although it would be the first time an officer has killed someone in his judicial district since taking the helm in 1988, the decision is aided by the fact that the New Milford Police Department has brought their cases to his office and the two have worked together for numerous years. In view of such a relationship, credibility could plague an investigation. He requests that the Chief State's Attorney utilize a prosecutor from another judicial district to "preserve a public perception of impartiality" or appoint a special prosecutor. John Bailey chooses the latter by appointing Waterbury State Attorney John Connelly.

A CHAMPION PROSECUTOR

A native of Waterbury, Connecticut, John Connelly joined the US Navy after high school, serving four years before being honorably discharged. He subsequently enrolled in a community college and earned an associates of science degree. Due to extreme merit, he went on to the prestigious Trinity College, in Hartford, to major in political science. In 1978, he earned his juris doctorate degree from the University of Connecticut School of Law. His first job was as legal adviser to the Waterbury Police Department. Connelly worked there for two years until appointed the assistant state's attorney for Waterbury. In 1983, his talent quickly reached the federal level when appointed as assistant United States attorney for Connecticut. In 1984, he returned home to serve as Waterbury state attorney. About half of Connecticut's death row inmates are there because of him.

The hard-nosed prosecutor wastes no time in accepting

the role to review a police-involved shooting. He quickly makes his presence known by visiting New Milford one day after the incident.

Reporters clamor around Connelly for answers.

"Attorney, can you confirm or deny that Franklyn Reid was shot in the back?" a reporter shouts.

"No comment," Connelly says.

Visiting Dr. Carver's office for a meeting, reporters again bombard him, only to be greeted with "no comments at this moment."

* * *

I land at the Wilkes-Barre/Scranton International Airport in Pennsylvania after spending hours reflecting during my flight from Florida. Two-and-a-half hours later, I finally arrive in New Milford. It's hard to comprehend that my brother is dead. Maybe he's temporarily sleeping, and when I see him, he will awake. Maybe this is a well-devised prank and we'll have great laughs when I get home. Or maybe, he is gone and this could be a turning point for something different.

I'm not sure where to channel my focus but preparation for a funeral is going to be top priority. It's life's way of helping us to say our final goodbye. I contemplate how that farewell could be impermanent, yet it acts as closure for many people. Some believe that "the end is the end," others find comfort in an anticipated spiritual reunion. It's a double-edged sword, sharpened with torment or acceptance. And no one can tell anyone else when to move on; this decision must come from within oneself. Surely, guidance from loving people can prove beneficial, but the ultimate catalyst resides in one's heart. I choose to assist others in healing their pain; and in time, my own closure will naturally occur. But since my brother's death is so, so fresh, these thoughts of moving beyond grief are premature.

Traveling north on Route 202 in my white Nissan Maxima, everything seems normal and quiet. Branches appear brittle but the chill in the air is refreshing, perhaps signifying the stench of death is fading. The commotion has passed, but a cloud of uncertainty dwells over the town. When I pass the actual scene, I see that a makeshift memorial occupies the leafy embankment, neatly decorated with a white cross, surrounded with beautiful flowers. It offers a timeless moment to slow down and visualize how lives changed at that location. I don't stop.

After reaching home, I park on the road since vehicles fill our small driveway. My parents are sitting in the dining room along with Peter (Dad's boss), his wife, and Marcus (Dad's coworker). Both Peter and Marcus offered to pick me up from the airport, but since I had my car, I'd graciously declined their kind gesture. I walk through the kitchen and everyone stands up. Looking at my parents, I could cry uncontrollably, but I don't. I have to mask my emotions.

Instinctively, my first thought...I want a drink. I drop my bags and hug Dad who is drinking Jamaican rum punch. He and I always indulge in a few drinks together, but this time feels different. Like most college students, I became a social drinker which increased my tolerance level. I embrace Mom who looks tired, but since they have guests, she doesn't want to sleep. The next few moments turn into a hug fest with Peter, his wife, and Marcus, as "my condolences for your loss" reverberates. Mom excuses herself, picks up my bags, and takes them down the hall to my room.

"Can I get you something?" Dad asks.

"A beer," I say.

He reaches in the fridge and grabs a Budweiser, which I open and chug. Less than thirty seconds later, the can is empty. I grab another and repeat, this time with a loud and long belch. I grab a third and chug halfway. For a few seconds I forget eyes are looking at me; but no one says anything. They just stare. Could alcohol become my grieving outlet? Mom rejoins the group; Dad continues small talk with his friends. While standing in the kitchen sipping my beer and listening, reality finally hits home. I grab a fourth beer.

Most children have special bonds with their mothers because of extraordinary past events or their unwavering love. (Though the same can also be said of fathers.) I look at Mom and think, *if it wasn't for you, I wouldn't be here today*.

One night, when I was four, my parents, friends, and I were walking home from our grocery store in Jamaica. I was lagging behind when suddenly a car flew around the corner. Everyone jumped out of the road. But I stood in the middle, frozen as the headlights approached me. Mom is not a fast runner but angels must have given her wings that night. She dashed toward me and a split second later, the car hit both of us. I was thrown down a ten-foot gully, landed on my head, and lost my two front baby teeth. Mom took the brunt of the hit and broke her right thigh in half.

Naturally, I want to support her during this traumatic time. There's something I know I have to get her to do.

"Let's take a walk to the site," I say.

"No, I'm not ready yet," Mom says.

"Well, we have to drive by that area whenever we leave the house unless you take the back roads."

"I would rather take an alternate route," she says.

"We both know that's inconvenient, especially since you like driving on the main road."

"Okay, my son," she answers, forever brave. "You're correct. Let's go."

Sometimes the best comfort is silence. Our few minutes' walk highlights that fact.

Arriving at the site, I quickly realize the incident took place in clear view of anyone curious to catch a glimpse. We gaze at the makeshift memorial, complete with leaves stained with tiny specks of blood. I feel an urge to know what happened as I step back toward Park Lane Road, away from my mother, for a complete view of the area. Witnessing her broken heart as she stares down on the spot, rips open mine. *Will this moment ease her burden or prolong her farewell?* I suspect closure is nowhere on her horizon but her inner strength is much in demand for dealing with the catastrophic shredding of the fabric of her family, as well as the forthcoming investigation.

* * *

After conferring with Carver on post-autopsy results, Connelly meets with reporters.

"I can confirm that Dr. Carver said the victim was shot in the back. It doesn't appear he had a weapon," Connelly says.

That news puts the department in absolute decision mode. Rather than waiting for the fallout to drip, drip, drip until the identity of the officer is revealed, images of Scott Smith, the face behind the shooting, are broadcast on television. The repercussion for such a revelation could usher in a period of unrest. A black man shot in the back by a white police officer is a recipe for revolt in the community—a call for justice that demands immediate action. A generation of young people could swarm the streets and use the incident as an opportunity to plea for change.

But just as the New Milford air is cool, so is the temperature of public reaction. The department played its cards right when they released Franklyn's criminal history. It was an attempt to get ahead of the story and win over public opinion. They effectively force-fed their beliefs to the media who ate it up and delivered it to countless others. Indirectly, they tamped down desires for public gatherings. However, the department is not immune from negative publicity, as seen through headlines such as, "New Milford Police Plagued by List of Recent Misfortunes," and "Killing Puts New Milford Police Department Under Fire." The mounting criticism, coupled with Connelly's confirmation, deepen curiosity about what really occurred in New Milford. Reporters seek answers and citizens express their thoughts. The National Association for the Advancement of

Colored People (NAACP) Chapter in Danbury, Connecticut, becomes inundated with telephone calls as discussions become tailored around the use of excessive force.

"The killing was unnecessary," Fran Smith, a New Milford resident and local black historian, says.

Others comment that officers are in the right to clean up lowlifes, like Franklyn, from the streets.

Lines slowly divide communities as the calendar page flips to 1999. The futures of two young men seemed bright, but they robbed each other of their destinies. Franklyn had planned to surrender in the new year; Smith's aspiration was to join the State Police. The department wants to put 1998 behind them and return to normalcy, but life's directional path appears to have alternative plans. The state of Connecticut lays the groundwork while the media spotlights the shooting, and countless others learn of it. Scott and Franklyn didn't ask for the public's eyes to be upon them, but they are. Could the situation have been avoided or was it a tragedy destined to happen?

TRYING NOT TO DROWN IN THE CRIMINAL JUSTICE SYSTEM

The eighties ushered in a tide of new beginnings, placing hip-hop music in the mainstream. Rappers exploded on the scene, bringing a new form of music to high school and college kids. Big, outrageous hairstyles rode the wave as youngsters swerved and grooved with the latest fashions and styles. It wasn't a black community thing; it was an *all* community thing that swept across the country. Kids wanted to be seen and heard by their peers; not for attention, but to indulge in a cultural phenomenon that identified their generation. Tinted windows and low-riding cars playing loud music were a couple of the "in" things that excited some and repulsed others.

Franklyn and his friends embraced that trend, especially when hanging out at Young's Field. His car windows were tinted; he had extra speakers in the trunk, ensuring his slow jams were heard. He Jheri curled his hair, a popular type of hairstyle with young minority men. The long, soft, wavy hair appeared greasy to some, but that didn't diminish Franklyn's boyish looks. He found love that sung wedding bells and got married at the age of eighteen. The honeymoon period didn't last long; a year later, divorce sung another tune that belted out irreconcilable differences. I recall it being a case of young lovebirds fading out of love. Franklyn was back on the market.

His troubles compounded in the early nineties as new relationships traversed uncharted territories with arguments and domestic disputes. When the conflicts couldn't be resolved, call the cops. If someone felt threatened, call the cops. If someone felt angry, harassed, or felt emotional pain had been caused, call the cops. With his run-ins with the department mounting, Franklyn had officially become a target for police scrutiny. There is nothing to gain in sugar-coating his history. Some arrests were due to his own poor choices or bad decisions; others were exaggerated to substantiate the artificial labels. The incidents escalated between 1990 and 1994, the college years of Scott Smith.

On October 29, 1992, Franklyn was pulled over by Officer Hoag for driving a Honda Accord with a suspended license. Hoag stated that a brief struggle occurred. Franklyn was arrested, and charged with driving with a suspended license and interfering with a police officer. Four days later, on November 2, 1992, Officer Kaminski spotted the same vehicle. He thought the tinted windows appeared much darker than allowable by Connecticut law. He tailed the vehicle to a residence Franklyn was visiting and informed him that the tint was over the legal limit. Franklyn stated that the Department of Motor Vehicles provided validation the tint was in compliance, though that validation wasn't in his possession. Kaminski called for backup and decided to arrest Franklyn for driving without a license. The officer stated Franklyn initially resisted arrest but eventually was handcuffed. Kaminski searched the car without a warrant and found a steak knife that Franklyn stated was used to splice speaker wires. He was charged for the weapon in the motor vehicle, criminal mischief, and interfering with an officer.

The litany of motor vehicle stops grew. An arrest for floor display lights was added. Franklyn fell into a trap that countless others are accustomed to—repeated court visits and ballooning legal fees. As part of a plea bargain at a December 1992 court appearance, he received a suspended sentence and placed on probation with all counts dismissed.

Commenting for the record, his lawyer stated that the root cause of Franklyn's run-ins with the law may have been a minority going up against a large majority in terms of law enforcement in a predominantly white community.

"I'm sure the court is wondering where this comes from, and it doesn't appear to be from substance abuse or the usual psychiatric kind of issues we see in this court, but really from more of a social issue, and to that extent I sympathize with Mr. Reid's position," Public Defender

Douglas Ovian stated. "At the same time, the fact is that he is fulfilling the prejudices he saw other people acting on by becoming a convicted person in his community."

Franklyn felt he was being singled out and profiled, leading to frustration that was unleashed when interacting with certain members of the department.

While working for Union Carbide and Manpower temporary services, he filed for fourteen weeks of unemployment benefits, receiving a total of $1,184 in compensation at the end of 1991. He was arrested on warrant, pled guilty, and repaid the amount in 1993.

Complaints stemming from arguments paved the way for further arrests. This time there were charges for him being threatening. New Milford had a small minority population that may have led to several race confrontations. However, no one died as a result of alleged words swirling back and forth. In some communities, ordinary people resolved these discrepancies by shooting at each other. In New Milford, the police department dealt with the situations through written statements from both sides and issued warrants. In fact, Franklyn's side was heard in virtually all minority-on-minority confrontations. He had a temper; there is no question about that. But people with tempers live to argue another day.

An incident resulting from someone deflating his tires at Young's Field led to a family friend being stabbed with a steak knife at his grandfather's house. Franklyn was arrested and charged with assault. In the end, however, the victim appeared in court stating the stabbing was an accident, supported by a notarized statement. Although various accounts of the incident were provided to police, the fact that Franklyn had stabbed someone established him as a menace to society, giving Litchfield's State Attorney's Office the silver bullet to finally get a conviction. Some in the department felt vindicated in their negative assessment of Franklyn, and coupled with his rap sheet, he was labeled one of the most dangerous people in the community.

New Milford Police also received a complaint that Franklyn had inappropriate contact with a minor. He was arrested and charged with sexual assault. In an effort to leave his past behind once and for all, Franklyn pleaded *nolo contendere*, meaning he neither admitted nor disputed the charges of sexual assault in the third degree and assault in the second degree. After the plea, Judge Walsh spoke directly to him.

"Do you understand that once I accept your plea, you cannot change your mind between now and the time of sentencing or successfully request to withdraw your plea of *nolo contendere*? You can't do that unless I permit you to do so. And that would only happen for a very good reason, and I see no such reason now or expect one to happen in the future. But I am the only one who can allow you to withdraw your plea."

Judge Walsh accepted the plea and the court found Franklyn guilty.

Prior to his sentencing date, a violation of a protective order surfaced for which a warrant was issued and served. However, at the same time, new information about the sexual assault claim surfaced, which could have invalidated the charge about to send him to prison. A motion was filed to withdraw his plea and vacate his guilty verdict but they were denied.

On March 24, 1995, prayers were answered for those who direly sought the incarceration of an identified dangerous criminal. Joyous celebrations probably erupted in some houses as victory was claimed in the name of justice. Franklyn had acquired a new label: convicted felon bound for prison life. When a back is against the wall, people often atone for past behaviors, whether self-inflicted or as the recipient of accusations. It's time to learn a lesson and move forward. It's also an opportunity for others to continue with their lives. Franklyn fulfilled all legal obligations while being gainfully employed up until his sentencing date. His employer stated his job would still be available, but Assistant State Attorney Guy Wolf had other plans. Franklyn's life path took a new direction in 1995 when he was sentenced to five years in prison, suspended after three years.

Taking a quick detour, I want to broaden the perspective on the race situation in New Milford. Although Franklyn's experience in town appeared to be racially motivated, my experience was vastly different. The idea of prejudiced people never crossed my mind. Or I was completely unaware of it? During high school, our home on Birchwood Drive became the hangout spot. No need for an invitation for friends or strangers; they just showed up, and the police never bothered us. My wrestling career flourished, thanks to the guidance of Coaches Joe Neff, Patrick Burns, and Daryl Daniels. I appeared regularly in local newspapers. I captained the wrestling team as we crisscrossed the state, competing for New Milford's pride. During senior year in 1996, the team went undefeated, and I became the first State Open Wrestling Champion in the program's history. I saw the largest segment of the community for who they were: good, kindhearted, and accepting. It makes me proud to call New Milford home.

My older brother, Dwight Jr., wasn't around long enough to see how he would have fared. In 1992, a friend from the department advised him to leave town or he would succumb to the same treatment as Franklyn. Dwight literally packed his car and left New Milford the next day, relocating to Mount Vernon, New York.

* * *

Our mother became the outspoken member of the family. She wrote numerous letters regarding Franklyn's treatment; most fell on deaf ears. She visited every agency only to be sweet-talked with empty words, but she never gave up. She exemplified the strength of a mother, a woman who refuses to sit quietly, regardless of the obstacles life erects.

The moment a prison gate closes and you look around the man-made structure, surrounded with barbed wire and fence, you realize time is your worst enemy. Prison has ways of changing people. Some inmates occupy their time by trying to be as productive as they can. Franklyn spent his wisely, reflecting upon the past and dreaming about the future. He watered the seed of religion, planted at a young age, nurtured by Pastor Britt. It flourished while in prison. He penned his thoughts about life on the inside, acknowledged his shortcomings, and professed unconditional love for God and family through his jailhouse diaries.

The first year of incarceration proved the most challenging. The twenty-four-year-old fell into depression and loneliness, which he tried to rectify by crying away his painful sorrows. The environmental adjustment of being told when to eat, sleep, wake, shower—things taken for granted on the outside—contributed to the young man's emotional state. Inmates like Franklyn have no choice but to learn to adapt in order to survive on the inside. He endured being locked up twenty-three hours a day, relegated to one hour outside his cell. In the real world, people look forward to the weekends; in prison, they were sometimes grossly dreaded. The water was often turned off, which created a filthy problem. If your bowel said it's time to release waste, well, inmates have a choice to hold it or crap in a bag and hold that until the water is turned back on. "Prison life is rough," Franklyn wrote on countless occasions.

One night in April 1997, a fire filled the prison cells with smoke. The guards left the prisoners. Franklyn wrote, "It's like they want the smoke to kill us." Shortly after, they were taken outside to stand in freezing temperatures from 10:30 p.m. until 4:30 a.m. On returning to their cells, the guards called in additional support. Franklyn wrote the inmates were pepper-sprayed, beaten, then placed on lockdown.

"After they treated us like wild dogs, they brought us food that is colder than snow to eat." The prisoners rebelled by tossing the food in the hallways, forcing the guards to clean it up.

Conforming became the way of life. With all that time, he read the Bible six times and rekindled his relationship with Jah, the short name referencing God. He placed faith in the Lord to guide, protect, and help him grow up. One night, while sitting in his cell, he wrote:

> Where in my life did I go wrong that I am now in prison? I know my mother and father raised me good; they taught me how to love and respect others and never pay back wrongs with wrongs.

He realized the first step was admitting to past, troublesome behaviors. He was a womanizer, addicted to one of God's greatest gifts.

> Women were my weakness in life. I always like to have more than one woman. However, now that I have been free from women for so long, I can overcome my weakness. I often wonder to myself, when I get out of here, if I can find one woman who I can love, respect, and spend forever with. I believe with the help of my God, the highest, I will be able to stay with one woman.

That addiction contributed to his domestic disputes, which dragged law enforcement into the fold when he was kept away from his greatest love: his kids. Franklyn admitted he was not the best father earlier in life, but everyone experiences mistakes. He felt prison was necessary for him to become accountable for those mistakes, to learn maturity.

The primary goal of most inmates is to get out of prison a better person, by recognizing what went wrong in order to redefine the future. He participated in various programs, received certificates in Addiction Services Tier 2, Training in Nonviolence, and Self-Motivation and Achievement Realization Technique (SMART). The SMART program focuses on principles and methods for developing higher levels of self-awareness, personal achievement, and success. In February 1997, the Shiloh Church of God in Christ outreach team awarded him learning certificates for Dual Diagnosis, What it Means to be a Father, and Domestic Violence, as well as one in recognition of Black History Month.

Franklyn understood the importance of education. He studied and took the General Education Development (GED) exam, a nationally standardized test used in Connecticut since March 1967. He failed the exam by one point. Steadfast in his pursuit, Franklyn committed to continue the educational dream after prison. He did not fulfill his desire.

* * *

Meanwhile, someone else's dreams were edging closer to reality. In December 1996, Scott Smith was officially hired by the New Milford Police Department. The department's newest member was sent to the highly regarded State Police Training Academy in Meriden, Connecticut for sixteen weeks. The trainee learned the duties and responsibilities of a police officer in lessons encompassing arrest procedures, defensive tactics, firearms training, medical response, and criminal and motor vehicle laws. He returned in early 1997 and completed another twelve weeks of field training, partnering with various members to gain additional experience and essentially fulfilling the department's one-year probationary period from his date of hire. He eventually achieved another milestone by becoming a patrol officer.

* * *

Days before Franklyn's release from prison, a new battle surfaced. Those who had rejoiced after his conviction, waited patiently to hand him over to Immigration and Naturalization Services. Attorney Joseph Tapper, who represented my brother, obtained his court transcript, and noted the court did not read him his immigration rights. The result was that his freedom path remained clear. That did not sit well with Assistant State Attorney Guy Wolf who was determined to pull every possible string, at any cost, to send him back to prison. His belief was that Franklyn was a menace to society, a violent criminal who didn't deserve to roam the streets, anywhere. As such, he stacked the deck with insurmountable choices and waited.

Prison did not dampen Franklyn's spirit. He reflected upon his three years in prison. "I'm asking God the Father to help me be pure and do what is right at all times." Freedom and he were reacquainted on April 28, 1997.

In an effort to correct the court's error, on May 2 in court, Wolf presented Franklyn with two choices: fight his case and the state would add additional charges he didn't know about; or stick with the original charges he was convicted of. With limited options and no money to fight the system, my brother and mother decided to stick with the original charges. It appeared that a play was already in motion. Franklyn's *nolo contendere* plea was vacated on April 18, 1997, ten days before his release date. Although he served his time, it appeared that the Fifth Amendment forbidding people from being tried twice for the same offense took a holiday. Franklyn was read his immigration rights.

He found himself in another repetitive cycle of persistent court appearances, but this time, he elected for a jury trial. My mother continued her caring role: she attended court, spoke with people in the justice system, and documented those interactions.

An honest conversation in January 1998 revealed new twists that dramatically blurred the line of impartiality. Christine Kennedy was assigned as Franklyn's probation officer. In January 1998, she visited his home and met with my parents. A pleasant, eye-opening conversation ensued in which Miss Kennedy stated that Wolf and a second state attorney named Shepack had placed her under enormous pressure to violate Franklyn's probation at any cost; they would take care of the rest when he returned to court. My mother asked to have his probation transferred, but Miss Kennedy stated that Wolf and Shepack would not approve her request. They detested Franklyn, she said, and all Jamaicans with intense passion and direly wanted him back in prison.

Over the next three months, a spin twirled in the desired direction of those attorneys. An allegation of harassment miraculously surfaced. At a March 23, 1998 probation visit, INS agents detained Franklyn. Miss Kennedy had called immigration services. When she met with my mother again, the friendliness of the January meeting had dramatically shifted. According to my mother, Miss Kennedy was argumentative and rude, a sign someone may have coerced her into a biased position from her initial impartiality. Regardless, Franklyn was released under a Notice of Custody Determination.

"Pursuant to the authority contained in Section 236 of the Immigration and Nationality Act and part 236 of Title 8, Code of Federal Regulations, I have determined that pending a final determination by the Immigration Judge in your case, and in the event, you are ordered removed from the United States, until you are taken into custody for your removal, you shall be released under bond in the amount of $3,000."

Franklyn had to answer for those unfounded harassment allegations. At an April 1998 court appearance, the prosecution pressured Franklyn to voluntarily call INS and deport himself; in exchange all charges would be dropped.

He refused. His bond was set at $10,000 and another court appearance was scheduled.

In June, the state claimed to have tapes of him making harassment calls. He denied this but was still charged with six counts of harassment. Those tapes never surfaced, but his bond ballooned to $100,000. At a second court appearance in June, his disposed charges appeared on the docket for plea purposes with the following message: "This case was sentenced and disposed on 3/24/1995. A violation of Probation proceeding (1st) began on 5/29/1998 Committed to Department of Corrections and Probation Ordered." His bond ballooned to $150,000. My mother demanded answers, but she was ignored. It appeared the financial squeeze was in full swing to send him back to prison, but my parents bailed him out by placing our house as collateral. A probation hearing was scheduled for September.

That summer when I came home from college, Franklyn and I embraced. He gave me six notebooks and a few pieces of art. "These are my jailhouse diaries and prison drawings; you should keep them," Franklyn said. I looked at the drawings, some on handkerchiefs, and flipped through the books and knew he had patiently spent a lot of time on them. I never asked why me, but he knew our mother and I are hoarders and would never discard anything remotely important. We spent quality time together and became regular gym rats at the local fitness center as I prepared for the upcoming wrestling season. Our family could see he was working to avoid a relapse into old ways. He continued his religious journey with Pam (his girlfriend), by reading the

Bible daily. He was content restarting life over on the outside. Although his employer had promised his job would be waiting for him, Franklyn did not return. He found employment at a fabric company. Soon after I returned to college in August, activities spiked in New Milford.

In early September, Miss Kennedy was visiting a client and saw Franklyn and his girlfriend sitting in his car. A confrontation occurred and Miss Kennedy felt threatened. She immediately went to the department and filed a complaint. In her statement, she said she was alarmed Franklyn's car had stopped so close to her and blocked her path. She felt intimidated at the obscenities hurled at her. Franklyn and his girlfriend's versions differed considerably.

According to their statements, Miss Kennedy walked over to his parked car. She stuck her head in the window and the ladies hurled remarks. An unbiased eyewitness saw the commotion and corroborated Franklyn and his girlfriend's versions with a written statement, but because Miss Kennedy's words carried the power of influence, her version was sufficient.

New Milford issued a Breach of Peace/Threatening warrant with a bond of $13,500, which a judge signed on November 2, 1998. The added ammunition was in play for his September hearing, which he did not attend due to conflicting appointments. Franklyn, not the most responsible person, wasn't always timely for his scheduled appearances, and frustration with the repetitive court cycle can become intolerable for some convicted felons.

As a result, that state bond ballooned to $205,000 for

failure to appear. Allegations of threatening surfaced on October 16, 1998, which Franklyn denied, but that didn't matter. The very next day, New Milford issued a warrant for threatening, which a judge signed on October 26, 1998. That mightily quick investigation and immediately issued warrant was a head-scratcher that galvanized a concerned mother to spread the word.

For years, she recognized the bull's-eye painted on her son. She did what many other mothers would have done—she let the mighty pen do her talking. She named names of those conspiring against her son, provided detailed accounts of events that transpired in 1998, and wrote letters to Attorney General Richard Blumenthal, Senator Joseph Lieberman, Chief State Attorney John Bailey, and Litchfield State Attorney Frank Maco. The financial squeeze became overwhelming and placed my family on a path toward bankruptcy, losing everything we owned. In one letter my mother wrote:

> Mr. Blumenthal, our son did not kill anyone; he did not commit treason nor did he bomb anywhere, for his bond to be that high. You can clearly see the malice, ill-will, and vendetta everyone has against our son. We are poor, powerless, and on the verge of bankruptcy. We don't have money to hire a real criminal lawyer to fight our son's case.

In November of 1998, the bond's woman called the house regularly and said that Franklyn must turn himself in or she would begin the foreclosure process in January

1999. With his back against the wall, knowing false and embellished accusations were going to do him in again, Franklyn penned a letter to Judge Walsh dated November 19, 1998. He singled out individuals and summarized his version of how events transpired throughout the year and promised to surrender. On December 27, 1998, my mother wrote Representative James Mahoney and recapitulated the year's events. He responded on December 29, 1998, the day Franklyn died.

Dear Ms. Reid:

Thank you very much for contacting me.

As much as I would like to assist you, there is a long-standing agreement between the Connecticut Members of Congress that we will handle matters only for our own constituents and will refer others to their own representatives.

For this reason, I have referred your inquiry to your Congresswoman, Nancy Johnson. Her office should be contacting you directly, but you may want to get in touch with her district office, at 480 Myrtle Street, New Britain, Connecticut 06053. Her telephone number is...

Although I cannot be of assistance to you in this matter, I am very glad that you thought of getting in touch with me.

ACT III SCENE I

CIVIC DUTY

Life has a way of placing people in the right place at the right time. We may witness kids playing, a fight, an accident, death, property destruction, overzealous individuals, a crime, or other incident in progress. Most of the time, involved parties are unaware that anyone is watching and recording with their eyes or devices. Depending on the situation's severity, law enforcement may need to get involved to reconstruct events with the aid of evidence and impartial eyewitnesses. Often, one individual glimpses a few seconds of an incident and moves on, then another person witnesses a few more, and so forth. When eyewitnesses are placed in a room to tell their versions, ideally, a scene is collectively portrayed which either supports or discredits a statement or report.

It's one's civic duty to provide clarity and truth to a situation when varying stories exist. One statement could make a difference to the deliverance of justice. Eyewitnesses stepping forward to collaborate or explain an incident form the backbone of the judicial system. But our minds may not always allow us to do what is right or needed. We contemplate the possibility of coming forward, but the event may be so overwhelmingly traumatic that we cannot process it and decide to keep the memory locked away.

Unbeknownst to Franklyn and Officer Smith, strangers were traveling on Route 202 to their morning destinations. Some stopped at the Sunoco station, idly waiting in their vehicles, pumping gas, or busy with attendants inside the store with its large windows. Curiosity was piqued as they glimpsed two men dashing from Sunoco and across Route 202 toward an embankment. Seeing a white man chasing a black man was unusual in New Milford. The commotion virtually halted traffic as the white man drew a gun. Some assumed kids were out playing as they passed the scene—before seeing a gun. Others worried a robbery was in progress. Several thought the commotion ended, seeing the white man in control of the black man. Some wondered if an injury had occurred, seeing the black man lying on the ground and the white man standing over him, while additional people rushed to the area. Many viewed bits and pieces of the incident, the images seeping into their memories, as life had situated them in the right place at the right time for a wrong act. Sooner or later, the "how" that proceeds "did this happen" will be answered.

Scott Smith utilized his allotted forty-eight hours granted to police officers, writing and meticulously revising his statement to ensure no detail was left out. His official affidavit on how events transpired, summed up in four pages, was delivered to Waterbury State Attorney John Connelly. Statements from Sergeant Cramer and Detective Shortt taken hours after the incident accompanied that document but did not stand alone. Strangers such as Diane Swanson, Abu Nassier, Gail Meehan, Dan Merton, Chris Gardner, William Earys, Francis Roger, and Leon Angelovich, stepped forward to share memories of what they saw. A four-year-old amongst other unnamed eyewitnesses also shared his visual recollection with investigators. Their statements, along with investigators' narratives, swell Connelly's investigative files. The initial evidence coupled with Dr. Carver's autopsy conclusion ruling Franklyn's death a homicide, appears to be pointing in one direction, but toxicology results are still pending.

Attorney Connelly is confronted with an agonizing decision that could challenge his strong core beliefs of right versus wrong. Should Officer Smith be charged with a crime? Was Mr. Reid's rights or a general statute violated? It's not a lighthearted decision to charge a police officer nor is it feasible to look the other way. The answer, written in black letters, crowds pages of white paper in front of him. The law, bound to protect its people from injustice, paves a path that leads to court. That doorway into a courtroom where a judge will become its gatekeeper can only be opened by Connelly's directive. He holds the authoritative power bestowed by Connecticut law to bring forth any charges.

The people and the media seek answers. After all, a

black man stamped with the label of criminal, was removed from society. However, isn't it also one's duty to remember he was a human being, too?

* * *

Honoring Franklyn's memory obviously occupies my thoughts. Closure will come when the ground six feet beneath the living becomes his final resting place. Pastor Britt knows the heartfelt journey the living must endure and how a funeral should proceed. He visits our home and offers suggestions in a soothing voice. The date is set for January 9, 1999. I want something as a remembrance.

Walking into Hat City, a tattoo parlor in Danbury Connecticut, I'm unsure of what to get but know it has to be traditional. Jimmy, the tattoo artist (a friend who gave me the marking of a horse in September 1997), is excited that I've returned.

"Look, I have your picture in my photo book," Jimmy says.

"There's that monster horse," I say, sharing a laugh.

"I know you came here for a reason. Remember? I said you would be back within two years?"

"Yeah, I remember."

"You're unbalanced!" Jimmy says. "People with a tattoo on one side of their body typically want another on the other side to feel balanced. Anything particular in mind?"

"I'm not sure yet. Let me flip through your books."

I look at skulls and tribal bands but nothing jumps off the page. Jimmy senses I'm having a hard time deciding.

"How about something like these daggers, cross, and hearts?" Jimmy suggests.

My eyes brighten after seeing such majestic art. I flip through pages edging closer to a decision until I find the ideal tattoo.

"This is it, Jimmy. I like the dagger that resembles a cross going through a heart."

While placing the image on my right shoulder, Jimmy realizes I live in New Milford.

"I read about a shooting there a couple days ago and someone died," Jimmy says.

"Oh, yeah."

"Have you heard anything about it?" he asks.

"Yeah, the person who died is my brother."

Jimmy stops and looks at me in shock.

"Oh man! I'm sorry to hear that! My condolences, brother."

"Thanks, I appreciate it."

"It's a sad situation all around, but I'm going to give you a piece of advice. Everyone is going to be falling apart around you. Someone has to be strong; you have to be strong."

The glint in my eyes is noticeable as those kind words transmit a warm comfort that my heart instantly embraces. I feel a connection with the man whose artwork will be a constant reminder of this moment for the rest of my life.

"I'll try to do my best," I say.

Jimmy isn't satisfied when he looks at the image.

"How about I add, 'In Memory of My' above the cross and 'Brother' through the heart?"

"That's a great idea!"

Jimmy places another image on my shoulder. The four-plus hours of needles penetrating my skin are a testament to keeping memories alive. It's a remedy others have embraced. Discomfort is temporary but the visible artwork is permanent.

I think about how Connelly could ravage emotions and unearth deep-rooted resentment. Which side will bear the brunt of his decision? No one knows, but the first thing I have to deal with is Franklyn's funeral. The media is invited. They're probably eager to record a group of minorities finally lashing out publicly against Smith and the department. When cameras are rolling, they want to show a bunch of savages acting like unintelligent fools to appease those who believe minorities typically hurt their own cause. Will their expectations be fulfilled?

SAYING GOODBYE

Before we go any further, we would like to thank all of you for your kindness, for your support, for your prayers, and for your attendance this morning, here at this worship service. We have come, first of all, to honor God and give God thanks for a life. We're keenly aware of the fact that God in the beginning created mankind and breathed into man's nostrils the breath of life. The Bible said he became a living soul.

Soulful words from Pastor George Britt as he officiates the funeral service at Northville Baptist Church.

We have come also to grieve together, to share our grievances, and to share our sorrows. The scriptures are very clear, and it says unto us, rejoice with those who rejoice, and weep with those who weep, and grieve with those who grieve. And bear ye one another's burdens so fulfill The Lord of Christ.

Family members, friends, dignitaries, and the media, have packed the house of God located on Little Bear Hill Road, a fitting location to deliver a message of peace, unity and compassion.

> We come also because we believe that the church is a place where it offers us an opportunity to come together in unity with every race, with every color, with every nationality. And God said in his word, Lord I pray that they may be one, even as we are one.

Outside, an overcast sky seemingly waits to pour tears from above as Franklyn's final journey is underway. Rain signifies cleansing, but the downpour is currently in a holding state, a command Mother Nature has delivered. The parking lot is at capacity but notably absent is law enforcement. Lillis Funeral Home alerted Sweeney that their services were not necessary today.

Franklyn's open casket is positioned in front, below the pulpit. Dressed in a black suit, both hands neatly crossed over his midsection and eyes permanently closed, the young man is surrounded with beautiful flowers and memorable photos. It's a sight we are all keenly familiar with. Some dread these moments; others celebrate a life gone to the other side. It's the last stare, touch, or delicate massage of the deceased person's cheeks and head that delivers a silent farewell. In some cultures, the living may choose to forfeit something to be buried with the dead. I had chosen to give up CK (Calvin Klein) One cologne as a parting gift.

My daily scent for two years transferred to my brother will never be worn by me again. I ensured the bottle was placed in his coffin.

Faces shuttered with sadness and tears belie hearts open to receiving glory in God's presence and his people. The sweet sound of music soothes troubled souls; some choose to sing along. Pastor Britt speaks of peace with faith.

I bring you these words: "How beautiful are the mountains of the feet of him that drinketh with tidings? The peace that brings good tidings of hope and publishes and tells the world the message of salvation. He giveth power to the faithful and to them that have no might, he increases their strength...God's grace is sufficient to carry us through every circumstance.

Mortimer Reid delivers a memorable eulogy. The eighty-seven-year-old says he collapsed after learning his grandson had died, but God gave him strength to travel from Jamaica. Wilbert Shaw brightens spirits and turns frowns into smiles by asking everyone to shake hands. For a minute, giggles and grins mask the presence of death with jubilee. But how surreal? Two grandfathers burying their grandson.

Cameras roll in anticipation the funeral will become a backdrop to unleashed, pent-up frustration or lobbed insulting remarks. In other words, minorities acting like rabid wolverines. Quite the opposite occurs. Anger is left out in the cold while love warms the hearts of those in attendance. But the police department remains on alert to swoop in if restoring order is warranted.

Six Reid boys (including three cousins), who grew up together in Maroon Town, Jamaica, carry one of our own. Passing through a gauntlet of clicking cameras, we make the final walk toward the hearse. The long procession of vehicles traveling south on Route 202 takes a quick detour onto Park Lane West to circle our home. Suddenly, raindrops fall.

The rainfall ends while mourners huddle together at Center Cemetery for closing scriptures. I recall familiar words from my grandfather's eulogy as a stark reminder that life is precious. *The Lord giveth and taketh!* My brother's casket, adorned with living red roses, descends into a moistened earth. I remain there until dirt fills his resting place.

The sound of music reverberates throughout the night at Birchwood Drive. The festivities exemplify feelings of togetherness sewn within our human spirit as people care for people. The next day those sentiments are reflected in newspaper headlines such as, "Saying Goodbye." The articles describe several hundred people coming together at a small white church, not in anger, not planning revenge, but in a celebration of life.

"We have to work together as a community," Mayor Arthur Peitler says at the funeral. "We have to give each other the tools, the love, the caring to make sure nothing like this ever happens again."

Peitler aims for unity to overshadow any perceived

division within the community. So far there have been no public demonstrations, but the press is keeping the story alive until groundbreaking news is released. It's bound to be explosive either way. But will Connelly initiate an investigation or will he jettison the decision on whether justice has been served into the court of public opinion?

ACT III SCENE III

THE CHARGE

News flash! Connelly receives a folder five days after the funeral. He quickly opens it and sees Franklyn's toxicology report. Pausing, he takes a deep breath before reviewing the results. After conferring with colleagues closely working the case, Connelly factors in the evidence and various statements before reaching an unprecedented decision. Tight-lipped and away from the media, an application for Smith's arrest is submitted to a superior court judge the next day on January 15, 1999.

Franklyn died Tuesday, December 29, and is buried on January 9. Smith is charged with murder in violation of Connecticut General Statutes Section 53a-54a on Tuesday, January 19. The court sets a bond of $250,000.

Connelly calls a press conference. Flanked by State Police and a roomful of reporters, Connelly holds up his right palm to represent Franklyn's back. His left hand forms a gun with the index finger representing the barrel and touches his right palm indicating how Scott Smith's pistol was placed against Reid's back.

"The officer intended to take the life of this person and took the life of this person," Connelly says.

By all accounts, Smith is Connecticut's first police officer charged with such an act in the line of duty.

"No simple shred of evidence brought about my decision to file the murder charge. But everything together, including Smith's own statement, indicates he was not in peril and therefore not justified in taking the life of Reid," he explains. "It's an intentional killing...I did not feel the shooting was justified."

"Do you believe Smith feared for his life?" a reporter shouts.

"I don't believe the facts and circumstances at this point in time demonstrate that," Connelly says.

"How will your decision affect law enforcement?" another reporter asks.

"Police officers have nothing to fear. At least 99.9 percent of police officers do their job properly. This will not affect their work," Connelly says.

The news unleashes accusations of betrayal and anger from some parts, praise for courage from others, and muted tongues unable to utter a reaction.

Stunned by the announcement, Chief Sweeney and Mayor Peitler hold their own press conference from the department.

"In thirty years, this is the lowest day in my career. The tragedy is complete. This was a tragedy for the Reid family,

Officer Smith, and now the New Milford Police Department," Sweeney says. "I am shocked and disappointed by the charges brought against Officer Smith. I am extremely concerned about the long-term ramifications for police officers across the state."

Peitler disagrees with Connelly regarding Smith's perception at the time of the shooting.

"He [Smith] perceived he was imperiled at that point. There are a lot of incidents in Connecticut where officers hesitated and ended up dead," the mayor remarks.

Sweeney poses an unanswered question. "If this case becomes a precedent, how will police officers safely perform their duties?"

His remarks could be the harbinger of what will galvanize support for the police force.

"How are your officers coping?" a reporter asks.

"We are telling them to believe in Scott Smith, believe in themselves, believe in their training, and believe in the system," Sweeney says. "Scott Smith should be viewed as innocent until proven guilty."

Hoping to protect the involved parties, the town, and the department, Mayor Peitler hands down a directive. Smith is suspended with no authority to act as a police officer.

Counseling is made available to members of the department. The emotional pain they are going through is no different than what my family has been experiencing. It feels like someone reached into your heart, ripped a piece out, leaving an aching void. When an incident touches those nerves, it connects like-minded people to stand up for their beliefs whether in law enforcement or not.

Attorney Allingham insists the shooting was justified and vows to vigorously fight the charge.

"My client will enter a not-guilty plea during his February 2 court appearance in Litchfield Superior Court," Allingham tells reporters.

His law firm, which lent assistance crafting Smith's version of events, staunchly supports the affidavit released to the media. But eyewitnesses are speaking out, essentially adding perspectives to a narrative by contradicting Smith's story. A community on the mend is virtually torn down the middle once again as unidentified residents react.

"Murder or self-defense?"

"Surprised he was charged with murder!"

"We don't really have all the facts!"

"Not the sort of thing you expect in New Milford!"

"It's not right to take a life!"

People freely express themselves without violence as both sides gain supporters. But the core reality, "A tragedy for all involved," is voiced by another resident.

Smith is devastated seeing his name mentioned in the same breath as the word "murder." How could a realized lifelong dream to serve and protect turn nightmarish by defensive actions? Shouldn't an officer's statement suffice as explanation and end an investigation so all can move forward? The rookie officer is perplexed to say the least. Accompanied by twenty-five colleagues, he surrenders to the State Police and immediately posts bail.

Although his lawyers are unwavering, Smith is confronted with a decision. Can Allingham play hardball as a formidable adversary capable of going head-to-head against Connecticut's top prosecutor, Connelly? Should he stick with him for representation?

Like everyone else, the news catches my family off guard. There wasn't any jumping around, no happy dance. Multiple reporters crowded our gate looking for a reaction, but they had plenty of groundbreaking information.

While watching the evening news, I think about the pending journey into uncharted territories. Trying to wrap my thoughts around "a first in Connecticut," I realize being seen in the shadows and heard from occasionally may become my role moving forward. The idea of Franklyn portraying the face of justice in one corner and Scott the face of exoneration in the other never crosses my mind. That decision rests with the state of Connecticut to do the right thing. John Connelly chose to seek answers in court, giving justice and exoneration equally deserved opportunities. Smith and Reid collided once while breathing air. Their next collision has left one without breath and the other gasping for air. In the interim, the call to action will run the gamut.

JUDAS! JUDAS! JUDAS!

A legal team shake-up has occurred. A formidable foe announces he will represent Smith before the first hearing. John J. Kelly, a former Connecticut prosecutor, now a criminal defense lawyer, has defended police officers charged with wrongdoing for over twenty-five years. Mr. Connelly and Mr. Kelly, both Irish Americans, are not strangers to each other. When Kelly was chief state's attorney in the mid-1980s, they clashed in the courtroom on several occasions. Their heated exchanges reached fever pitch when Kelly tried blocking Connelly's reappointment as Waterbury state's attorney in 1990. Although unsuccessful, both attorneys adhered to the principle of professionalism, as they had numerous times since. They don't expect personal enmity to tag along in a potentially high-profile case.

Capitalizing on Chief Sweeney's press conference message, virtually all department hands are aiding Smith. His colleagues, friends, and family, have established a defense fund since Connecticut police officers are required to foot legal expenses if charges are brought against them. Solidarity is an admirable quality. Law enforcement departments statewide receive fliers asserting:

> Police are an endangered species; let's protect the thin blue line that keeps utter chaos from taking over normal life! Officer Scott Smith, who is facing murder charges for shooting an armed felon on duty, has his first court appearance on Tuesday, 2/2/99. Anyone familiar with the case will realize that this could be any one of us.

The flier solicits donations for Smith and states that the warrant does not justify the arrest of a police officer for murder. It asks fellow brothers to gather in Litchfield on that date. Could their brazen spin display disdain toward Connelly?

Litchfield is nationally famous as one of the most beautiful residential communities in America. It is considered New England's finest surviving example of a typical late-eighteenth-century New England town. The quaint picturesque surroundings of endless trees, colonial-type structures, and mom-and-pop shops epitomize the definition of a New England suburban community. But the peace and quiet around the courthouse is about to dramatically change.

* * *

"Judas! Judas! Judas!" reverberates loudly as Connelly enters the courthouse. Thunderous "boos" accompany the cries, piercing through a heavy rainstorm outside court. A sea of umbrellas tries to withstand Mother Nature's torrents. The department's call to action amasses over one hundred and fifty police officers from across the state and beyond. Their staging area, a local inn designated as "rendezvous alley," is outfitted with makeshift tents offering coffee and donuts. Three buses and a stretch limousine transported those officers, many in uniform to the heckle zone.

Connelly is target number one, a bull's-eye for the raucous jeers. But he is not intimidated. "I hope those officers aren't 'on the clock,'" he retorts before entering the stone-walled courthouse.

Judas betrayed Jesus. That act eventually led to Jesus's crucifixion. For all intents and purposes, Connelly is similarly branded a traitor, a Benedict Arnold of police officers, for bringing charges against Scott Smith. Smith himself is excused from appearing at his own arraignment. But that doesn't dampen spirits of those present; their chants are heard inside the courtroom while proceedings are underway.

Attorney Kelly does not enter a plea. Instead, he requests a probable cause hearing. Judge Alexandra DiPentima sets the hearing for March 16, 1999, and orders Smith to appear. At that time, she will decide if the evidence supports a murder charge. Court is dismissed.

Once again, Connelly is booed by an unrelenting throng after emerging first. The media surround him.

"What is your thought about the protest?" a reporter asks.

"I am sure if the police officers and others knew the facts and understood the law, 95 percent of them would not have been here," Connelly says before boarding his caravan.

Minutes later, Kelly emerges and is showered with cheers and chants of, "We support Scott Smith." The disparagement zone is virtually transformed into an alley of praise. Standing tall, Kelly assures the gathering that he will reiterate Franklyn's violent criminal history, his attempt to grab a knife on a prior arrest, and that his telling others he would never be taken alive, played a role in his ultimate demise. Those words officially invite hearsay evidence to be presented in court.

Several minutes later, my parents, grandfather, Pamela, and I, emerge from the courthouse. Cameras click and flash, capturing our startled, grief-stricken expressions. We look out over the dispersing crowd, immediately crippled with the fear of possible intimidation. Perched on the steps, few in numbers, I know our momentary flinch may be temporary once the day's event is reported by the press and TV crews.

The demonstrators undermine confidence in the same criminal system they send countless others to, while promoting an atmosphere that police officers are above the law. There wasn't any public demonstration after Franklyn's death. My family remained on the sidelines so the process could play out—fortunately, in our favor thus far. The result: one of their own is facing criminal charges. Their response:

let's demonize the system for taking a bold stance. Their emotional reaction could galvanize a potential counter-grassroots movement. Their demonstrations continue the following day.

A second organized rally commandeers Connecticut's capitol. An official podium, suitable for important speeches, rests atop the steps looking down at approximately two hundred officers and supporters who gathered in Hartford for another solidarity showcase dubbed, "Back the Blue." The day before, Mother Nature rained unrelenting tears; this day a bright sunbeam's rays create a beautiful backdrop. The riled crowd bursts into cheers when the event's host, WZMX-FM 93.7 disc jockey Sebastian, calls Connelly a "jackass" and suggests he step down. Using his radio station pulpit as a way of promoting Smith's cause, he insults Connelly's intelligence as a prosecutor gone amuck.

"This man is trying to make a fool of you and is really trying to make a joke and mockery of the entire police force in Connecticut."

Sebastian suggests prosecutors should have police experience first; he doesn't know Connelly was once in charge of the State Police. Sebastian's tirade continues as he attempts to poison a prospective jury pool.

"I'm positive, without a shadow of a doubt, that there is no way a sensible jury can convict him [Smith] of murder."

In simple terms, gasoline is poured on a small fire which now blazes out of control with zero involvement from my family. Department members appear in uniform selling twenty dollar T-shirts for Smith's defense fund. The spectacle of draconian remarks continues. If Smith is convicted, New Milford Officer Duda tells the crowd, "the thirty thousand cops in the state of Connecticut should all turn in their badges and guns, and the governor can call in martial law, and we'll see how the public likes it." Although camaraderie brings feelings of unity, panic that a proven process might not deliver a favorable verdict cannot be dispelled. The message seeks to rebuke a criminal system by warping one isolated incident and rubber-stamping law enforcement's disapproval of the judicial process.

Although no legislators appear, Governor John Rowland voices support for Connelly and vows not to get involved.

"Clearly the officers have a right to protest. I've got a lot of faith in the judiciary system and that everybody will have their day in court," he comments hours later.

Connelly echoes Governor Rowland's comments from his office. But first, he refuses to step down. He chooses to step up for justice.

"They're sworn to uphold the law. The case is in the court system now. They should have faith in the court system—the system they ask the public to have faith in. Police officers are not above the law."

He reiterates that Smith broke the law.

"Based on the facts that we gathered, there was no way that I, as a prosecutor, could say this shooting was justified."

Personally, I have no objection to people standing up for a cause as long as all sides are fairly represented. Equal opportunity is what most would call it, but at this point, we are not experiencing equality. Why? Because one perspective wants to be seen as the only perspective: that a cop who followed Chief Sweeney's 'Philosophy of Force,' killed a criminal and is being unjustly persecuted. End of discussion!

However, recipients of that message respond, "Hold on a minute. Other viewpoints warrant discussion." Smith's public displays of support and our shocking appearances galvanize Reverend Cornell Lewis and the local NAACP chapter to react. While Connelly is ridiculed, respondents have a window of opportunity to add an opposing stance. A prayer vigil is scheduled two days before the probable cause hearing that will determine whether there is sufficient evidence to substantiate Connelly's charge against Smith.

A "Rally for Justice" temporarily spikes New Milford's minority population as the town green hosts community church leaders, activists, and over one hundred and fifty ordinary citizens. A larger-than-life gazebo unites blacks, whites, Hispanics, young and old, not to demonize law enforcement, but to highlight a troubling issue—the treatment of minorities by police officers. Candles are stuck through gold paper cups labeled with the day's theme. They are lit as a powerful reminder that prayers can mend fences by channeling human energy to identify root causes as well as help people seek common ground to discover sustainable solutions. Supporters join hands with my family, praise Connelly's decision, and vow their presence in Litchfield.

The next evening, the NAACP holds an open forum at the Danbury Public Library. Chief Sweeney joins his counterparts from Newtown, Brookfield, Bethel, and Danbury to discuss policies, procedures, and training. My dad and Pamela are in the audience as ordinary citizens voicing their concerns about racial profiling and unnecessary police stops of minorities. Personal stories wrapped in civility give credence to the First Amendment's freedom of speech.

A practical response is forthcoming from the chiefs, "We are unaware of any biases against minorities. If discovered, we vow to swiftly discipline involved officers."

Diversity within their respective departments could aid the solution, but that diversity is greatly lacking. They admit hiring minorities to work in predominantly white communities is an issue in itself. As such, their officers receive training in race relations and various equality issues intended to assist with their interactions with minorities. Although Franklyn and Scott have contributed to the current state of emotions, Sweeney cites them as part of an ongoing case he chooses not to discuss. Rightfully so; hours later, Smith will be standing before Judge DiPentima who holds the future direction of the case.

JUSTICE—EXONERATION?

Did Connelly err in judgment and rush to charge Smith? Depends on which protesters you ask outside of Litchfield's courthouse. Dueling rallies shatter the town's quiet serenity. Approximately one hundred officers gather to support Smith. Students from Western Connecticut State University and supporters of my family show their own strength in numbers.

Officer Smith, dressed in a dark suit, blue shirt, and patterned yellow necktie, glances at both rallies. His senses are bombarded with conflicting attitudes: applause on one side and chants of "No Justice, No peace," on the other. Some banners proclaim, "We support Scott Smith;" others demand "Justice for Franklyn Reid." Both sides stand together, at times disrupting each other with their side's point of view.

Inside, testimony from pivotal eyewitnesses, members of the New Milford Police Department and the State Police, along with evidentiary exhibits and Dr. Carver's autopsy results, attempt to inform Judge DiPentima why she should uphold the charge, lessen it, or drop the charges entirely.

The hearing spills into Day Two, and competing protestors are present for the most important ruling to date. Inside the courtroom, everyone seems to be standing on eggshells while Judge DePentima speaks.

In determining that probable cause exists that the defendant had the conscious objective to cause the death, the evidence and testimony elicited by the defendant on cross-examination does not negate the element of intent to cause the death of the deceased. The evidence presented is sufficient for a person of reasonable caution to find that the deceased died as a result of the injury intentionally inflicted upon him by the defendant.

Mixed emotions swirl throughout the courtroom, as those in attendance realize the judge's ruling before she officially discloses it.

The court finds that, based upon the evidence presented by the prosecution and pursuant to the applicable law, probable cause exists that the defendant is guilty of the crime charge: murder.

Gasps crack the silence. Smith's supporters appear visibly shaken and emotionally distraught that the plague of injustice continues its insurrection against law enforcement. Franklyn's supporters are pleased. Outside, applause or grumbling sum up reactions. Officer Smith arrived in court in high spirits, hopeful that justice would end his persecution. Now, facing prosecution, his demeanor alters.

How could an honorable judge grant rights to a dead man whose worthless criminal life is a stain on society? Perhaps those supporting the officer believe everyone should feel proud knowing that the hand that gripped a gun signed Franklyn's death warrant and successfully served it with a bullet. Accountability does not matter when it symbolizes "good" in society. Why couldn't the judge end a potentially destructive precedent that may have grave consequences in the law enforcement community? Reid was tried in the public arena, their harsh judgment saying, "You deserve death, you, son of a bitch." No doubt, some who feel betrayed by the traitor Connelly equate *him* to a son of a bitch. The defense and one side of protesters embrace that perspective; but holding to the law with unflinching honesty has played its role.

Connelly takes no joy in prosecuting one of his own. Society is filled with characters, mostly good, some not so good. But Franklyn was a human being granted the rights written in our laws. Those who reserve judgment also hold that value highest.

* * *

Chief Sweeney abruptly resigns a month after Smith's pretrial hearing. The timing may appear as if a captain has abandoned his damaged ship and its crew. It may create more difficulty for those remaining to weather the storm. We're not at sea, but the issues facing the department continue to rock the ship.

However, Chief Sweeney was presented with a once-in-a-lifetime opportunity. After spending thirty years in law enforcement, eleven as police chief, he accepts a private school job, an opportunity he couldn't refuse. The often soft-spoken chief is lauded for developing community police programs, a youth investigative unit, reestablishing a K-9 patrol, and establishing the Drug Abuse Resistance Education (DARE) program in New Milford schools.

"He is a very fine gentleman and a well-respected police chief in the state. He ran a good department, and I hope we'll continue to have the benefit of his counsel after he retires," says Wethersfield Police Chief John Karangekis, head of the Connecticut Police Chiefs Association.

Sweeney recommends Major Colin McCormack to be his replacement. An eighteen-year law enforcement veteran and the department's second in command, McCormick doesn't think the public will perceive Sweeney's resignation as triggered by the recent department turmoil. People, however, will always draw their own conclusions.

The shorthanded squad is in desperate need of personnel. Mayor Peitler and Sweeney (who remains chief until August 1999) agree to lift Smith's suspension under the premise that enough time has passed. Although on paid leave since the shooting, he returns to work doing administrative duties. Despite the murder charge, "There is a definite need for his services in that capacity," McCormack says. "We operate under the premise that people are innocent until proven guilty."

My family adds their perspective by stating the obvious:

it's a slap in the face and disgraceful, sentiments echoed by the NAACP and distraught citizens. I am 100 percent sure that families across our great country who've experienced a similar predicament would wholeheartedly agree. I view this as a professional decision, one that could be rescinded later.

Either way, Smith is ecstatic to be back in the department. Connelly clears a major hurdle toward trial, forcing Kelly to bring his A-game. But one hurdle remains before the trial can begin. It needs a new judge.

HONORABLE JUDGE CHARLES D. GILL

Judge DiPentima relinquishes her bench, effectively paving the way for a new judge. Experience and fairness are vital for a new hand of justice willing to accept a role that others may squirm away from.

At least one incident occurs in every high-profile trial that serves as a lesson for future trial judges about the importance of having firm control of activities and people in the courtroom. The assigned trial judge must define how the courtroom will function when the case is tried. Plans must be made for security while court is in session. Who will sit where during the trial must be determined, as well as the circumstances under which persons will be allowed to enter and leave the courtroom. Reserved, press, and open seating should be delineated meticulously. The sheriff's deputies responsible for screening people before they

enter the courtroom and enforcing the seating require-
ment should be well briefed concerning their duties and
responsibilities. Safety for the non-interference of jurors'
roles requires special care to ensure zero contact with lit-
igants, counsels, or any form of outside distraction. Their
accommodation must be suitable and the judge's directives
communicated with crisp clarity.

The trial judge's expectations, both within and outside
the courtroom, should be clearly articulated. If television
cameras are allowed in the courtroom, their placement
and ground rules governing their operation should be
established. Likewise, the permissible use of still cameras,
microphones, and other forms of media technology must
be defined and understood by respective users. A litany
of responsibilities accompanies the territory of being
entrusted as the law's gatekeeper.

The Honorable Charles D. Gill volunteers to serve. A dis-
tinguished résumé endorsed by his predecessor makes him
the ideal choice for the job. "He is someone who can handle
a high-publicity case with confidence," Judge DiPentima
remarks. "He is a very fair-minded, clear-thinking judge,
but most importantly, he is willing to do it. That helps."

Unless you are a nominee to the US Supreme Court, the
public knows very little about the men and women called
judges, who have the trusted task of providing justice to
all. We read about criminal trials, verdicts, and sentences,
without knowing the human dynamics of the final arbiter
in these cases.

Judge Gill grew up in the Newhallville section of New

Haven, Connecticut. As a young boy, "Charlie" delivered newspapers. His mom was a registered nurse and his dad was a self-made man. Fatherless at the age of nine, his dad had obtained two degrees in engineering over a fourteen-year period by working days and going to New Haven College (now a university).

Judge Gill's father eventually became the superintendent of engineering for Olin Mathieson Corp (previously Winchester Repeating Arms). In their "blue-collar," sometimes rough and tumble neighborhood, his dad became a respected "white-collar" man. Ironically, he was also a ballistics expert. Along with another man, he enhanced the science that identified Smith's fatal bullet as being fired from his issued firearm.

Judge Gill's dad's interest in law enforcement grew, and he served as the president of the New Haven Board of Police Commissioners for sixteen years and as a consultant to the FBI. Judge Gill learned a lot about police work through him. Likewise, one of his closest friends and relatives, his cousin, Peter Gill, was a captain in the New Haven Police Department, whom Judge Gill considered a true hero. His brother, Bob Gill, was a lieutenant in the New Haven Fire Department. Bob was decorated for saving the life of a fellow officer by refusing to let go of his hand as they both fell through a melted tar roof in an arson fire set during the tumultuous 1970s. Bob eventually had to retire as a result of burns he sustained in that incident.

Some may ask how an Irish Catholic judge with strong law enforcement ties running through his family could be fair and objective. An example of his lack of bias was evidenced when he reached across diverse lines and became an NAACP member. At one point, Judge Gill was also the only white member of ME-KE-LA, a black association working for social justice. He was honored to speak in church at their leader's funeral. His judgeship hadn't isolated him; he has mentored troubled young men for many years. One mentee, an African American boy incarcerated at age fourteen, found guidance and hope in this man. The fatherless teen yearned for knowledge and continued his educational pursuits. On the grand stage of Wilbur Cross High School, the new graduate proudly accepted his diploma from Judge Gill. One's actions can have a profound impact on the lives of many, producing unexpected opportunities. A glimpse of Judge Gill's private life reveals his hands of justice understand all sides.

Former Litchfield County public defender Carl Eisenmann echoes strong accolades, calling Gill a very amiable person. "But when he's on the bench, he is every inch, every millimeter, a total judge. He's an excellent jurist."

Between April and December 1999, media coverage dwindles. Thanks to local newspaper reporters, however, interest is kept on life support, occasionally boosted with significant newsworthy developments. While the legal battleground prepares for eventual confrontation, people's attention naturally withdraws from cumbersome processes such as Motions for Discovery and Inspection. What the heck does that mean? Sounds like a snooze fest if you're not in the legal profession. Boredom does not sell. *Law and*

Order grips its audience for an hour, and likewise, the public would rather tune in once the story's ready for consumption. Usually this is when a trial begins, but hurdles still stand in the way.

Litchfield State Attorney Frank Maco had requested a special prosecutor and change of venue almost immediately after the shooting. Connelly's appointment satisfies the former, leaving pursuit of the latter at his discretion. The state contracts with pollster G. Donald Ferree, Jr., of the University of Connecticut, to gauge awareness in Litchfield and Fairfield County by conducting a public opinion survey. Prepped with pre-selected questions, volunteers randomly call ordinary citizens.

According to General Statutes Section 51-353, "Any judge holding a criminal session of the superior court may, upon motion, order any criminal case pending in the court to be transferred to the superior court for any other judicial district."

In an unprecedented move—bolstered by the public opinion survey results but largely attributable to pretrial publicity—the state files a Motion for Change of Venue, citing Connecticut Practice Book (judicial conduct rules for the superior court), 41-23 (1), "That a fair and impartial trial cannot be had where the case is pending." The defense fiercely disagrees, claiming the defendant did not consent [Practice Book 41-23 (2)]. Kelly motions for dismissal, but Judge Gill denies until December 7, 1999.

At that Change of Venue hearing, the state presents 113 exhibits into evidence which include four television tapes, numerous newspaper articles, the survey results, and a diskette containing data from an internet website called "Officer Needs Assistance." Sergeant Duda, the architect, created another avenue to disseminate favorable information about Smith's self-defense claim while selling merchandise for his legal fund. Judge Gill personally reviews all evidence beforehand, some on multiple occasions. Those hours spent are already paying dividends, saving precious time.

The half-filled courtroom watches Connelly give a compelling argument regarding why his motion should be upheld, by focusing on Chief Sweeney's public actions.

Sweeney takes the stand and defends his department's press release of Franklyn's criminal history immediately after the shooting. He doubles down on his comments concerning police ramifications following Smith's murder charge announcement. (Sweeney was not trying to avoid trial. Connelly was using his actions as support for change of venue.)

Connelly chastises him for permitting his officers to appear in uniform at the first police rally and allowing merchandise to be sold out of his department. Connelly then calls Sergeant Duda to the stand to give an explanation for his website, which he believes is inflammatory, biased, and prejudicial. The day-long event ends without a decision.

Two days later, Judge Gill rules. He utilized survey results in Litchfield County: almost 100 percent of respondents did not see the website; 98 percent were not asked to contribute to Smith's defense fund; 54 percent could forget anything heard about the case if asked to serve as a juror; and a whopping 60 percent believed the state must prove intent to kill instead of wound.

"The negative publicity, thus far, does not reach the legal standards of inherent prejudice and the creation of a circus-like atmosphere. The survey confirms this conclusion. Adding to this is the protection of the individual *voir dire* process in Connecticut. The latter combined with this court's detailed screening of prospective jurors, further leads the court to conclude that both the State of Connecticut and Scott Smith can receive a fair trial by an impartial jury in the judicial district of Litchfield County."

The defense sought dismissal but that was denied; now, however, they celebrate victoriously. Peers living around Smith will hear and decide his fate.

ACT IV SCENE I

———

A HISTORIC TRIAL BEGINS

Tom Misczuk, from Fox 61 News, arrives at our home to conduct an interview on the eve of the trial. Looking relaxed, Dwight and Pearlylyn sit on a couch in the living room. I stand behind the cameras looking on.

Later that night...

"Officer Smith, involved in a police shooting one year ago, had been charged with murder, and tomorrow his case goes before a judge," says Brent Hardin from Fox 61 News at 10.

Tom Misczuk reports the very latest from the New Milford Police Department entrance, "State Prosecutor John Connelly says New Milford Police Officer Scott Smith's story is unbelievable, and that's why he's being charged with murder; and tonight, the father of the man Smith killed in the line of duty, says it is his understanding that the State believes it has a very, very strong case."

"There was no need to shoot him in the back at point

blank range, no need for it," viewers hear Dwight say from his interview earlier.

"Prosecutor John Connelly's case is that New Milford Police Officer Scott Smith committed murder. That Smith had twenty-seven-year-old Franklyn Reid of New Milford completely under control, one day, thirteen months ago, on the ground with a gun pointing at his head. Also, that it is unreasonable to believe that Smith feared for his life because he thought Reid was going for a gun," Misczuk adds.

"It's virtually inconceivable that the man was presenting a risk to the officer," says attorney Norman Pattis, a specialist in police brutality and misconduct cases, in a separate interview.

Misczuk reports, "Officer Smith's attorney has said Smith's actions are completely justifiable. Meantime tonight, Franklyn Reid's mother said she knows her son was wanted on misdemeanor charges, but she wants to know why Officer Smith would presume he had a gun."

"I want everyone to realize that he was a human being, and no human being should ever die the way Franklyn Reid died out there. This was an execution murder," Pearlylyn claims in her interview.

"This is the first time in the history of Connecticut that a police officer has been charged with murder in the line of duty," Misczuk concludes.

While watching the news, I realize tomorrow, February 23, 2000, won't be anything like what we've experienced thus far. This is not the climax of a public story. It's simply the culmination of events that's led to a new chapter to seek the truth. And given the emotional unpredictability, it has all the ingredients to create a circus-like atmosphere outside the courthouse. Inside, the rule of law should take precedence, to allow the case to be heard before a jury. The emotional toll the families have experienced over the last thirteen months may, unfortunately, be magnified.

The quiet town of Litchfield has once again become a media hub as satellite trucks from local news stations Fox 61, ABC, CBS, and NBC, line the street leading to the courthouse. Newspaper reporters from the *New York Times*, *Danbury News Times*, *Hartford Currant*, *Republican American*, *Litchfield Times*, and *New Milford Times*, to name a few, are present for this historic trial.

My parents, grandfather Wilbert Shaw, and I arrive at court. Dressed in business attire, we slowly walk toward the building through a barrage of clicking cameras. Reporters shout questions at my mother. Calmly, she offers a few words that may make the newsreel at the end of the day. Suddenly they disperse; we continue up the steps toward the security check.

Surrounded by family and lawyers, Officer Smith arrives. They, too, walk toward the courthouse through a crowd of reporters. "No comment" is heard.

It's one of those rare occurrences, two forces coming together, ready for battle. But we are not forces. We are two families approaching from opposite directions, taking the same entrance into the courthouse to seek justice. We are merely spectators, as Courtroom 2 will become the legal battleground pitting Prosecutor John Connelly against Defense Attorney John Kelly. Dignitaries, supporters, and legal scholars, have waited for this day. Numerous eyes are eager to witness a dramatic courtroom spectacle.

At the top of a narrow stairway, two entrances lead into the courtroom. The door on the left is restricted for lawyers, court personnel, sheriff deputies, and others granted authorization. The door on the right welcomes spectators. Admission is free, no tickets required, just first come, first served. Inside, the dark wooden decor reminds us of the classic appearance of a courtroom. No fancy gadgets or exquisite seating, just squeaky wooden benches for spectators; exceptionally crafted tables; and movable, cushioned wooden chairs for the attorneys. There are no high barriers to separate authorized personnel from the audience, just a waist-high railing.

The wooden jury box on the right will become the temporary home for twelve jurors and four alternates who will hear the case in its entirety and decide the fate of Scott Smith.

The packed courtroom stands as Judge Gill enters. Before his bench can warm, counsel have preliminary matters to discuss before the jury is ushered in. Since this case has garnered much attention from broadcast and print media, Attorney Kelly requests Judge Gill to ask the jurors if they followed the court's directive not to read or watch anything about the case since jury selection. He agrees to do that.

Additionally, both counsels discuss and agree on a

Motion of Sequestration. Judge Gill rules: the court is going to order that all witnesses in this case are sequestered. This means you cannot be in the courtroom while another witness is testifying, nor can you discuss your testimony with any other witnesses. If there is anyone here in the courtroom that is under subpoena in this case, or is going to be a witness and is not subpoenaed, at this time, they should leave this room.

Looking around, it appears no one falls under his order and courtroom occupants are just that, courtroom occupants.

"Bring the jury in." A phrase surely to be repeated numerous times, kick-starts the trial. Fifteen jurors consisting of nine men and six women, enter the courtroom. It's the great unveiling, gone is speculation about its composition. Reporters quickly jot down notes to remember the mixture of jurors; only one member is black. Numerous citizens were summoned and scrutinized extensively, but these fifteen were selected to render a unanimous verdict. That's the uniqueness of our justice system, everyday people deciding a trial's outcome regardless of the plaintiff or defendant's prestige. It doesn't matter which side has support. Ordinary folks feel the system is working when cases that deserve a trial are brought to a trial.

The human spirit embraces the search for answers to unknown questions, mysterious circumstances captivate the imagination. It's for that reason that a judicial system depends on a jury to listen to both sides, weed out what doesn't make sense, and allow truth to flourish. But wait a minute...there are supposed to be four alternates. We're down one already?

The jury listens as the clerk reads the state oath pertaining to criminal cases. Each juror stands and validates their honoring of it by saying, "I do."

Judge Gill addresses the issue of the missing juror. "One of the alternate jurors had an unforeseeable work emergency that could be significantly detrimental to the business where he is employed. I have interviewed him, and it's a cogent reason why he cannot do both this service and his job. He has been excused."

It is also an ideal opportunity for Judge Gill to bring up Kelly's concerns and remind the jury what they must adhere to.

"You are going to hear this probably a hundred times from me, that you are not to talk about this case with anyone, or allow anyone to discuss it with you. You shouldn't see or hear anything about it on the radio, on the television, in the newspapers, or even on the internet, because as you know, you have to decide the case solely, exclusively, based upon what you actually see and hear within the four walls of this courtroom."

Satisfying Mr. Kelly's request, the judge adds, "*Is there anyone who has not followed that or had a problem with that?*"

None of the jurors respond, signifying they abided by the court's directive since jury selection in January 2000.

Like the first day of class when a professor gives an overview of a curriculum, the trial's framework is provided. Though most people have probably watched trial proceedings on one of the many legal shows on television, this is what will unfold. Following a consistent template, the state, also referred to as the prosecution, will call their witnesses to the stand one by one. They will testify, and after their testimony, the defense counsel will have an opportunity to cross-examine them. At times, the state's attorney may ask additional questions of a witness, and sometimes the defense counsel will do the same. Eventually, Mr. Connelly will stand up in front of the jury and say, "The state rests," which means the prosecution has presented all the evidence it intends to produce during the trial.

Following the state's presentation, the defense will call their witnesses, and Mr. Connelly will cross-examine them. The state has the burden of proof, meaning the defense doesn't have to prove anything and is not obligated to present evidence. There will come a point in time when Mr. Kelly will say, "The defense rests."

During the trial, the lawyers may object to a question or answer, asserting that it is improper or inadmissible as evidence. Judge Gill will make a decision to agree with an objection (sustain it), or overrule an objection, meaning the question or answer is allowed and deemed admissible.

There may be times when lawyers and the judge ask the jury to be excused while legal issues are sorted, a perfectly normal practice in all trials. Once both sides tell Judge Gill they rest, the lawyers will give their final closing remarks.

Judge Gill instructs the jurors on trial procedure:

The arguments to you or to me are not evidence in the case, these are advocacy positions. The state, Mr. Connelly, will make his argument first, and then Mr. Kelly has an opportunity for the defense to make its argument. Then the state has an opportunity to give one more, final argument to you. So you will hear three arguments. After that is done, you will hear my instructions on the law. After that is done, you will retire to the jury deliberation room and start to deliberate.

He underscores the jury's sole obligation to seek truth and justice:

My responsibility is to conduct the trial in this case in an orderly, fair, and just manner. I have to rule upon any questions of the law that are presented by the attorneys in the course of their representation of their respective clients, and of course, I have to instruct you on the law at the end. It is your duty to accept whatever law I give to you as the law you apply in this case. On the other hand, it is the function of the jurors to determine the facts. You are the sole and exclusive judges of what the facts are. You alone, determine the weight, the effect, and the value of the evidence as well as the credibility of each witness. You must consider and weigh the testimony of all the witnesses who appear before you, and you alone, are to determine whether to believe any witness, and the extent to which any witness should be believed. It is your responsibility to resolve any conflicts in the evidence that will arise, and to determine where the truth lies. You are entitled in the course of evaluating the evidence to draw any and all inference which you find reasonable and logistical from the evidence you have heard.

The final formality: the clerk reads the charge.

This is in docket number CR18 97546, in the Superior Court of the State of Connecticut, Judicial District of Litchfield. John A. Connelly, State's Attorney for the Judicial District of Waterbury, accuses and charges Scott Smith, of New Milford, Connecticut, with the crime of Murder, in violation of Connecticut Statutes Section 53a-54a section (a), in that on December 29, 1998, at approximately 11:20 a.m., at or near the intersection of Route 202 and Park Lane West, in the Town of New Milford, Connecticut, the said Scott Smith with intent to cause the death of Franklyn Reid caused the death of Franklyn Reid by shooting him in the back with a handgun. To this information, ladies and gentlemen of the jury, the defendant has pleaded not guilty. It is your duty, therefore, to inquire whether he is guilty or not guilty; and if you find him guilty or not guilty, you will say so by your foreperson, and say no more. Kindly attend to the evidence.

It's time.

"We're prepared to start the trial. The state may call its first witness," echoes throughout the courtroom.

ACT IV SCENE II

———

COMMUNICATION

Prosecuting Attorney Connelly recreates the scene for the jury using town maps and photos. He leads with a pivotal topic—communication.

State police had seized a Dictaphone which recorded and time-stamped every New Milford Police Department phone and radio conversation. While mounting a case against Smith, Connelly and State Investigator Peter Keegan took the contraption to Barbara Snyder, a member of the FBI who specializes in audio/video forensics. They asked her to disjoin conversations between 11:00 a.m. and 12:02 p.m. on December 29, 1998. Ms. Snyder produced four cassette tapes and transcripts to allow both sides to verify or disprove testimony regarding officers and personnel. Although the state marked them as exhibits, the defense could reference them whenever they chose.

Connelly's tactic is to bring the jury back to the moments before and after Smith discharged his firearm.

The state calls Dispatcher Alex Correa to the stand. Attorney Connelly distributes transcripts for the jury to follow along while the courtroom listens to Ms. Snyder's tapes. The definitive reason Detectives Shortt and Jordan, and Officer Smith left the department was due to information regarding Sergeant Cramer's situation.

The witness validates communication with officers.

Defense Attorney Kelly's strategy: cast doubt—anywhere and everywhere—over the state's case against his client. He plays hardball during cross-examination. He hones in on what was not heard on the tapes and asks Correa, "Was any type of broadcast put out that Sergeant Cramer was in foot pursuit of Mr. Reid?"

"I don't believe so," Mr. Correa reports.

Connelly calls Cramer to the stand and asks, "Did you ever get in a foot pursuit for Mr. Reid?"

"No, personally, no," the sergeant answers. "I stayed with the vehicle, but I was kind of looking in the area to see if he hid in some bushes."

Connelly asks, "What was your plan as far as the car and Franklyn Reid?"

"Tow it, hold it, and once he turned himself in, we would release the car," Cramer responds.

"That's a pretty good plan?" Connelly poses to Sergeant Cramer.

"It works at times," Cramer replies.

Then, Connelly adds, "It works because people need their cars, and it's his mother and father's car?"

Cramer agrees.

Connelly presses Cramer. "Did you know, as the patrol supervisor that day, that Detective Shortt and Officer Smith were out looking for Mr. Reid?"

"I can't remember," Cramer says.

His response jolts Connelly. "Do you recall hearing a radio broadcast by anyone or anyone telling you?"

Stonewalling, Sergeant Cramer does not recall if the detectives "signed on" to inform other officers of their intentions, prior to the foot pursuit. Connelly replays the dispatch tapes again and points out there are no transmissions from Shortt and/or Smith.

Connelly questions Cramer about when he arrived on the scene. He reminds Cramer that he is a supervisor. "Why didn't you ask Officer Smith what happened?"

"I knew he had just been involved in a shooting. His mind probably wouldn't have been clear, and I felt it was better that the detectives spoke with him," Cramer explains.

His response prompts Connelly's voice to rise. Incredulous, the prosecutor states, "You drive up to the scene, and he is a young officer! He doesn't have seventeen years at the department. He has about a year and a half at the time. You see a dead man, and you know he shot him. You don't say, 'Hey Smitty, what happened?'"

"No, because I knew he was upset, and I wanted to make sure he was okay," Cramer says.

Connelly tries a humanistic approach. "So here you are, a sergeant at a potential homicide scene, and you don't go up to Officer Smith and say, 'Smitty, what the hell happened?'"

"I did not," Cramer asserts.

"Police officer, line of duty shoots a man, and you get on the telephone and claim that this was an accidental shooting?"

"I speculated that he accidentally discharged," Cramer says.

His response fires up Connelly whose tone echoes throughout the courtroom. "You see a man with a bullet hole in the back, and you know that one of your officers had shot him?"

Immediately, Judge Gill interrupts. "Excuse me!"

Attorney Kelly chimes in. "Can he talk to the witness rather than shouting at him?"

Judge Gill agrees. "Volume has to come down, Mr. Connelly!"

If anyone is standing outside in the corridor, I'm sure they heard the prosecutor.

He speaks softly. "A man is shot by a police officer, and you are trying to guess what happened?"

"I didn't know what happened. I kind of speculated that the gun may have gone off in a struggle," Cramer says.

Although Cramer had a plan, he did not expect Franklyn to surrender, a point Defense Attorney Kelly highlights during cross-examination to cast doubt on any assumption that other officers were out of line for coming to assist. Cramer's main concern was the incident's aftermath and the need to ensure the area was sealed off and evidence protected.

"I'm not a detective; neither are my men. Their job is

not to investigate what occurred," the sergeant says to Kelly, regarding any concern about compromising the investigation by asking Smith what happened.

Cramer sums up his tenure at the department. "There have been incidents where police have fired weapons, but nobody has ever been shot on my watch. Not since I have been there, at least by the police."

While the veteran exits the courtroom, ending the first day of testimonies, I admire his steadfast resolve in leading the coordination efforts. He endured difficult questions and Connelly's vigorous tone under oath, but he managed to cross the finish line to a degree unscathed. Although he was first to alert dispatch about a white car, he did what most officers would have done. He effectively followed the playbook of protocols. The common-sense approach of communicating, requesting assistance, and devising a plan fits his status of being a veteran police officer. The unexpected event had surely caught everyone off guard. Maybe Cramer's not talking to Smith had been a way to psychologically retreat, to protect himself, by not wanting to know what happened. It's up to the jury to decide and believe what is accurate as the trial progresses. In my view, he is a symbol for the badge that he wears. Hats off to you, sir!

ACT IV SCENE III

"WE GOT HIM"

The next day, the familiar courtroom scene feels like déjà vu. Along with my parents, I'm sitting in the same spot as I did the previous day. Across the aisle, Smith's family is sitting with members from the department. No words are exchanged between the families as we resume our rightful roles of spectators in a packed courtroom.

Shortt testifies he spotted a black male walking in the vicinity of Sandra's Cleaners while Smith drove the undercover Ford Escort north on Route 202. The officers turned around, pulled into Sunoco gas station and identified Franklyn.

Connelly asks, "Do you recall whether he was carrying anything?"

"I didn't see him carrying anything. I was trying to see if it was him," Shortt says.

Believing Franklyn would run, Shortt told Smith to pull up close to him but did not specify the driver or passenger side.

Connelly asks, "Wouldn't it have been better for you to tell him to pull up on your side, so you can get out, because he's driving?"

"If he pulled up on the passenger's side of the car, he would have hit the gas pumps," Shortt says.

Perplexed at what the officers did, Connelly points out that they are in a moving vehicle.

"If it's a two-man car, the passenger most likely would be able to get out of the car quicker, but you have to work with what you have," Shortt says.

Connelly reminds him it's a busy gas station next to a major road in broad daylight.

Shortt states Franklyn ran in a northwestern direction after both officers exited the car. Initially, he engaged in foot pursuit but gave up and returned to the car, leaving Smith alone and yelling at Franklyn. Shortt decided not to yell as he believes Smith would have drowned him out. He demonstrates the volume he heard in a very loud and powerful tone. "Franklyn! Stop! Police!"

Connelly appears apprehensive. "It was a loud yell?"

"I would say it's pretty loud," Shortt responds.

Connelly asks, "Franklyn and anyone else in that gas station area should have heard it?"

"I can't say how other people hear anything, but I imagine they would. I heard him," Shortt says.

Shortt believed the chase would go a long distance and decided it best to cut Franklyn off with the car.

Connelly seeks clarity. "You knew who Franklyn was and you let Officer Smith continue on his foot chase by himself?"

"Officers get in foot chases with people every day of the week by themselves," Shortt says.

Connelly agrees. In fact, it's not a crime. He recapitulates the detective's action so there is no doubt as to what he did. "So, you let Officer Smith who has less than two years in the police department, less than *two weeks* in the detective bureau, run after Franklyn Reid himself? You gave up the foot chase?"

"I gave up, to continue the chase in the car, which is a lot faster than the foot chase," Shortt says.

Connelly transitions to Shortt's time in the car but notes the detective could have instructed Smith to return to the vehicle and continue pursuit. "Do you recall what you said to headquarters on your first dispatch?"

"I called headquarters and said, '54 to headquarters, we're in foot pursuit of Reid, Route 202 northbound near Sunoco; we got him,'" Shortt says.

Connelly revisits the dispatch tapes he played for the jury. He indicates no hesitation in Shortt's stated words. "You are not going to give false or missing information to dispatchers, because you knew other police officers are in the area looking for Mr. Reid. So as far as you were concerned, 'we got him' means you got Mr. Reid?"

"No, what it means is at first I called in that we were in foot pursuit. I looked at Mr. Reid and Officer Smith and saw that they had stopped running and Officer Smith was then in contact with Mr. Reid. There wasn't a distance between them. That is when I said we got him," Shortt explains.

Dispatcher Correa had asked if Franklyn was in custody,

but Shortt says he was preoccupied, trying to get where the men were and didn't immediately respond. Correa called a second time.

Connelly asks, "What did you say?"

"I said, yeah, standby," Shortt says.

Connelly asks again and Shortt affirms.

After turning right onto Route 202, Shortt states Officer Smith was grappling with Franklyn but he was engrossed in the car.

Connelly asks, "Were you paying attention to the action?"

"Not really, I am driving the car, trying to communicate with headquarters, doing a lot of things, trying to get there. I see them in glances. I don't see the entire incident," Shortt says.

Looking perplexed, Connelly asks, "What were you doing in the car that you couldn't rivet your attention to this chase?"

"Trying not to get hit by other cars," Shortt says.

Puzzled at the detective's action, Connelly asks, "In that little car, how fast were you going for nearly a hundred feet?"

"I don't know how fast, but I know when I went to stop the car, it started to slide. I tried to pull it off onto the curb so it wouldn't get hit by other passing cars."

Connelly presses further. "What was your main concern? What was happening to Officer Smith and Mr. Reid, or whether or not your car was going to skid?"

"My main concern was what was happening with the officer, and that I would try to get through the situation without anybody else being injured."

The detective says he was busy taking the standard shift car out of gear, engaging the emergency brake, and getting his radio. Then he heard something.

Connelly asks, "Just prior to the gunshot, where are you looking?"

"I am in the car, I am grabbing the radio, and I heard the gunshot. Specifically, whether I'm looking at the steering wheel, the dashboard, the radio, I couldn't tell you," Shortt says.

At that point, Shortt gets out of the car and sees Franklyn laying on his stomach and Smith standing, holding his weapon. Shortt claims that was the first time he saw the gun.

Connelly says, "You heard the shot, ran across the street, and you see Officer Smith standing there with his service pistol out. What did you say to Officer Smith?"

"I don't say anything. I looked at Mr. Reid to see what his injuries were," Shortt replies.

Shortt says he didn't ask Smith what happened because "it was apparent" he shot Mr. Reid.

Connelly digs deeper. "You're a cop for fifteen years; this is a homicide; Officer Smith is standing there with his gun out over a person who is lying on the ground. You don't say to him, 'Scottie, what happened?'"

"No, I could see what happened; he shot him," Shortt says.

In a sincere tone, Connelly asks again. "As a human being, you see a man with a gun in his hand; you know it's Officer Smith; you see a man lying on the ground. You weren't curious as to what occurred?"

"Of course, I'm curious as to what caused the shooting, but at this point, I don't ask that question," Shortt says.

Connelly ties the alleged grappling between Reid and Smith with Shortt's concern whether Smith had sustained a stab wound, but Shortt claims it would have been noticeable and didn't ask. Connelly presses on regarding when he asked Smith what happened, but Shortt's "days later" response suggests concern took a holiday. So while a bullet settled in Franklyn, the officers must have been momentarily crippled by an awkward silence.

Shortt claims he never saw Franklyn run back onto Route 202 and didn't see the two men facing each other. But Connelly brings up the statement he gave investigators hours after the incident. Initially, Shortt could not determine if it was an entrance or exit wound. Why is that important? An entrance wound to the chest suggests both men were facing each other at some point within those forty-one seconds.

Connelly asks, "If you never saw Mr. Reid and Officer Smith facing each other, why would you think the wound in someone's back would be an exit wound, that is, where the bullet comes out?"

"I didn't see the entire incident. I didn't see the point when the shot was fired. I don't know whether he was facing him or behind him at that time," Shortt insists.

By the time Shortt had called for an ambulance and asked for supervisors, Detective Jordan had arrived on the scene. Franklyn's hands could have had a direct impact on why he was killed. If hands are in front and hidden, logic dictates that once a person is shot in the back, that individual falls forward onto his hands.

Detective Shortt cannot confirm for certain where Franklyn's hands were. He stated they were either off to his side or underneath him. Connelly believes, at a pretrial hearing, the detective confirmed Franklyn's hands were out by his side. Shortt doesn't recall saying that, although he's not 100 percent sure.

Following the detective's detailed recollection of events, it's time for Kelly to cross-examine.

After receiving information from dispatch, "I made a decision to assist Sergeant Cramer in the foot pursuit," Shortt explains. "Another officer needed assistance in capturing a person who was wanted."

Shortt believes it was a wise decision to instruct Smith to pull their surveillance vehicle as close as possible to Franklyn who was going to bolt. He confirms he ran approximately "thirty-five to forty-five feet" before disengaging foot pursuit, as both men started pulling away from him.

Kelly digs deeper as Shortt recalled that traffic was moderate to heavy. "Why didn't you just, without looking, drive onto Route 202 and take a right?"

"The car we were in didn't have any lights and sirens that I could use to warn people of my location. If I had pulled out, I would have caused an accident," Shortt says.

Kelly explores the major point that Franklyn resisted arrest. Demonstrating for the jury, Shortt reenacts the four seconds of grappling he witnessed, with Mr. Kelly playing the role of Franklyn. According to Shortt, Officer Smith grabbed Mr. Reid on the shoulder and it appeared Mr. Reid pulled away. It was at that time, Shortt had his first communication with dispatch. There were no punches or swings thrown at Smith to suggest any type of confrontation.

Shortt believes he made his best effort to leave his vehicle quickly but the car slid and settled about thirty to forty feet away from the men on the opposite side of the street.

While Shortt's reenactment with Kelly could bode well for Smith, Connelly notes that Shortt never mentioned the two men grappling to dispatch, nor had he reported it to Sergeant Cramer at their impromptu briefing, only that there had been an accidental discharge.

Shortt appears eager to leave the trial and incident behind him. His words are left for the jury to analyze.

ACT IV SCENE IV

MEMORY LANE

Chief Sweeney, who recently shunned the spotlight for private employment, reemerges as he approaches the stand. Prosecutor Connelly is prepared to jog his memory and secure his decisions and actions on a host of issues.

Connelly returns to the same query he had put to Shortt. Why didn't anyone question Officer Smith at the time of the incident?

"You were not concerned or interested as to what happened? You knew somebody was shot, correct?"

"That is what I was told," Sweeney says.

Connelly paints a visual. "When you got to the scene, you knew that one of your officers was involved in a shooting of a man named Franklyn Reid, and that man was being worked on by medical personnel, and you didn't ask Officer Smith what just occurred?"

"That's correct," Sweeney responds.

The chief had other pressing issues which required his

attention, such as notifying the state. Connelly brings up that awkward conversation.

"When you told Attorney Wolf that the person who was involved was Franklyn Reid, what was Guy Wolf's response? How would you describe it?"

"Unprofessional," Sweeney says.

Connelly repeats Sweeney's testimony. "So, you just told Guy Wolf that Franklyn Reid was the victim of a police-involved shooting, and you described Mr. Wolf's response as unprofessional; is that correct?"

"That's correct," Sweeney says.

Sweeney confirms he authorized Smith's departure to seek counsel which leads Connelly toward the preservation of evidence. He suggests a crime scene can consist of the incident area, physical evidence, and a person. Sweeney agrees.

Kelly interrupts. "Objection, leading the witness."

Judge Gill, however, sees the approach differently. "This is preliminary and is overruled."

Sweeney describes the kind of physical evidence that should be collected from a person involved in a shooting. "You want to determine if he or she has fired the gun."

Connelly refers to a type of test commonly performed after a firearm is discharged. "As an investigator, gunshot residue tests on the hands have to be done quickly. If you wash your hands or wipe your hands on a towel or cloth, gunshot residue could be missing?"

Sweeney confirms this. Connelly inquires about other items, and Sweeney mentions clothing.

Connelly summarizes. "So, it's important in a shooting case to get the suspect's clothing, to look for gunshot residue, blood splatters, rips or tears in the clothing, correct?"

"That's correct," Sweeney says and nods in agreement.

Connelly's questioning is aimed at having Sweeney explain standard investigation procedures so the jury has an understanding of evidential values as a precursor to the prosecution's next question.

"Did you do anything like that before you let Officer Scott Smith walk out of the New Milford Police Department?"

"No, I did not," Sweeney says.

His response sparks a merciless retaliation from Connelly, whose voice level increases. "Did you see if his hands were checked for gunshot residue at all? Did you check if his clothes would be taken from him so they could be preserved as evidence?"

"No, I did not," Sweeney says.

Connelly asks, "Why didn't you do that, Chief Sweeney?"

"It was not my personal job to do so," Sweeney says.

Connelly is unrelenting in seeking answers. "Your job is to find out what happened at the time you are securing the crime scene. State police haven't arrived yet, but you let Officer Smith walk out of that police station carrying potential evidence with him. Isn't that true?"

Kelly has had enough. "Two objections, Your Honor, argumentative and yelling at the witness!"

Judge Gill sees it differently. "Overruled!"

That timely interruption forces the question to go without a response as Connelly transitions to the department's use of deadly force policy which was in effect on December 29, 1998. The defense, the chief, and others stated publicly that Officer Smith followed the *Philosophy of Force*, written by Chief Sweeney. The state believes otherwise. Connelly proceeds to read passages but Kelly intercedes.

"Excuse me, Your Honor, I'm going to object. We are now reading from a document that is not in evidence. If he wants to introduce it, that is the proper way."

Before Judge Gill rules, the state accedes. Sweeney authenticates his document which becomes evidence, allowing Connelly to continue.

"Physical control of subjects being taken into custody is vital. However, equally vital is the control of our emotions while this is accomplished. Personnel are reminded; only the amount of force that is necessary to effectively make an arrest is standard in which we use force, under code of law. The use of force is a conscious, controlled decision. We must readily acknowledge and be cognizant of our duty to decrease our level of utilized force as soon as it becomes appropriate. When we use force where we have relinquished control of our emotions, the judgment will be made that too much force was exercised."

Sweeney acknowledges the passage, possibly foreshadowing a prosecution tactic to use against Smith.

Mr. Kelly cross-examines. First, Sweeney cites Smith's shaken appearance as to why he didn't interview the rookie officer and tells Kelly he wanted to "ascertain what the facts were."

From the defense's viewpoint, an individual has a right to seek counsel. Kelly's client was not immediately arrested or charged with a crime. He asks, "Did you think you had the right to prevent Officer Smith from speaking to a lawyer?"

"No, sir," Sweeney says.

"Did you think you had some obligation to restrain Officer Smith at the New Milford Police Department, rather than letting him speak to an attorney?"

"It was a request to speak with an attorney," Sweeney says.

Kelly revisits the issue of the *Philosophy of Force* policy. "You were asked about the philosophy, and it was read to you. Is that the total material that you prepared and distributed to members of your department concerning their use of force, including deadly force?"

Connelly quickly objects. "I didn't ask him what the policy on use of deadly force was, but on philosophy of force, not any rules or regulations."

The audience fixates on the attorneys, as Kelly rebuts in defense of the document's entirety. "It is also part of a larger document, Your Honor, and I think I'm entitled, if one page had been introduced, either through this witness or any other witness, to inquire about the remainder of it. It doesn't stand in isolation; it is not a vacuum."

Although the lawyers find themselves debating about the document, Connelly is aware the jury is paying attention.

"If Mr. Kelly is going to make a statement, I ask that the jury be excused," Connelly asks of the court.

Judge Gill steps in. "I think if the state is going to be putting in evidence, exhibits, they put them in during their case, so I am going to forestall you at this point in time. By agreement, you put one exhibit in during the state's case, but the usual procedure is that any exhibits that will be admitted, you put in *your* case."

Kelly wants to broaden the scope on allowable questioning.

Connelly fires back. "It's beyond the scope. All I asked about was the philosophy of force."

Kelly concedes and tries a backdoor approach by asking Sweeney to divulge all sources he relied upon as the basis for developing the Department's Philosophy of Force document.

Connelly interrupts again. "Objection as to relevancy! Every source that he has?"

In a general sense, Sweeney explains that his philosophy was developed using model policies published by the International Association of Chiefs of Police that dealt with force, as well as various readings in professional journals and manuals.

Kelly asks about the type of training Sweeney made available to officers on the various uses of force. Connelly objects again—for going beyond the scope—but this time Kelly takes a firmer stance.

"We were asked about his philosophy; we were asked about police use of force. I'm just following up on questions. That door was opened," Kelly says.

Connelly does not view it that way. "Your Honor, if Mr. Kelly's going to give speeches, it's improper."

The lawyers' combative face-off intensifies.

Kelly shouts, "I am making an argument."

"Make them outside the presence of the jury," Connelly retorts.

Judge Gill intercedes. "Hold on one second. I am going to allow one more question, Mr. Kelly. I'm telling you right now, the area of police training and police *standards* are not standards that are going to be told to this jury. They are going to be told about the *law*."

Kelly concedes, giving Connelly another opportunity at Sweeney, who acknowledges that a person has a right to have an attorney present during questioning.

Connelly sees another opening and asks, "The person doesn't have a right to have an attorney present to hide or destroy evidence, do they?"

"Objection! Argumentative!" Kelly hollers.

Judge Gill forcefully rules. "Sustained and I demand it be stricken!"

Seemingly unfazed, Connelly accelerates his barrage of questions. "You knew when you let Officer Smith leave the department that Franklyn Reid had died?"

"I believe so," Sweeney says.

Connelly responds. "Sure, you did! You knew that Franklyn Reid had died from a single gunshot wound to his back. You knew Officer Smith was the one that fired that shot, correct?" Sweeney affirms, as Connelly inserts, "This is homicide," which echoes throughout the courtroom.

Kelly bellows, "Excuse me, Your Honor, can he dispense without the shouting?"

Judge Gill speaks. "Mr. Connelly, this is why we have microphones, so you don't have to shout."

Realizing he got a bit carried away, Connelly apologizes and continues. "In all your years as a police officer, have you ever driven a suspect in a homicide to a lawyer's office?"

Kelly flies out of his chair. "Objection!"

Judge Gill agrees. "Sustained. I ask that it be stricken, as it's highly improper!"

The ruling perplexes Connelly, but Kelly says, "No foundation for it."

Questions arise regarding who told who they were taking Smith to seek counsel. Was it Detective Jordan, whom the chief instructed to take Smith back to the detective bureau, lock the door, and have no one enter or leave; or was it Officer Marino who arrived at the station soon after the shooting? Sweeney recalls it was Officer Marino.

At any rate, Connelly continues using both officers as he digs deeper. "Chief Sweeney, isn't it true that when Detective Jordan first told you that he was going to take Officer Smith to an attorney's office, you told him not to do it?"

"I don't remember Detective Jordan saying he was going to take—"

Connelly interrupts. "How about when Officer Marino said it, then, didn't you say, 'That is not a good idea. Don't do it; state police haven't arrived yet?'"

"My only comment was that we had to fulfill our statutory obligation to notify and have an investigation," Sweeney says.

Connelly repeats his question. "You didn't tell Detective Jordan and Officer Marino, 'It's not a good idea to take him to the attorney's office,' and they told you, 'Chief, I don't care what you said, we're doing it.' Isn't that true, chief?" His voice booms through the courtroom.

Frustrated, Kelly implores the judge to intercede. "I think Your Honor has an obligation to tell Mr. Connelly to stop bullying witnesses. That is number one. Number two, it is repetitious. He is not getting the answers he wants, so he's bullying the witness."

Judge Gill rules. "I understand your objection with regard to volume. I insist that the volume be kept down, low, and do not argue with witnesses. The words are the words. The jury will hear them whether they're shouted or not. The second part of the objection is overruled, and I will allow that question to be asked and answered."

"I would say again that I do not remember comments to that effect," Sweeney testifies.

The heart-pounding, edge-of-your-seat exchange is reaching the end. Kelly's cloud of doubt struggles for a foothold, but he reverts to a *right every American citizen has*.

"I'm not under arrest and the police want to talk to me. I can still say I want to consult with an attorney?" Kelly asks.

"Yes," Sweeney answers.

Connelly finishes with evidence.

"You could have seized, taken into custody, Officer Smith's clothing before he left the police department, isn't that true?"

Sweeney concludes his testimony. "Yes."

The battle for justice rages on as the former chief

appears relieved to step away from the stand, possibly testifying for the last time about this dramatic case. It equates to turning the page or closing a chapter in his illustrious career at the department. Although my family never met the chief, I feel he performed his duties well by standing up for the men and women who served. Supporting our brave officers on a daily basis is honorable, which I wholeheartedly endorse, but there are instances where a mediator is called upon to decide right versus wrong. The law and our court system are that mediator, and this is one of those instances.

* * *

Every murder case has a forensic pathologist to testify as to the cause and manner of death. They perform an autopsy and are referred to as coroners or medical examiners. Dr. Wayne Carver's last name fits his profession well. The tall man of substantial proportion enters the courtroom. I'm curious whether the jovial, bearded gentleman will fascinate the jury with shocking testimony. Connelly appears to have a good number of exhibits on the desk. The defendant may hear some gruesome details and quite possibly see photographs of the repercussions of his actions. To what extent will Dr. Carver magnify our collective emotional distress?

ACT IV SCENE V

98-14113

"Good afternoon, Dr. Carver. Fit in that chair all right?" Connelly asks.

The almost giant of a man is looking uncomfortable.

"No worse than other ones," Carver replies with a smirk, knowing the slight discomfort is temporary.

In practically all cases involving outside witnesses, attorneys typically establish credibility through presenting background information—a process called *voir dire*. The idea is to educate the jury on why he/she qualifies as an expert witness. Whichever side that brings in the expert—state or defense—leads the qualification process. The opposing side may challenge credibility by questioning the witness' background before their testimony is presented in trial.

Dr. Carver, by any argument, is a qualified expert. He has performed over four thousand autopsies. He's been called upon twice to testify in New York, Massachusetts, and Rhode Island, as well as approximately sixty times in Illinois, over 350 times in Connecticut, and twice in federal court.

Connelly asks, "Have you been qualified as an expert witness in the area of Forensic Pathology?"

"Yes," Carver replies.

Franklyn's injury prompts Connelly to ensure no ambiguity exists. While he organizes exhibits, Dr. Carver confirms it was a gunshot wound.

"It was just over the center of the back and slightly skewed to the left side of center, between the upper portions of the shoulder blades, and about ten inches from the top of his head," he explains.

Dr. Carver identifies a photograph of Franklyn as the person on whom he performed an autopsy on December 30, 1998. The number 98-14113 shows under Franklyn's neck. "That is a number assigned to the investigation of Mr. Reid's death in our office. It simply reflects the fact that he was the 14,113th death reported to us in the year 1998," Carver tells the court.

Connelly closely examines the neck region and points out red and white objects which are the plastic outer portions of intravenous catheters.

"They are designed to go inside a vein to deliver fluids, blood, or drugs, directly into the bloodstream," Dr. Carver explains. He asserts they were attached when he received Franklyn's nude body.

Connelly displays another photo and notices an abrasion along Franklyn's forehead. Dr. Carver reveals that damage to the outer layer of the skin can happen from squashing, stretching, or scraping it off. "The under layer is more resistant to tearing when it's stretched more so than the outer layer. When the outer layer is damaged, it would no longer do one of its primary jobs, which is to waterproof you, so the underlying tissue weeps, and dries after a while, and as it dries, it turns dark so you can see these things," he says.

Connelly interrupts. "I'm sorry, someone is coughing. Can you say that again?"

Carver repeats the explanation.

Sounds plausible. I've observed Connelly's subtle approach of having witnesses repeat answers of importance which carry great weight, so the jury can hear it twice. Could this have been one of those moments?

(Judge Gill was in sync with my thinking. He believed Connelly was wisely using an old lawyer tactic to reemphasize an important point.)

Connelly asks, "Is this type of abrasion consistent with a person's face, let's say, being on the ground and then turned sharply to one direction?"

"Yes, if small, sharp objects had come in contact with the skin while on the choppy ground, then that seems to flow in the realm of possible occurrences," Carver responds.

A premortem injury occurs before death when the heart is still beating, causing the wound to bleed. In a postmortem, there is no heartbeat, so no bleeding. Dr. Carver characterizes Franklyn's linear abrasion as perimortem which occurs at or about the time of death.

Connelly turns to Franklyn's back as Carver differentiates an entrance wound from an exit wound. Carver's examination revealed the bullet never left Franklyn's body, as Connelly displays heart-wrenching close-up images of the wound. The deep hole takes your breath away; tears are hard to hold back.

My mind wanders to analyze my surroundings. I feel my breathing deepen as I glance left. Grim-faced and emotionally sad are how I'd describe the courtroom occupants, mingled with a heightened state of anticipation. Observing Smith, he appears stone-faced. What are you thinking at this moment, Scott Smith? If I could only hear your thoughts or feel your emotions, maybe I could figure out if we have something in common as you sit there, seemingly staring into space. Our paths have never crossed, but life has pitted us on parallel tracks, traveling through a trial searching for justice, although what we seek differs considerably. You're looking for vindication, while I'm looking for answers. We could view our journey as an opportunity to reflect on what happened, cast its occurrences in the distant past while showcasing it as a beacon for change in hopes of avoiding such incidents in the mysterious future. Many Scott Smiths have sat in your chair; countless Wayne Reids have found themselves in mine. And plenty of Franklyn Reids have brought us here. Some people are fortunate and blessed by the greater power to have their case displayed on the grandest stage of them all, the public domain. What an awkward feeling though, that a personal link could be forged for the greater good of and by the people.

I look at my mother sitting next to me. I can see her occa-sionally quivering lips and the glistening in her right eye, staring forward with sadness. I know her feelings because I've endured similar moments over the last eighteen months. It's the memory of the loss of a person's life. Time tries to heal the pain, but like a circle, the pain returns with the advance of the calendar. Old wounds reopen when a birthday passes or a holiday or an anniversary. In our case it's that infamous December day. That's the gift of emotions: they find a way out when calamity wanders into our thoughts, and that makes us human. I look in Smith's direction once more with another thought. Could this be another common link between us? We are in court being reminded of the same person.

Suddenly, Connelly's voice rivets my attention so sharply, I'm sure my eyes must be bulging out.

While loudly tapping the wound with his index finger, he says, "The hole, it's dark around the edges. You can see it on the close-up. There appears to be some red. Could you tell us what that red mark is?"

"Those are abrasions where the outer layer of skin has been damaged," Carver responds.

Connelly follows up. "Let me ask you this. Can you give an opinion with reasonable medical certainty as to what caused that redness, the abrasion around the bullet wound in Mr. Reid's back?"

Anticipation of Connelly's lead-up swells, knowing the seconds ahead could change the dynamics of which direc-tional path the trial may take. Smith is especially eager to learn that course.

"That is the result of energy associated with the discharge of the weapon, and the pattern of it is due to the weapon being closely applied to his body, and the interrupted nature of it is consistent with there being cloth or clothing between the weapon and his skin."

Connelly yearns for simplicity. "Now, doctor, did you, in your autopsy report, classify that wound to Mr. Reid's back as a contact wound?"

"Yes, I did," Carver says.

Looking relaxed and walking the floor, Connelly is not ready to relinquish this climactic moment. "Would you educate the ladies and gentlemen of the jury as to what a contact bullet wound is?"

Smith's eyes are locked on Dr. Carver, knowing what he is about to reveal.

"That is one in which the muzzle of the weapon, the end of it, is in contact with the surface into which it's fired."

Connelly stops in front of the jury and reverts to that old lawyer's tactic. "I didn't hear it! Again?"

"It is a wound in which the end of the weapon is in contact with the surface into which it is being fired," Carver repeats.

Sighs and looks of shock crowd the small courtroom. I glance at Smith's face, seeing his right profile. The bombshell medical confirmation appears to have zero effect on the officer. Why is that? Could that fact be something you already knew which is why you can't produce a reaction? I know the folks next to me—my and Franklyn's parents—are feeling uneasy and uncomfortable as the timeline of their son's inevitable end is reconstructed before their eyes.

Directly across the aisle to their left are Smith's mother, father, and sister. The family appears distressed. If Carver's confirmation had favored their son, I'm sure the Reid family would have reacted in a similar matter. It solidifies life's unintended consequences that brought both families into close proximity as empathy for the defendant and the deceased, respectively, is the bond linking us together at this moment.

Connelly reiterates, "So, in other words, Doctor, is it fair to say the gun that caused this wound to Mr. Reid's back was pressed up, flush against Mr. Reid's back?"

"Yes," Carver says.

The idea of a contact wound may have shocked some but Connelly digs even deeper by focusing on the interior of the bullet hole and whether anything else was discovered. Dr. Carver reveals that black soot lined the cavity of the skin. "That soot comes out of the muzzle of the weapon when it's discharged, so it's part of the pattern of being in contact with the skin," he explains.

The prosecution's demeanor during his questioning of Dr. Carver differs considerably from his questioning of Chief Sweeney. No shouting or yelling—and not a single objection from Kelly thus far. Essentially, the chief medical examiner is captivating the courtroom by further confirming the presence of gunshot residue that comes from the barrel of a gun. Knowing the soot didn't miraculously appear, Connelly wants to know if gunshot residue was embedded in Mr. Reid's back and what caused it.

(There's that old lawyer tact again, Judge Gill had

thought. A similar asked and answered question highlighting its significance.)

"The weapon was in contact with the surface (Franklyn's back) that it was fired toward," Carver says.

Connelly asks about the bullet's direction through Mr. Reid's body. "It went from the back of the body toward the front, from the left side of the body toward the right, and from above to below," Carver explains.

Connelly clarifies that in his autopsy report, the doctor had said, "slightly" from left, veered right and downward.

"Yes. In terms of going down, the bullet ended up under the skin of the front of his chest," Carver says.

Connelly asks about immediate paralysis. "Once that bullet severed Mr. Reid's spinal cord, Mr. Reid could not move?"

Carver's response is choppy and halting. "Well, everything below the damage he could not—I mean he never—lost contact with everything below the level of injury, so he cannot move those things."

My mother abruptly stands up and dashes from the courtroom, trying to control her emotions. Surprised heads turn. It catches everyone off guard. The only thing anyone can do is watch. It's the strain of seeing close-up photos of her son's injury and hearing the gruesome details that pushed her emotions over the edge. People are told to control their emotions in a courtroom setting, but sometimes the human spirit dictates what the body is able to accept.

Connelly quickly refocuses the courtroom by asking

Carver about the amount of blood that seeped from Franklyn's wound, seeing he had been instantly paralyzed.

"I would not expect a large amount of blood to come squirting out of Mr. Reid," Carver says.

Connelly asks, "Bleeding would only come to the surface if Mr. Reid was rolled over on his back?"

"Eventually it would get to the surface, but turning him over on his back would make it a very efficient process," Carver explains.

Carver's shocking testimony and credible forensic evidence could be quickly overshadowed if "substances" such as illegal drugs or alcohol contributed to Franklyn and Scott's confrontation. Could Franklyn have been under the influence at the time of his death? That answer could potentially change the trial's direction related to culpability.

"When conducting an autopsy, it's protocol to send bodily fluids and tissues to a toxicological lab to examine for the presence of alcohol, drugs, or poisons," Carver says.

With that, Connelly arrives at a moment of truth. "Did Mr. Reid's body or his blood contain any alcohol?"

A heart-pounding, split-second pause.

"No, it did not." Carver's answer echoes throughout the courtroom.

Connelly asks, "Did you find any heroin or cocaine in Mr. Reid's system?"

"No, I did not," Carver says.

Connelly asks, "Did you find *any* drugs in Mr. Reid's system?"

"We found some aspirin-like drugs in his urine. We did

not find it in his blood," Carver says. "He had had some aspirin, but long enough before his death that his body had almost completely gotten rid of it."

Connelly sums up Dr. Carver's testimony. "Is there any question in your mind that the redness around the wound, soot, and the gunshot residue inside the wound, that would indicate anything other than that the gun, or the muzzle of the gun, was pressed up against Mr. Reid's back?"

"No," Carver says, which led him to confirm Franklyn's cause of death resulted from a gunshot wound that passed through his back to his chest.

During Dr. Carver's examination of Franklyn, he removed the bullet and bullet fragments. He labeled the projectiles and packed them in a tin can, sealed with Scotch tape, and gave them to the detectives who were present at the autopsy.

Connelly wraps up without leaving any stones unturned or cans unopened. After identifying the canister, Dr. Carver opens and displays its contents while describing them. The larger piece is the main portion of the bullet. It's a type of bullet called a semi-jacket, which means a portion of it is covered with copper. He states that the smaller projectile is a "piece that breaks off from this type of bullet as it traverses through tissues."

Connelly requests a moment to review his notes. He thanks Dr. Carver and gestures to Kelly to assume the floor.

It's challenging to refute medical testimonies, but it is the defense's obligation to find inconsistencies, highlight them, and somehow cast doubt. He chooses the abrasion, or in other words, a scratch, to pose a few scenarios.

"If somebody had said to you, is that the result of him falling? Would that type of scratch be consistent with a fall?"

Dr. Carver acknowledges the possibility, if something sharp and pointy had glanced him on the way down.

Kelly asks, "Would it be indicative of having been in a fistfight?"

Connelly interrupts. "Objection, Your Honor. It's hypothetical. There is no evidence to that."

Kelly clarifies. "I'm asking him to exclude things, that is all."

Judge Gill agrees with Kelly and overrules Connelly.

Carver responds. "This is not the type of injury that I would characterize as the pattern of a fistfight. Although, if a fistfight got interesting enough, this could be part of it, but it's not characteristic of a typical fistfight injury."

Kelly follows up. "How about if someone said it would be characteristic of being pistol-whipped?"

Connelly interrupts again. "Objection, there is no evidence, whatsoever, that Mr. Reid was pistol-whipped on his forehead. The state is not claiming that."

Kelly retaliates, "I don't care what the state is claiming; I'm entitled to include or exclude from questions what it is consistent with. That is all."

Judge Gill rules. "I'll allow the question."

Carver answers undeterred by shenanigans, "This is not the pattern of a pistol-whip."

Kelly poses a third scenario: if the injury could be caused by being placed in an ambulance?

Dr. Carver states, "It's not supposed to happen, but it certainly could."

Kelly inquires if any angle was involved in determining the bullet's path based on the gun being in contact with Franklyn's clothing, as indicated by the doctor.

"It was not exactly ninety degrees to the skin, but in terms of the ability for soot to escape, and go out over the skin's surface, it was close enough that there was no gap for it to go out," Carver says. However, he is unable to determine if Franklyn was stationary or moving at that time.

Regarding the left to right direction of the bullet, Kelly asks, "If we presumed you were a person holding a handgun and my back was to you, would it be consistent with me making some movement from my stationary position to my right or shifting to my left?"

Dr. Carver affirms with reasonable medical certainty that if the starting position was exactly ninety degrees to the surface of Kelly's jacket, the scenario holds water. Carver explains that dealing with people who are dead, measuring from the top of the head is more precise since all things that can cause death are in the upper half of a body. He reiterates the wound on the back was "ten inches from the top of his head," and the bullet on the front was "under the skin at a point fourteen inches from the top of the head."

Kelly momentarily reviews his notes while doubt possibly latches onto the bullet's track. He turns the floor over to Connelly who's primed with irrefutable evidence.

"In what cases do you see gunshot residue in the bullet hole?" Connelly asks.

"Only ones in which the muzzle of the weapon is in contact with his clothes," Carver says.

Connelly takes direct aim at doubt by attacking Kelly's argument about whether Franklyn was standing up or on the ground at the time he was shot.

"Doctor, on the position of Mr. Reid's body, the example I gave you would be Mr. Reid lying on the ground, the gun pressed up against his back, and the shot being fired. That is consistent with what you found in your autopsy?"

Carver agrees which prompts Connelly to continue. "In this injury to Mr. Reid, you can't say whether or not Mr. Reid was lying on the ground, whether or not he was standing up?"

"That is correct," Carver says.

Connelly adds, "What you can say, though, is that whoever pulled the trigger of that gun had the muzzle of that gun flush up against Mr. Reid's back?"

"That is correct," Carver says.

Connelly asks, "It's also consistent with somebody lying on the ground with their hands behind them, being held by another person, and that person pulling up on him and perhaps turning slightly to their left because of the tug of the arms?"

Kelly quickly objects to the question's form, but Judge Gill overrules him.

Carver responds. "If the weapon is still perpendicular to the ground, yes."

Kelly takes the floor. "Doctor, did you find in the course of the autopsy you conducted anything consistent with the cause of death to Mr. Reid as being held on the ground with his hands behind his back, someone putting a handgun against his back and shooting him?"

Dr. Carver acknowledges the last part—"the handgun shooting him"—which gives Kelly a chance to substantiate Officer Smith's claim by refuting the irrefutable.

"I take it, Doctor, you don't know whether or not the gun was placed there or Mr. Reid backed into it?"

"No, I do not," Carver says.

Connelly stands up with a final question. "Doctor, that red circle around the wound—that is not a situation where someone backed into a gun, but where the gun was actually pressed into the person's back?"

"At the time it is discharged, it's in tight contact with his back," Carver concludes.

My mother quietly rejoins the courtroom. Her moments of solitude pulled her from the brink of emotional collapse. Remembering Franklyn's first smile, first word, first plane ride, teaching him how to drive, traversing through the legal system, identifying his body, and listening to the description of his final moments, defines a similar pattern for most parents. She must brave her journey to the end, and maybe one day another parent will remember her courage and find their own inner strength to struggle through the difficulties of losing a loved one. Life is precious but at times it isn't pretty. Some may say it's unfair. But collectively, courage is drawn from each other whether we're famous or just average human beings.

ACT IV SCENE VI

———

EYEWITNESSES

Francis Roger, the last person who had a face-to-face conversation with Franklyn before he was shot, shares precious moments which embody the spirit of goodness and acts of random kindness embedded in the hearts of most people. Walking toward her house from her daughter's beauty shop, Mrs. Roger noticed a stranger standing in her yard. Unafraid of the young man's presence, she approached the fellow.

Mrs. Roger describes Franklyn's demeanor as friendly. Connelly asks her to tell the jury about her unexpected interaction with Mr. Reid.

"He asked to use the telephone, and I took him into the house. I know that is not the best thing to do with people you don't know, but my husband was in his shop, going back and forth to the garage. He saw us. My daughter was talking to one of the other girls, in the doorway of her shop where I just left; and they all were watching. So, I knew they knew, and I knew he knew that they were watching."

Inside her home, Mrs. Roger stood approximately three feet from Franklyn and observed him. She thought he was nicely dressed and didn't notice any marks on his face. Franklyn informed her that his car had a flat tire, and he was going to Sunoco and wanted to call his girlfriend.

Kelly cross-examines Mrs. Roger and asks her to tell the members of the jury what she heard.

"He dialed and when someone answered he said, 'Yo' and asked the person to please meet him at the Sunoco station."

* * *

Mr. Daniel Merton sat in the passenger seat of a pickup truck at the Sunoco gas station while his boss pumped gas. While on his cell phone, Mr. Merton observed a black male leisurely walking uphill toward the gas station. It appeared a bit unusual, but nothing too out of the ordinary. While still on his phone, Mr. Merton's boss suddenly pointed out that the black male had started running. Merton became riveted to what transpired next. According to Merton, the black male (Franklyn) was wearing a white shirt and carrying a coat draped over his shoulder. He ran toward Route 202. The white male in plain clothes (Smith) chased him.

Connelly asks, "Did you hear him [Smith] yell 'Franklyn! Stop! Police!?'"

"No, I did not," Merton says.

As the chase ensued, Merton exited the truck and watched the men approach the main road. "The black man darted into the road. I remember him looking back and the next thing, they both ended up on the other side of the road." Merton admits he missed portions of the incident due to traffic. He eventually saw the black male on the ground but was unsure how he ended up there. Approximately a minute or two later, he observed another officer (Detective Jordan) performing CPR.

Kelly wants to head off a potential conflicting account of Shortt's testimony. He inquires if the witness saw how the chase began.

Merton is unable to determine where Smith emerged from, and he doesn't recall seeing two men leaving a car. "When I finally got sight of what was going on, he was already chasing him, and it seemed he was close enough where I wouldn't have known where he came from," Merton says. He reaffirms he did not see two white males chasing the black male. Mr. Merton's examination by the attorneys ends, and he appears grateful to leave that December morning behind.

* * *

The next witness, Mr. William Eayrs, was traveling northbound on Route 202 in his Jeep Cherokee with his wife, son, and two nieces. As he approached the Sunoco gas station on their right, they observed unusual activity. A thin black male ran along the sidewalk in the same direction they were traveling with a tall white man chasing him. Mr. Eayrs thought a robbery was in progress. Suddenly, the black male darted left into traffic and made it safely to the other side of the street. The white male followed the black man into the street, but stopped on the double yellow lines in the middle of the road.

Connelly asks, "What was the white male doing?"

"He stopped in front of my car; had a gun pointing at the black male. They're talking, but we don't know what they're saying," Mr. Eayrs says.

At that point, Eayrs thought the white male was a police officer. Connelly asks Eayrs to reenact his visual in front of the jury box. The prosecutor plays the role of Smith, the witness the role of Franklyn. As Connelly demonstrates, according to Eayrs, Officer Smith had both hands clasped around the gun, pointing it at Mr. Reid. Mr. Eayrs holds both hands up, explaining that was how Mr. Reid stood as he faced Officer Smith. Traffic had stopped in both directions as the officer walked toward Mr. Reid.

Connelly asks, "When the white male is pointing the gun, where is the black male?"

"The black male is on the left side of the road just standing there," Eayrs says.

* * *

Connelly turns the floor over to Kelly. Inconsistency descends like a cloud on the courtroom. Detective Shortt testified he never saw the officer and suspect facing each other, and the first time he saw Smith's pistol was after the shooting. Kelly focuses on Franklyn's anticipated move.

Eayrs thought the black male wanted to run back across the street.

Kelly asks, "What gave you that impression?"

"He made a lunge to go there. But, by that time, the white male had a gun on him," Eayrs says.

Mrs. Eayrs wanted to wait around, but they didn't know the individuals and it appeared the commotion was over. The family continued their journey.

I feel the temperature rising. A bead of sweat slowly drips down my forehead. Some of the jurors appear to be feeling the heat as well.

* * *

The next day, Judge Gill addresses the courtroom.

"I have a note from jurors that I am going to address. It dealt with the temperature of the room yesterday. We were unable to get the air-conditioning on to cool down this room because it's an old unit. Frankly, when it's on, it sounds like an automobile idling in here. So, what we have done is try to use low tech rather than high tech. When you are not here, we open the windows and turn the fans on."

The state calls Mr. James DeMaria as its first witness of the day. DeMaria, a truck operator, was traveling southbound on Route 202, heading toward New Milford to retrieve construction equipment. The driver of the low-bed tractor-trailer was approaching the Sunoco station when he saw two people run across the road approximately two hundred and fifty feet ahead of him. Losing sight of them,

Mr. DeMaria drove on. A moment later, he saw the same two people now running northbound toward his truck. DeMaria thought kids were fooling around. Traffic slowed and the distance between the runners and DeMaria's truck decreased.

Connelly asks, "Tell the ladies and gentlemen of the jury: when you were abreast of the two men and looked to your right, what you saw."

"When I looked out of the passenger's side window as I'm driving by, I saw the black male on the ground, and the white male standing next to him. He (the black male) was on his back, kind of propped up on his elbows. I saw his face and he was alive," DeMaria says.

Connelly reverts to a demonstration for the jury, this time enlisting State Inspector Peter Keegan to demonstrate the position of the black male. The inspector sits on the floor. With Judge Gill's permission, the prosecutor asks Mr. DeMaria to step down from the stand and position Inspector Keegan as he saw the black male on the ground. The witness instructs Mr. Keegan who is sitting on his butt to lean back on both elbows and bend his knees up, which formed a triangle from the side view.

Officer Smith, the jury, judge, personnel, and those in the front row (including me), have a clear view of the demonstration. I hear curious audience members stand up behind me to get a better view.

DeMaria could not say with certainty where the black man's hands were, although Connelly reiterates, he was leaning back on both elbows. Mr. DeMaria confirms that

Franklyn's feet were pointing toward Route 202 and his head was looking away from the road.

Connelly asks, "Where is the white man?"

"He is to the right side of the black male, just standing next to him," DeMaria says.

Connelly displays an exhibit, a photograph of the embankment which shows lots of dead leaves and the blue tarpaulin Inspector Pudlinski had borrowed from New Milford police officers to preserve the integrity of the scene. DeMaria indicates Franklyn and Scott were in the middle of the blue tarpaulin. He thought the early morning action had ended when a gun came into play.

* * *

Kelly assumes control of the floor.

He offers a sketch into evidence, which the witness confirms is an accurate representation of what he saw on that December day. Franklyn's position was like someone lying on the beach, looking relaxed. Although Mr. DeMaria stated he was approximately fourteen feet away from the men when his truck was abreast to their location, he can't say for certain how Franklyn ended up on the ground. He doesn't recall seeing them grappling, Franklyn lying on his stomach, or hearing a gunshot.

* * *

Mrs. Gail Meehan testified she was a passenger in a vehicle

driven by her husband, with her family in the back seat, when they left a local bank and drove southbound on Route 202 toward New Milford. A flatbed tractor-trailer directly in front of the family (driven by Mr. DeMaria), began to slow as it approached the Sunoco station. As her husband reduced his speed, Mrs. Meehan noticed a man standing on the roadside a small distance ahead. The trailer was not carrying a payload and afforded an unobstructed view. She alerted her son that something was happening in front of them.

Looking nervous on the stand, Mrs. Meehan identifies the flatbed truck from a photo Connelly displays.

He asks, "Did there come a point in time when you saw some activity on the grassy area off the road to your right?"

She takes a deep breath.

"I looked over to my right and saw one person standing. From where I could see, I was only looking at his back and it looked as though someone else was there on the ground. I didn't realize until I came up a little bit closer that there were two people to the right of me."

While her husband crept slowly toward the commotion, Mrs. Meehan assumed the person standing was a plainclothes police officer. The individual on the ground was wearing a woolen hat but the head was turned away from her, facing south on Route 202 in the direction they were driving. Edging closer, Mrs. Meehan realized it was, in a fact, a white police officer, based upon his stance. She assumed whoever was on the ground was someone the officer apprehended. But her assumptions shifted as they got even closer and could see the people clearly. According to the witness, the person on the ground was on his stomach and the plainclothes officer was over him.

"He had his left foot on his back, and the boy on the ground had his hands behind him secured by the officer's left hand," she says.

As soon as Mrs. Meehan was almost perpendicular to the action, the person on the ground turned his head in her direction, now facing north on Route 202. It was at that moment she realized it was a black male and confirmed the woolen hat was, in fact, his hair. She states the black male's feet were perpendicular to Route 202 and he was lying flat as she looked at him.

Connelly stops in his tracks from walking the floor and asks, "You looked right at him? He moved? He was alive?"

"Yes, I saw his eyes," Mrs. Meehan responds.

For a precious second, the eyes of two strangers met; my brother and Mrs. Meehan were staring directly at each other. Life had placed Mrs. Meehan at the right place at the right time to capture that exact moment, without knowing what the subsequent seconds would bring. Did Franklyn know his end was near? It is said people know when they are going to die. It's unexplainable and one of the greatest mysteries of our time; but that glimpse, that momentary connection could have been Franklyn's farewell to life.

I feel chills run up and down my spine. My moist eyes are glued on Mrs. Meehan as I listen to her words. *You were potentially the last person to see my brother alive. God bless you for being here today!*

Once again, Connelly turns to his trusted friend Inspector Keegan, and enlists his services to demonstrate what the witness saw. Connelly wants the witness to play the role of the officer, with Inspector Keegan as the black male, and reenact what she saw.

A slight issue arises. The witness is wearing high heels and prefers not to take them off, which is understandable. She prefers to explain the position. Judge Gill permits her to step down from the stand. Inspector Keegan lays face down on the floor in front of the jury box. The witness points and states the officer's foot was in the center of Franklyn's back. She reaches down, takes both the inspector's hands, places them behind him, and indicates the palms were facing up.

A good demonstration but it seems to lack dramatic effect.

"I don't know how I'm going to do this, judge. I want to make sure everybody sees," Connelly says.

The prosecutor decides to play the role of Scott Smith and steps on Inspector Keegan's back. Connelly proceeds to recreate the positions under the direction of the witness. As demonstrated, Officer Scott Smith was crouched down with his left foot on Franklyn's back, using his left hand to hold both of Franklyn's hands behind him, palms up.

Kelly interjects, "May the record note, Your Honor, Mr. Connelly's left foot is directly in the center of the back of poor Inspector Keegan."

A worthy reenactment by a team player. Connelly asks, "Are you all right, Inspector Keegan? I'll buy you lunch!"

Connelly directs attention back to the witness. "This is how it appeared to you?"

"I was there, yes," Mrs. Meehan says, nodding in agreement.

The stunning visualization is hard to watch and makes it harder to comprehend what happened seconds later. I glance in Smith's direction again. What are you thinking at this very moment? If I could only look into your eyes, I would know. It is said a person's soul can be seen through their eyes. What would I see in yours?

Mrs. Meehan testifies her attention was focused on the sight of the two men when something abruptly entered her peripheral vision. She glanced to her left and saw a small car (driven by Detective Shortt) rapidly approaching.

Connelly asks, "What happened next?"

"The car jolted up on the curb a bit and stopped. As I turned left, the door flung open, but nobody had come out, so I went back in this direction," Mrs. Meehan says.

Connelly displays a photo of the embankment, the car on the opposite side of Route 202, and the Sunoco gas station in the background. "You saw the door open?" he asks.

"Yes," Mrs. Meehan says.

"You looked back toward the police officer and the black male on the ground?"

"Yes," Mrs. Meehan repeats.

"Where were the black man's hands? Still behind his back?"

"I believe it was still behind his back."

"Being held by the police officer?"

"Yes," Mrs. Meehan confirms.

"Did you hear a gunshot at that time?"

"No, I did not."

Connelly reiterates, focusing on the most crucial points. "As you sit here today, Mrs. Meehan, there is no question in your mind that the officer's foot was on the black man's back, and the black man's hands were behind his back with the officer grasping them with his left hand?"

"From what I saw, that's what happened," she says.

Mrs. Meehan insists the flatbed truck did not block her view from seeing activities in front of her. As they approached the scene, she says, traffic slowed dramatically because of the commotion, weather conditions, and the slow movement of the tractor-trailer. That afforded Mrs. Meehan adequate time to view significant portions of the incident, approximately twenty seconds from her first observation up until she was abreast with the two people. The entire sequence of events from when Detective Shortt first alerted dispatch to requesting an ambulance took forty-one seconds.

Kelly is eager to discover holes and discredit the witness's story. He chalks up the previous demonstration as an awkward position but undeterred, Mrs. Meehan insists the officer was in control of the black male.

Although the prosecution glazed over the undercover car, Kelly digs deeper.

Detective Shortt testified that the car slid while trying to stop, but the witness's observation differs. In stark contrast, it appeared the car did not have any trouble coming to a stop. As previously stated, the driver door was flung open, which didn't happen on its own. Mrs. Meehan states the officer [Smith] glanced over his left shoulder to view the surveillance car while holding the black male [Franklyn] in the previous demonstrated position.

Mrs. Meehan had no favoritism toward Franklyn, Scott, or the police department. It's fortunate the longtime New Milford resident saw something and felt it was her civic duty to step forward in hopes of providing clarity to a tragic situation.

* * *

The next witness, Mr. Leon Angelovich, was traveling north along Route 202 in his oil truck when traffic slowed near the Sunoco station. Leon spotted a Ford Escort off to the side, in the direction he was driving, with its flashers on. Another car whipped by his truck in the opposite lane and veered into a driveway. The driver (Detective Jordan) hurried to exit and ran in a northerly direction toward Smith; another man (Shortt) followed suit. Eventually a third man (EMT Michael Gabriel) ran toward the three men.

Sitting in the witness box, Mr. Angelovich states he didn't see a person lying on the ground until the men stopped running. He recalls it didn't appear anyone was in the car with flashing parking lights, confirming Shortt was one of the four men. When he finally saw the body, Franklyn was laid out in leaves with his hands in front of him and his head turned to the side. Mr. Angelovich puts his hands up and out in front of him, indicating to the jury how he saw Franklyn.

Connelly asks, "Do you remember how you described it to state police in your statement?"

"It looked like he was flying," Leon responds.

Connelly repeats in a somber tone, "It looked like he was flying."

Leon states one of the men around the body was bending down which, from his perspective, made him think that the man (Detective Jordan) was checking to see if the person on the ground was okay.

Connelly wants other pertinent information. "I don't care about the men; I want to know the position of the body and where the arms were?"

"The arms were straight out in front of him."

"Belly down?"

"Belly down."

Connelly asks again, "Belly down?"

"Belly down," Leon repeats.

If jaws could drop, I believe a few just did. Repeated damaging eyewitnesses are strategic brilliance by the prosecution, but they cause emotional turmoil for the families. It doesn't matter what side you're sitting on, defense or prosecution. The Reid family now has vivid images of Franklyn's last moments, while Smith's family has heard described the dramatic events that culminated in this trial.

* * *

Kelly's challenge is to discredit and cast doubt on Angelovich's story, but it appears he doesn't have any groundbreaking questions to fluster the witness. He simply repeats what has been asked and answered. Referencing a photograph of the Ford Escort and the blue tarp, Kelly wants the jury to know where Angelovich spotted the body. The witness points to the middle area of the blue tarp. With that noted, the defense is on the verge of wrapping up cross-examination.

Holes can't be found in a story if they don't exist. Mr. Angelovich was traveling by the area, performing his routine duties, when he saw something which created a memory. As he steps away from the stand, I nod my head to him as a gesture of goodwill for putting up with the disruption of his life over the last two years. Maybe he saw me, maybe not.

* * *

Mr. Abu Nassir was working the cash register inside Sunoco. Employees typically keep watchful eyes in and around their establishments as patrons pump gas or grab refreshments. The entrance of Sunoco is constructed of glass, and cash registers are situated so cashiers can look directly outside at the pump bays and Route 202 beyond. While attending to customers, Abu noticed a black male emerge from the rear of the building, walking with a red jacket. He occasionally focused on the young man, following his movements because it's unusual to see someone walking through the station. Then Abu saw a car pull up and the driver exit and approach the black male, who kept walking. He assumed the driver might be a police officer looking for someone.

Under questioning, Abu states that the mouth of the driver was moving, and he assumed words were said to the black male although he couldn't hear or make them out. Both men quickened their pace as Abu continued stealing glances while ringing up customers. Next he saw the white man (Smith) reach for something in his pocket as both men miraculously crossed Route 202 without causing an accident. Connelly asks few questions until he hears the words, "The man seemed captured."

Connelly interrupts. "Let's slow down. Who was the man that seemed captured?"

"The black male was captured by the gentleman who was chasing him," Abu says.

Connelly instructs the witness to stand up and demonstrate what he saw. Abu stands up and raises both hands chest high.

But could Abu actually see what the two men were doing when they were so far away across Route 202? The Sunoco employee says that while the two men were small and distant, he could still see Smith's back and Franklyn's front facing toward the gas station.

According to Abu, "The black man was standing, appearing to be captured, and not running."

Reaffirming a crucial point, Connelly reenacts the previous demonstration, hands up, as the witness confirms that was what he saw.

Abu turned away from the two men to attend to a customer. When he looked back outside, the situation had changed dramatically. "I saw the white man (Jordan) pushing on the other man's chest like CPR," he said. Abu said he did not hear a gunshot.

Connelly displays the same photograph of the scene he showed to prior eyewitnesses and asks Abu to confirm where he saw Franklyn lying on the embankment. As did Leon, Abu points to the middle area of the blue tarp. Using that location, Connelly once again turns to Inspector Keegan and enlists his services for another reenactment. The prosecutor chooses one frame of the witness's testimony to reenact for the jury. He has Inspector Keegan lay on the ground, playing the role of the black man. The witness steps down from the stand and, through a series of questions, assists in positioning the inspector. Franklyn's head was slightly up toward the embankment, lying flat on his stomach. Abu could not see where the black male's hands were.

The witness continues playing the role of the white man. He stands over the inspector, bends down, and pretends to hold something in his back. Connelly relinquishes the floor to Kelly who is eager for cross-examination.

Abu saw portions of the incident—when Franklyn entered the gas station, Officer Smith getting out of the car, the chase, hands up, and CPR performed. His testimony was based on direct examination by Connelly related to the statement he gave the State Police hours after the shooting. The level of detail was astonishing and corroborated other eyewitness testimonies. In a great number of cases, statements are precursors to eventual testimonies, if called upon or subpoenaed. As a result of what was seen, a question can be asked a hundred different ways, but the answer essentially remains the same.

* * *

Kelly asks the witness for the length of his interview by the State Police and the last time he reviewed his statement. It appears Kelly was alerted to something during Connelly's time on the floor. He revisits Detective Shortt's role leaving the surveillance car, then retrieving it. Abu says he didn't see anyone exit from the passenger side of the vehicle.

While Smith and Franklyn had feet to the pavement, Abu confirms the car was following them. Whether a cloud of uncertainty surrounds Shortt's initial reaction, it's an undeniable fact that he eventually commandeered the car to join pursuit.

Kelly says, "So, it's clear to us, the first time the second white male got out of the car, was when the other white male and the black male were already across Route 202?"

"Yeah, he looked a little bit older than the first man," Abu says.

Kelly is not disputing the witness's testimony except for his reporting which led to the last demonstration. He asks Abu if he has his statement, which he confirms.

Kelly then asks, "Where in your statement did you tell

them (the investigators) you saw the white man straddling the black man holding something to the black man's back?"

The witness skims through his two-page statement.

Kelly asks again, "Can you point, for me, anywhere in it where you told that to State Police?"

Abu tries to explain.

Judge Gill chimes in. "He wants to know if that is in your statement or not. That is all."

Kelly is trying to show the prosecution's demonstration was inconsistent with Abu's prior statement.

Connelly intervenes. He has no objection to placing the document in evidence so the jury can draw their own conclusions. Abu's statement is read aloud. It clearly states the black man was face down. While not directly referencing Smith's position, it clearly corroborates earlier witnesses' testimony that Franklyn was lying on the ground face down.

* * *

Longtime New Milford Community Ambulance volunteer, Mr. Michael Gabriel, is the next to testify. He describes being at home when his pager went off for an unknown medical emergency at Park Lane Sunoco. The emergency medical technician (EMT) jumped into his truck and rushed to the site, arriving within ninety seconds. He turned onto Route 202 and surveyed the area to identify the unknown medical emergency. Looking in a northwesterly direction across the busy road, Mr. Gabriel observed an African-American male lying on the ground. He initially thought the person had been hit by a car. As he parked next to Sunoco's entrance, he noticed a black Ford Escort ahead of him. He glanced across the street again. This time there was activity around the individual we know to be my brother.

Mr. Gabriel tells Connelly he saw Detective Jordan roll the body over and start chest compressions as he was getting out of his truck.

Gabriel grabbed his bright red medical bag, which held bandages, braces, and a two-way portable radio, and proceeded across the street. He met Detective Shortt in the middle of the road, initially not recognizing the plain-clothes police officer. Shortt briefed him on the situation.

"I grabbed my two-way radio and advised dispatch that we had a possible gunshot wound," Gabriel says on questioning.

Gabriel rushed to aid Detective Jordan. His BVM resuscitator failed to operate properly while Jordan was yelling to assist Franklyn with breathing. Gabriel had a pocket CPR mask which he placed over Franklyn's mouth and nose, and proceeded to breathe air into Franklyn's lungs. Approximately three minutes later, a second EMT, Kim Silvernail, arrived on scene. They stopped, rolled the injured man onto his right side, and examined his body.

"We saw what appeared to be a gunshot toward the center of his back," Gabriel says.

Silvernail applied large bandages to the wound and placed Franklyn on his back again. He relieved Detective Jordan from doing chest compressions.

"I believe at that point, Kim took a knife and cut the victim's shirt," Gabriel says.

While waiting for paramedics, Silvernail and Gabriel continued CPR.

Connelly asks, "Did you see any weapons on the ground around where this man was? A knife, a gun, anything like that?"

"No, sir, I did not," Gabriel says.

∗ ∗ ∗

Kelly focuses on the disturbed area around Franklyn as he attempts to connect with Detective Shortt's grappling claim but Gabriel suggests an alternative version. During attempts to save Franklyn's life, many personnel surrounded him, equipment was thrown on the ground, and the body was rolled over and eventually removed from the scene. Gabriel acknowledges he caused some of the disturbance around Franklyn in the process of rendering medical assistance. Photographs taken after the fact, suggests validity to the witness's claim.

Kelly walks toward Gabriel in front of the jury box with a photograph depicting the witness's red medical bag, its equipment, colored gloves, and another red object. Within the middle of those objects is the disturbed area; Gabriel confirms that's where Franklyn had lain.

Death can come suddenly and unexpectedly. Professionals like first responders, paramedics, doctors, nurses, and a host of others do their best to prolong life. They often win temporary victories, but eventually death triumphs. As Gabriel concludes his testimony, I'm reminded to thank those who tried to save my brother's life. I appreciate their services, their professionalism, and their sacrifices.

In retrospect, the unpredictability of life caused each of the eyewitnesses to cross paths and witness what they saw or heard. Whatever doubts the jurors originally had as to what happened slip away as the evidence and testimony presented by those eyewitnesses paints a clearer picture of the tragic event. The time is now counting down to when Officer Smith will testify in his own defense. His version, however, will have to wait a little bit longer.

ACT IV SCENE VII

———

FOOTPRINT

Sergeant Hyatt's objective for visiting Sweeney's department was to interview the officer involved in the shooting and collect evidence. Hyatt had spoken with Smith's attorney, Tom Allingham, and proposed a meeting with Smith but he was denied access. He had to apply for a warrant to collect a gunshot residue test and specific items that Smith wore at the time of the shooting. Now he was on the witness stand.

Connelly asks, "You knew the law says it may take ten days to execute a warrant. You wanted to execute that warrant immediately for the reasons you stated about the potential loss of evidence from the clothing and from the hands, correct?"

Hyatt agrees.

In cross-examination, Kelly reminds the jury that Smith never denied firing the fatal shot. He asks Hyatt, "Would it be fair to say that as far as police work is concerned, its (the residue test) value lies in the fact that it can help point in the direction as to whether or not someone has recently fired a handgun, or has touched a handgun that has been fired?"

Hyatt agrees, which bolsters Kelly's intent to derail the importance of the test.

"If the person admitted they fired a handgun, the gunshot residue test loses some of its significance, does it not?"

"I think it holds the same significance," Hyatt says.

Kelly argues that Smith followed through with the investigator's request—maybe not immediately, but eventually.

Connelly counters that untimely investigation overshadows cooperation. The duel between time and evidence remains unresolved as both attorneys leave that decision for the jury.

* * *

Edward McPhillips, a forensic firearm's examiner from the Connecticut State Police Forensic Lab, testifies about the operation of Smith's Heckler & Koch duty firearm. He states there are two actions required to fire the weapon: squeezing the grip with eight pounds of pressure, followed by pulling the trigger with three and a half pounds of pressure. Those actions cannot be performed in reverse order. McPhillips test-fired Smith's handgun eight times and noted it did not malfunction.

* * *

State Trooper James Lynch testifies he was tasked with collecting evidence and had visited the hospital twice. He accompanied Sergeant Hyatt to view the body and confirm identity on their first visit. "When I went into the room, Franklyn Reid was deceased, lying on his back. The clothing on the upper portion of him was soaked with blood and cut on the chest portion," he says. "His pants, boots, everything, was still on his person, at that time." Lynch explains he had the daunting task of removing that clothing.

On the second visit, Lynch confirms he removed three layers of shirts from Franklyn's upper body which were stuck to his skin.

Wearing gloves, Connelly displays a thermal shirt as Lynch affirms it was closest to Franklyn's body, soaked in blood. The second layer was a short-sleeved T-shirt; the third, a knit "Air Cargo" shirt. Both were removed. The front of all three garments were cut down the middle and the backs were intact with a bullet hole. Knowing the jury won't have the clothes during deliberation, Connelly displays photographs which are identified as actual images of the physical evidence seized from Franklyn's body.

Lynch continues to describe the clothing on the lower portion of Franklyn's body without interruption from the defense. "There were basically three layers, including boxers, sweat pants, and a pair of blue jeans," he says. He searched the pockets and found a toothbrush, address book, ballpoint pen, Apex pager, and thirty-five cents.

"So, Mr. Reid had a total of, as far as money goes, how much?" Connelly asks.

"I believe it was thirty-five cents," Lynch says.

* * *

As Lynch exits, I recall how not long ago, Franklyn and my wardrobes were virtually inseparable. The middle school years of dressing in properly fitted clothes had transitioned in the nineties to baggy attire, fashionably ripped, and bright in color. Countless parents and teachers uttered the phrase "pull your pants up" during that era.

Franklyn was a twig of a kid, but that didn't stop him from wearing oversized pants. He figured out how to sport the big jeans without having them fall off his tiny waist—wear extra layers. Franklyn's layering included his underwear (or they could have been mine), a pair of my practice wrestling shorts, jean shorts or sometimes sweatpants, and baggy jeans. If the jeans were still loose, a multicolor Jamaican belt did the trick. Although I was proportionately larger than Franklyn, I couldn't fit in his jeans, so I imitated the multiple layers, sporting this fashion most of my high school years, eventually giving it up before entering college in 1996. It didn't matter the season or the reason, wearing layers of clothing became a part of our identities. After listening to Lynch's testimony, it brought tears to my eyes and a smile, knowing big brother died wearing a style we both enjoyed. I guess that's another unintended consequence of trials that involve death—visits down memory lane.

* * *

The state prepares to call their final witness. Former FBI Special Agent William Bodziak, who specializes in footwear and tire impressions has testified in federal court over one hundred and fifty times. The description of his qualifications educates the audience but, most importantly, the jury.

Footprint impressions discovered at a crime scene are categorized as two-dimensional (most common) or three-dimensional. The latter are impressions in sand, soil, or snow that display some sort of depth. The former is created when a shoe or boot transfers a substance like dirt, grease, or blood from one surface to another and leaves an impression. A footwear impression can be recovered from a scene by photograph or by plaster cast. If feasible, obtaining the original item that potentially caused that impression can aid in the process.

At the laboratory, there are four areas of examination: first, the suspect's footwear and its patterns. If the designs don't match the photograph or impression, it's eliminated from consideration. If there is a match, the second area examines the actual size of the patterns and designs. The third area examines the designs for evidence the footwear had been worn, leading to the final area, which looks for uniqueness such as cuts, scratches, or any foreign objects wedged in the shoe's tread.

While Bodziak speaks, I reflect upon the prosecution's witnesses. I think about the amount of time, effort, and resources the state of Connecticut has invested in this case. Putting aside specifics that occurred and looking at it from a general point of view, police officers are investigating other police officers. A unit from Connecticut State Police led the investigation, conducted interviews, and collected evidence. Although it's their responsibility, they essentially investigated one of their own with professionalism and in accordance with the law.

I am pleased the same investigators have testified. New Milford police were approached and they aided the investigation process but their commitment toward Smith was unwavering. Regardless of circumstances, they stood by Smith's side just as my family and supporters stood by Franklyn's, even after both men were publicly crucified by some in the news media. Franklyn was labeled a violent criminal because he had run-ins with the law and spent time in prison; Smith's story was improbable. Franklyn's past collided with Smith's future and the trial's publicity is the consequence we must endure. Despite differences that exist in facts and opinions, everyone has a right to agree or disagree because that's who we are: diverse people living in one of the greatest countries on earth with the freedom to peacefully express ourselves and choose sides.

* * *

Mr. Bodziak identifies a long-sleeved, blood-stained thermal shirt and an Air Tech shirt with holes on the back side—the items Trooper Lynch removed from Franklyn's body. The black and once white actual shirt with red stripes shows a noticeable jagged cut down the middle front area.

Bodziak next identifies Officer Smith's Timberland

boots. He says, "The bottom of it (the boot) has a pattern which consists of individual design elements sometimes referred to as lugs, which go around the perimeter of the boot on both sides." Distinct circular designs run in the center portion from the middle toward the front, some recessed due to wear and tear.

Bodziak produces a transparency of the examined left Timberland boot, with an arrow indicating the circular designs. Connelly directs him to the jury box for up-close views of the exhibit.

"It's made by applying fingerprint powder to the bottom of the boot, then pressing that against an adhesive material, which retains and enables a transfer of that detail to a clear material," Bodziak explains.

Connelly brings another exhibit depicting the Air Tech shirt as Bodziak reports a shocking discovery.

"This is a picture of a portion of the stained area on the back of the shirt. There are two arrows pointing to circular designs which can be seen, which I observed on that shirt," he says.

Connelly reacts and asks, "On the shirt, itself?"

"There were circular patterns and some other patterns which were similar to the designs on the Timberland boots," Bodziak confirms. "It had a real consistent edge characteristic all the way around that reflected it was made by a man-made object, as opposed to a drop of blood that may have wicked through the clothes," he adds.

During his examination, Bodziak used a 2X magnifier to observe patterns on the shirt. Other circular areas were discovered but not as well-defined. Bodziak places the transparency of the boot atop the photo of the shirt.

"Those are circular designs that correspond with the circular designs of the same size on the Timberland boot."

Connelly poses a hypothetical question. Referring to an individual lying on the ground, stomach down, wearing the Air Tech shirt, and a second person wearing the Timberland boots with mud on them, stepping on the individual's back, he asks: "Could you give an opinion with reasonable scientific probability, that once the shoe is removed, mud is left on the shirt, and the shirt now becomes covered with blood; would the footwear impression still be left on the shirt?"

"That certainly is possible, yes," Bodziak says.

* * *

Kelly can't even wait for Connelly to sit down before letting the court know this is the first time speaking with the witness. He seeks a definitive answer as to whether Smith's footwear caused the impression on the shirt.

"Maybe not specifically this boot, but one could have been the cause of it," Bodziak says.

Kelly attempts a different approach by focusing on a literal definition. In part, positive identification means a shoe made an impression; whereas positive elimination means a shoe could not have made that impression.

Regarding those categories, Kelly asks, "The mark that you claim you identified, were you able to reach a conclusion that one of these boots was involved? Was it the left or right?"

"I couldn't say if it was the left or the right, it could be either, in the context of limitations of this examination," Bodziak says.

"So no one is misled, you are not saying that either of those two boots made the mark on this shirt?"

"That is correct," Bodziak says.

Kelly is looking for a conclusive response to discredit Bodziak's analysis by asking how he could know Smith's exact boots made that impression when countless replicas exist in the world. He directs Bodziak to the jury box.

I suspect Bodziak wasn't expecting to shuffle back and forth from the stand, but he looks comfortable in that role. On the other hand, Officer Smith appears taken back by Bodziak's level of detail. After all, this is the first time he's listening to Bodziak testify as to what he did or didn't do, based upon evidence. It will be interesting to hear his version when he takes the stand.

Bodziak points out distinguishing characteristics on the right boot—changes in rubber designs and patterns—due to erosion over a period of time. "Some of these design elements are worn almost to the point where they are down to the base of the rubber," he says. Regarding the circles on the left boot, "You can still see all of them. There are a couple that are worn almost smooth," he adds.

Noticeable nicks can be seen on the heel of the left boot and cuts on the rubber in the sole area of the right boot. Bodziak concluded that the circular designs found on the shirt correspond only in shape and size with the sole of the two boots in evidence, but Kelly requires clarification while the witness returns to the stand.

"It was your opinion from what you observed, that you are not making a positive identification that whatever is on that shirt has been caused by either the left or right boot?"

Bodziak agrees, prompting Kelly to inquire if what he observed on the shirt was a footprint impression.

"I can't imagine what else it could be, sir, under the circumstances," Bodziak says.

Kelly asks, "What are the circumstances, sir?"

"That the person was stepped on from the back," Bodziak says.

Those damning words seem to irritate Kelly. "You take this as a fact?"

While pointing to a photograph of the boots, Bodziak replies, "There is nothing else I'm aware of that would leave those circular patterns other than footwear."

Kelly is dissatisfied. The courtroom has found itself in the middle of a game about words and their intended meaning. He asks, "Is it your testimony that what is on the back of that shirt is positively an item of footwear?"

"I can't imagine what else it could be."

It's apparent Kelly wants Bodziak to say footwear impression, but he's not getting his way. He tries another approach by directing the witness to look at his report.

"Objection!" Connelly calls out.

Kelly fires back, "This is cross-examination."

Judge Gill intervenes. "Hold on, look at his report again for what and where?"

Bodziak offers to read his conclusion but Kelly snaps at him, "If I want you to, I will ask you!"

Judge Gill interrupts. "Now, that is argumentative."

The dust-up favors Kelly. Bodziak commences reading but Kelly suddenly interrupts him.

"Is it your testimony, that you cannot answer my question—whether or not you concluded that you observed that on the back of that shirt was a footprint impression without reading your report?"

Bodziak is not getting caught up in fiery exchanges. "I can tell you I concluded that, but you wanted me to explain where in the report that I mentioned this, so I have to read the whole thing. I don't have it committed to memory."

He reads in part:

"My results are a circular design is present in at least two locations on the back of the shirt. This design corresponds with the respective size and shape of the circular portion of design found on the Timberland boots. This design is possibly the result of contact with the Timberland boots, or similar boots having a similar circular design."

Kelly's ears are open, listening for "footwear impression." He's adamant to challenge Bodziak but there's no mention of that terminology.

"I don't use the term 'footwear impression,' but in the five paragraphs I just read, I pointed out all the similar features between this and the Timberland boots, which are footwear," Bodziak says.

The next few minutes are contentious as Kelly demands to know why Bodziak didn't use the term "footwear impression" in his report when he specializes in footwear and tire impression and will be teaching a seminar on that subject to Connecticut State Police? Connelly repeatedly objects to the questioning, and the resulting order echoes throughout the courtroom: Sustained!

The audience witnesses a slight breakdown of cordial proceedings. I view it as the surfacing of the raw emotions both attorneys have invested in this case. It's what turns lawyers from Dr. Jekyll into Mr. Hyde. One minute they use compassionate words in soothing tones; the next, they vocalize aggressively to strike fear in our minds. Lawyers probably consider commanding a courtroom as a treasured prize. But, since we're not in the Wild West, Judge Gill keeps law and order so cooler heads can prevail. I still hear the echoing of his voice ringing in my ears: Sustained! Sustained! Sustained!

Following this dramatic legal volley, the courtroom needs a break to digest what just transpired, but Connelly has one more surprise for the court.

He rises from his chair and says, "Your Honor, at this time, the state rests."

Those words end one side of this memorable trial. Undoubtedly, the wheel of change is already in motion, but after the showmanship those magnificent lawyers, the quality of witnesses who testified, and the trove of evidence presented, I'm sure others will look back and emulate the bravery of Mr. Connelly and the resilience of Mr. Kelly.

However, that could be unnecessary if society recognizes issues in their early stages and seeks resolution.

My mind returns to the sorrowful task at hand—deciding the culpability of the person who shot and killed my brother. And there is Kelly, eyeing Judge Gill, ready to deal the state's case a fatal blow.

Franklyn and Scott may not have lacked opportunities, but many brothers and sisters of all origins and colors live in poverty without education, essentially locked out of the American Dream. They reside in rundown communities where hustling is survival, crime is the norm, and untimely deaths are a part of everyday lives. Kindhearted people in those communities band together to provide opportunities for children and adults with outreach programs, places to practice religion, and playgrounds and parks for peaceful gatherings. But the obstacles are often too great to overcome, the walls too high to climb, and the bridges too long to cross.

They live where jobs are scarce, making it a struggle to maintain living quarters, keep food on the table, and kids in line. At times it's a juggling act where the balls cannot be kept in the air. Even when people are depleted, they still desperately want to help and support their communities, but their ability to do so is limited. Criminal activities, violence, and drug use spike as youngsters join gangs because they seek attention and lack the education to sustain employment. Seeking a sense of belonging and family, they perceive street life as the way to bridge the income and acceptance gap, and that creates divided communities. Walk on this side of the street but stay away from the other side. Feel free to travel in this area of town, but don't dare venture over there. Underlying issues fester and grow exponentially over time. But those loving people never give up; their unconditional will is unwavering regardless of circumstances. All they are asking for is a helping hand over that wall or across that bridge. Sadly, some in power have written those communities off as lost causes, branding them the forgotten people living in the United States. That is the reality of *their* American Dream.

ACT V SCENE I

EYEWITNESSES

As is customary, the defense can motion for acquittal after the prosecution rests its case. It's possible that Judge Gill's decision could halt the trial in its tracks. My dad has held the notion that the shooting may have been accidental and a jury would be sympathetic toward Smith. After seeing the jury composite, he affirms his belief that Smith will not be found guilty. My mother believes otherwise. She places her trust in God and will accept the verdict or any premature decision by the court.

The jury is dismissed, and Kelly lays his claim.

"Now that the State has rested, consistent with the provisions of Sections 42-40 and 42-41 of the Connecticut Rules of Court, I move for a Judgment of Acquittal in this case. I realize the claim of the Defense is self-defense, and based on that, despite the fact that the State has the burden of disproving the defense, Your Honor might conclude there is sufficient basis for this trial to go to the jury. Our position however, is that looking at the quality of the State's evidence, or lack thereof, and the tremendous amounts of inconsistencies and speculation testified to by those witnesses, there is not a sufficient basis for this case to proceed to the jury, and our motion should be granted!"

Connelly rebuts...

"Your Honor, the evidence that the State has presented to the jury up to this point has been overwhelming to convict Mr. Smith, not only in the eyewitness testimonies but the physical evidence in this case, which corroborates many, if not all, of those witnesses. Therefore, Your Honor, the State would ask that the Motion for Judgment of Acquittal be denied!"

Short, simple, and to the point, Judge Gill rules.

The Motion for Judgment of Acquittal is denied. The court finds that the evidence thus presented would be reasonable to permit a finding of a guilty judgment by a jury.

My parents are relieved the trial will continue but Smith's family was hoping for the alternative.

* * *

The next day, Diane Swanson, a Sunoco employee for fifteen years, is the first eyewitness Kelly calls to the stand. Connecticut State Police interviewed her hours after the incident for approximately an hour and forty-five minutes.

Kelly kicks off. "Ms. Swanson, are you nervous?"

"Of course," the lovely, elderly lady says.

Based on the magnitude of the case, it must be challenging for eyewitnesses to step forward into the spotlight. This woman, wearing her glasses, appears ready to get this over with, quickly. I recognize Ms. Swanson from frequent visits to Sunoco for gas. She may not know me, but I've seen her from time to time. Pam knows Ms. Swanson from being a regular patron and recalls asking to use Sunoco's phone to call my dad minutes after my brother was shot.

Before proceeding, Kelly offers soothing words to put Ms. Swanson at ease. "If you don't understand any question I ask you or you want it repeated, just tell me and I'll do so, okay?"

She nods in agreement.

Kelly asks, "On December 29 of 1998, in the morning hours, were you working at the Sunoco station?"

"Yes, I was," Ms. Swanson says.

"Were you the only cashier on duty?"

"No. Mr. Abu Nassir was with me."

"Can you tell us, on that date, what your primary responsibility was and what his primary responsibility was?"

"He was the cashier and I was the gas attendant."

Kelly suggests that something occurred that morning which attracted the witness's attention.

He asks, "Would you tell the ladies and gentlemen of the jury what that was?"

She takes a deep breath. "I was standing in the gas station and saw a gentleman coming up the hillside, from the side of the station. He stopped in front of the store and was just standing there, kind of looking up and down the road, like he was looking for something or someone."

Kelly asks, "Do you recall how he was dressed?"

"Dark pants, light shirt and jacket."

"What do you recall concerning the jacket?"

"He had it over his shoulder," Ms. Swanson says.

"Did you recognize him?"

"Not at first, but then after I looked again, I knew who he was."

"Did something else happen?"

"I noticed this black car come flying in the driveway and it came right up to the front of the store and stopped. A gentleman driver got out, and as soon as he got out, Franklyn started running," Ms. Swanson explains.

"When the individual got out of the automobile, did you know who that was?"

"After a couple seconds, it dawned on me; I had seen this man before," Ms. Swanson says.

"Did you know what his occupation was?"

"A policeman."

"Would you tell the members of the jury what you saw?"

"I looked out and saw him [Franklyn] in the middle of the road with his hands up in the air, but he wasn't standing still. He was like, trying to dodge cars."

Ms. Swanson lost sight of the commotion due to a stone wall and tree. She quickly moved to another part of the store for a better view but to no avail. She hurried back to the front of the store.

Kelly asks, "What happened next?"

"I looked out, and I could see a body laying across the side of the road on the other side."

"How much of the body could you see?"

"The whole thing."

"Could you tell if the person was on his stomach or his back?"

"On his stomach," Ms. Swanson says.

"Would you describe what you saw?"

"I saw this person straddle over him and reach down with their right hand to the left side of the neck."

While the witness testifies, Connelly is reviewing a document from his file.

Kelly continues. "Shortly thereafter, did someone arrive at the gas station that you knew?"

"Yes, Pam. I don't know her last name," Ms. Swanson says.

"Did she arrive on foot or in an automobile?"

"In her car."

Ms. Swanson went outside after Pam arrived.

Kelly asks, "What did you do?"

"I went over to her. I didn't know what had happened, and I knew she was upset and she had her kids with her, so I figured I'd be out there to help her."

Connelly takes the floor with document in hand, presumably Ms. Swanson's statement.

"You told State Police, in your statement, which you gave just an hour or so after the incident, that he was carrying the jacket, correct?"

"Yes," Ms. Swanson says.

"You never said over his shoulders?"

"No, I did not."

The witness may have been nervous to correct Mr. Kelly but Connelly doesn't shy away from adding clarity. He brings up another point.

"The first police officer who was chasing Franklyn, when you saw him, he was bending over, talking to him, correct? Or it appeared he was talking to him?"

"Yes, sir."

Finished testifying, Ms. Swanson appears relieved and quickly scurries out of the courtroom. Potentially, this is her final time reliving this case.

Kelly calls Christopher Gardner, his second eyewitness. The self-employed homebuilder had stopped at Sunoco.

Kelly asks, "Were you there alone or with anyone else?"

"With a helper, Dan Merton," Gardner says.

"What was your purpose in being there?"

"Getting gas."

While fueling, Mr. Gardner noticed a black male walking up the hill toward Sunoco. He glimpsed him for a few seconds.

"Did you notice him do anything at that time?" Kelly asks.

"To the best of my recollection, he was removing a nylon windbreaker," Gardner says.

Mr. Gardner stopped paying attention until approximately thirty seconds later when he heard a voice yelling.

Kelly asks, "Could you hear what was said?"

"No."

"Did you hear anything else?"

"Yeah. There was a distinct sound of like sneakers slapping pavement. It was really loud, boom, boom, boom, boom, boom, like that. Real fast," Gardner explains.

"Did you look to see where that sound came from?"

"Yeah, I saw a black guy running across the lot and another guy chasing him."

Mr. Gardner alerted his helper while viewing the commotion. He saw both men dash across Route 202.

Kelly asks, "What did you see next?"

"He [Franklyn] definitely came back into the middle of the road, stopped, and raised his hands up," Gardner says.

"What did you see next?"

"Within the next few seconds, the other guy [Smith] caught up and apprehended him. I don't know the right word, but it seemed like he had control of him or was grabbing him and escorting him out of the road."

"When you say grabbed him, what did you see?"

"It didn't look like there was any struggle, the black guy was...his attitude might have been: 'Okay, I give up.' And the other guy might have been: 'Okay, let's get off the road.'"

Mr. Gardner went inside Sunoco and paid via his credit card. A few minutes later, he came outside and looked across the street again.

Kelly asks, "What could you see at that point?"

"I remember there was a guy in dark clothes laying on the ground. There was a guy giving him CPR and some guy on a walkie-talkie. It looked like a real confusing situation," Gardner explains.

The defense's selection of Ms. Swanson and Mr. Gardner to testify suggests a stark contrast to reveal inconsistencies with the prosecution's eyewitnesses. A tit for tat that offers conflicting eyewitness accounts so that Kelly can use his greatest weapon: doubt. He may continue to elevate Franklyn's jacket as crucial evidence but whose testimony will he try to discredit next?

ACT V SCENE II

UNIDENTIFIED IMPRINT

Later in the morning, Kelly aims to show Mr. Bodziak's results were inconclusive since he couldn't definitively prove that Smith's boots caused the mark on Franklyn's outer garment. He calls Kenneth Zercie, a second footprint impression expert who works in the Connecticut State Police Forensic Laboratory.

"On December 29, 1998, where did you go?" Kelly asks.

"I was directed by the commissioner of the Department of Public Safety to respond and offer any assistance to the Western District Major Crime Squad at the scene of a police-involved shooting in the town of New Milford," Zercie says.

Zercie spoke with investigators but the scene was mostly processed.

Kelly asks, "Was certain clothing brought back to the state laboratory by you?"

"Yes. The evidence officer had prepared several of the

items for transport. I took custody of those items...primarily the clothing of the victim, firearm, and several other pieces of evidence recovered at the scene, and transported those to the lab when I left the scene that evening."

Kelly reintroduces Smith's footwear which was collected on December 30, and transported to the lab. He asks, "Would you identify what they are?"

"The two items consist of one pair of Timberland boots which my initials appear on."

Mr. Zercie informs the jury he received a specific request from the state on March 16, 1999, to examine Franklyn's shirt for any footprint impression and compare it against the Timberland boots for a probable cause hearing. At that time, he examined the boots for the first time.

Kelly asks, "Did you reach a conclusion with reasonable scientific certainty as to whether or not those boots in front of you made an impression on the shirt that you examined?"

"I could not identify Smith's boots as causing the impression, but I cannot eliminate them either," Mr. Zercie reports.

Connelly is fired up for cross-examination. He puts on gloves and displays Franklyn's outermost layer of clothing. "What is that?" he asks.

"It's a garment that I received from the crime scene, presented at the laboratory on the night of the twenty-ninth, taken out of its initial package, placed in a secure area for drying as it was saturated and apparently blood-stained."

Connelly asks, "You took photographs of it as soon as possible, correct?"

"They were taken the day after and several times after that, yes, sir."

"Stand up and point out to the ladies and gentlemen of the jury, the patterns that you saw."

"There was an area (he points to the lower quadrant of the garment), that shows some discoloration and difference."

"When you first saw this, the pattern was much brighter?"

"Yes, Sir," Zercie admits.

Connelly shows a few pictures taken by Zercie's office of the area he identified. Looking at one picture, Connelly asks, "That's a real close-up of that pattern area, correct?"

"Yes, sir."

"So, you were well aware of a distinctive pattern on the back of the shirt, correct?"

"We were aware of the gunshot-type defect and that there was some type of pattern present, yes, sir."

"Did it ever cross your mind that perhaps you should ask, as a footwear examiner in this case, to look at any shoes the officer was wearing?"

"I didn't recognize the pattern as that of footwear."

"So, you were just going to leave it there and not do any further examination?"

"I could not identify what the mark was. I would have no idea where to start," Zercie says.

Connelly wraps up. "In the photographs of the shirt, do you see similarities between impressions on the shirt and similarities to Officer Smith's soles of his boots?"

"Yes, sir."

After listening to the morning testimonies, it doesn't seem Smith's case is being bolstered. I imagined the defense would reveal groundbreaking evidence to damage the state's case, but that did not materialize—yet. Outwardly, Smith looks calm, showing no emotion. Maybe he feels exoneration will find him, once he testifies.

Kelly has shown great restraint throughout the trial. Unlike Connelly, Judge Gill has not chided him for shouting. Although Zercie hesitantly confirmed similarities between the pattern on Franklyn's shirt and Smith's boot, Kelly remains steadfast.

Judge Gill dismisses court for an hour lunch.

* * *

During the afternoon session, Kelly calls EMT Kim Silvernail to testify. After arriving at the scene, Silvernail says he observed somebody lying on the ground. Kelly asks, "What did you do?"

"I put on some gloves and looked through the equipment that EMT Gabriel had there. I took over the left-hand side where Detective Jordan was, to take over his CPR."

"What did you do?"

"Initially, I took a pocketknife I had and cut open his clothing."

Kelly seeks confirmation of a crucial piece of evidence. "Did you notice any articles of clothing?"

"There was a jacket that was on my left-hand side, next to him [Franklyn]," Silvernail says.

"How close to him was it?"

"Next to me, it was inches away from him. Six inches maybe."

"What did you do with it?"

"I pushed it out of the way before I rolled him," Silvernail says.

Connelly takes the floor.

"Mr. Silvernail, when myself and Inspector Keegan interviewed you shortly after the incident at the State Police Barracks in Southbury [Connecticut], and I asked you specifically about whether or not you saw a red and blue jacket when you arrived at the scene, what did you say?"

"I don't recall what I said," Silvernail says.

"You don't recall what you said?" Connelly asks incredulously.

A few awkward seconds of silence.

Connelly refreshes his memory after no response. "You said you didn't see a jacket, isn't that true?"

Looking a bit nervous, Silvernail says, "I don't recall if that's true."

Connelly takes a step toward the witness box. "Didn't I show you pictures of the area where Mr. Reid was lying with the medical debris in the area, and I pointed out to you a red object on the ground and said, 'Mr. Silvernail, do you recall seeing that object when you first arrived?'"

"I don't remember what my response was..." Silvernail repeats.

Connelly, getting frustrated, repeats, "Your response was, 'No, I didn't see a jacket.'"

"I don't recall saying that."

The courtroom is in awe witnessing a fascinating spectacle under oath. Mr. Silvernail appears to be sweating; Smith appears pleased.

Refusing to depart without an affirmative answer, Connelly reminds Mr. Silvernail about another meeting they had at the Danbury Courthouse with Inspector Keegan and Attorney Lipsky when asked about seeing the jacket.

"I don't remember you asking me that question, particularly," Silvernail says.

Connelly fires back, "Wasn't your response, 'Everybody's asking me about the jacket and I don't remember seeing it'?"

"I was referring to everybody asking if I took the jacket off or if it was already off."

Connelly asks, his volume elevating, "Mr. Silvernail, you never saw the jacket, did you?"

"Yes, I did."

"You did?" Connelly asks rhetorically as his voice echoes throughout the courtroom.

"Yes," Silvernail quietly says.

Kelly interrupts. "Objection, Your Honor. I ask that the witness not be yelled at again. There's no indication he can't hear."

Judge Gill intercedes. "Okay. I understand. Volume, Mr. Connelly."

In order to make an additional point, Connelly goes along with Mr. Silvernail's storied version of moving the jacket and asks, "Did you have blood on your gloves?"

"I don't recall," he says.

This is significant because Kelly believes that since tiny specks of blood were discovered in the pocket area of Reid's jacket, it bolsters Smith's claim that Franklyn was reaching for a weapon. If Mr. Silvernail admits his glove was bloody and he did, in fact, move the jacket, Kelly's claim would be just that, a claim.

Connelly attempts once more with a backdoor approach. "Who was the first one to ask you where the jacket was located when you arrived at the scene?"

"I believe it was you," Silvernail admits.

"That's right. I did ask you that and what did you say?"

"I don't remember exactly what I said."

"You didn't say to me that the jacket was right next to Mr. Reid, did you?"

"I don't remember you asking me that. You asked me if I took it off."

"I have no further questions," Connelly concludes.

Apparently, Connelly's last question is what the witness confirmed to Kelly who retakes the floor. He directs the witness to the first meeting he had with Connelly.

"Did you tell them you had moved the jacket?" Kelly asks.

"I don't recall if I told them that or not."

"Do you recall if they asked you whether or not you moved the jacket?"

"I don't recall that specific question."

It appears Silvernail has fallen victim to a case of amnesia. It's obvious he came to court to avoid answering virtually all questions Connelly had about seeing the jacket. But he did confirm being Scott Smith's neighbor. The choice of whether to believe if his poor memory is due to a question never asked or to willfully not wanting to hurt Smith's case is up to the jury.

Meanwhile, an epic courtroom showdown is brewing.

ACT V SCENE III

———

IN HIS OWN DEFENSE

The next day, Officer Smith takes the stand. He had listened and watched Connelly systematically shred his self-defense claim. Kelly's strategy is to cement Smith's version of the event in the minds of the jurors to create doubt about the state's case. He leads with Smith's law enforcement knowledge about a five-step model known as the Use of Force Continuum.

Kelly asks, "Would you explain the training you received concerning that?"

"The bottom of the model is a compliant person, and that is the vast majority of people we deal with. The next step would be passive resistant. They are not actively resisting you but they are not compliant, such as a protester. They are sitting on the ground, they refuse to move. You tell them to move; they are not actively resisting you but they are not complying with your order. The reasonable police officer's response could be hands on, like contact controls, basically, grabbing ahold of them and moving them. At this level you can use OC spray, which, in other words, is pepper spray. Some people know it as mace, it's a little different than that.

"The next step up would be actively resistant. They are doing something physically to resist your efforts to arrest them. They are not assaulting, punching, or kicking you; they are pulling away. You can use compliance techniques such as wrist twist, arm bars, pressure points. The next step up would be assaultive bodily harm. They are punching you, kicking you, biting you, things like that. At that level, you can use all the techniques and OC [spray], as well, but you can also use what is known as the PR-24 [side-handle baton]. You can use the PR-24 for arm bars, pain compliance, as well as strikes to certain areas of the body, depending on how assaultive the person is.

"The final stage of the top of the model would be basically serious physical injury and/or deadly force. This person may have a weapon, a knife, gun, threatening your life at that level. You are allowed to use what's called deadly physical force, which includes the firing of a firearm. At that level, you can use the PR-24 to strike lethal areas such as the head or the neck."

The well-spoken officer, looking relaxed, speaks in a confident tone.

Smith explains officers are taught to lay a person prone or on their stomach. Once laid out, officers use commands to make them spread their arms out like an airplane and turn the palms up.

"The reason why you tell them to turn their palms up, is

so you can see there is nothing in their hands. You tell them to look away from you and spread their legs. Once you see their hands are free, if you have your firearm out, you would now holster that weapon. You would move in, kneel on the center area of the back, put one handcuff on the hand you have control of, give an order to have the suspect bring the remaining hand that is not cuffed toward the center of their back, and handcuff that hand."

The officer had received firearm training through a series of lectures and target practice with and without ammunition using his Heckler & Koch service pistol. Edward McPhillips had testified that two distinct actions are required to initiate fire of the H&K: squeezing the grip with eight pounds of pressure, followed by pulling the trigger with three and a half pounds of pressure. Smith disagrees.

"If you have to use deadly force to defend yourself... it will work in reverse order. You can squeeze the cocker [grip] then pull the trigger, or you can pull the trigger, then squeeze the cocker," Smith says.

With that, Kelly directs Smith to discuss how he became acquainted with Franklyn.

Smith begins to describe a roll call in early 1997 when he was first briefed about Franklyn.

Judge Gill interrupts. "Ladies and gentlemen, I'm going to allow some testimony from Scott Smith concerning what he heard at the roll call. Ordinarily, that is hearsay evidence. A person can't testify as to what someone else told them, in court. There is an exception. This allows it to be admitted for you not because what was ostensibly said to him was true, but that it was said to him. This is allowed for state of mind, which I will explain later."

Smith recalls that a shift supervisor stated Franklyn, a convicted felon, was released from prison and had returned to the New Milford area. He had resisted arrest, was known to carry weapons, had stabbed and severely injured someone, and all officers were advised to use extreme caution when dealing with him.

"During the same roll call, one particular officer, I don't recall who it was, said he found a knife in his vehicle, and he does resist arrest," Smith says.

Kelly brings up the first time Smith met Franklyn. In late 1997, Smith, along with another officer, were dispatched to Franklyn's grandfather's home in New Milford to investigate a complaint regarding a stolen television. While there, Franklyn showed up.

Kelly asks, "How long was he in your presence?"

"Approximately ten to fifteen minutes."

"Were you in uniform?"

"Yes, I was."

"How close did you get to him?"

"Five, six, seven feet," Smith answers.

Kelly aims to establish that Franklyn knew Officer Smith as that investigation ended and both young men parted ways without incident. Kelly brings up another occasion. On October 16, 1998, Smith along with two officers attempted to serve Franklyn with warrants at his parents' home in New Milford.

Kelly asks, "Prior to going to that location, did you have a conversation with Officer Wheeler?"

"Yes, I did," Smith says.

"And what did Officer Wheeler tell you?"

Connelly objects. "Your Honor, it's offered not for the truth of the matter?"

Judge Gill reminds the jury. "This is another hearsay situation. He is going to testify as to what somebody else told him, and that situation, again, I'm going to allow him to answer that question not because what was said to him was true, but because—for the truth of, as you find it, that it was said to him. Okay."

Smith explains. "Officer Wheeler said, 'Hey, Scottie, you know who we're dealing with here?' I said yes. 'You know, he will run, he will fight, and he does carry weapons.' He said, 'Scribby and I...went to arrest him one time... While Officer Scribner was trying to handcuff him...Franklyn reached quickly into a front pocket, I [Officer Wheeler] got there first, grabbed his arm.' They handcuffed him, and they ended up finding a knife in his pocket."

Kelly asks, "So you went to a specific location?"

"Yes, we did."

"Tell us what happened when you got there."

"I went to the front door and knocked on the door."

"Did anybody answer your knock?"

"Yes."

"Who did?"

"Mrs. Reid, and I believe Mr. Reid was there, but I'm not too sure about that," Smith says.

"Tell us what you said."

"I identified myself, said I was looking for Franklyn Reid; we had arrest warrants for him; was he home?"

Suddenly, Connelly intercedes. "This was on October 16?"

"That is correct," Kelly answers.

Kelly turns to Smith, "Did you arrest Franklyn Reid on October 16, 1998?"

"No."

While hunting for Franklyn on December 29, 1998, Smith expressed to Shortt concern for Cramer. "There was nobody speaking on the radio, and it struck me, I hope Sergeant Cramer is okay, because the last thing we knew, he was in foot pursuit with Franklyn Reid. You would expect to hear some type of radio transmission, updates, status, so I was concerned," Smith tells Kelly.

"As you approached Sandra's Cleaners, did something occur?"

"Yes."

"What?"

"We were heading north on Route 202. Detective Shortt looked to his right and said, 'Hey, is that him?' I said, 'I don't know.' We thought it was worthwhile to turn around and check and see if it was him or not," Smith explains.

"Did you turn around?"

"Yes, in the intersection of 202 and Park Lane West. The traffic was too heavy to make a U-turn in the middle of the road."

"And about how far would you have to go past the Sunoco gas station to turn around?"

"Approximately a tenth of a mile."

"What did you do next?"

"By the time we got in the area of the station, I saw a black male walking across Howland Road up into the Sunoco parking lot. As I'm pulling in, Detective Shortt said, 'Is that him?' I said, 'Yes, that is Franklyn Reid.' I rolled down my window. I don't know if it was all the way or partially," Smith says.

Kelly asks, "How close did you get to Mr. Reid?"

"I would estimate, ten to fifteen feet."

"What occurred?"

"He had walked between the first set of gas pumps and the building where you go in to pay for your gas. We were pulling in behind him as he was walking, and he was looking over his shoulder at us. Detective Shortt said, 'Get as close to him as you can. You know, I think he is going to run.' I felt the same way. I pulled the car...within ten to fifteen feet...and stopped."

"Do you recall how he was dressed?"

"Baggy clothing, blue jeans, nothing more specific."

"Do you recall anything else about him concerning clothing?"

"He was carrying a light jacket or sweatshirt. I'm not sure how he was carrying it, but I believe it was in his right hand."

"What did you do next?"

"I stopped the car. I immediately opened my door to get

out, and as soon as I did that, Franklyn Reid started running in the opposite direction."

"What was your intent when you got out of the car?"

"To catch Franklyn Reid and arrest him."

"Could you describe the manner in which he ran?"

"Very fast."

Kelly asks, "Did you say anything?"

"I started yelling, 'Stop, police. Stop, police.' I believe I called him by his first name."

"What did you say?"

"Stop, Franklyn."

"Without offending anyone's ears, can you demonstrate to the jury the manner in which you yelled those words to Mr. Reid?"

Smith proceeds and yells his command very loud. *"Stop, police! Stop, police! Stop, Franklyn!"*

His tone echoes throughout the courtroom. I am sure anyone around Sunoco would have heard the officer, but apparently no one did except Shortt.

Kelly continues, "Did he stop?"

"No, he did not. He ran across Route 202. I slowed momentarily because I thought I was going to get hit by traffic. I checked both ways very quickly to make sure it was safe for me to run across the road." Smith says he continued the chase running *very fast* while yelling his command.

"Where did you see him go?" Kelly asks.

"We were still in the road...there is a white line on the road...so basically running along the roadway, right side. He turned left onto a grassy area alongside the road."

"What did you do?"

"I turned left as well, still yelling, 'Stop, police. Stop, police.'"

"Where did you see him go?"

"He ran right back into the middle of Route 202 without even looking."

"What went through your mind at that time?"

"Just did not make any sense to me. I am trying to take this guy into custody. First, he runs into traffic without looking. Now he looks like he is going to turn left to walk into the woods. Now he turns sharply right, running back into the middle of traffic. It was so irrational to me. At that point I have no idea what he was doing, thinking...It didn't make any sense for him to go back into the middle of the roadway."

"What did you do at that point?" Kelly asks.

"Things were very—happening very quickly now. We just finished running...I see that he is standing there with his back mostly to me, and I can't see his hands...He is looking over his shoulder, staring at me."

Kelly wants a demonstration. "Would you stand up and attempt to demonstrate the position you saw him take in the middle of Route 202?"

Smith stands in the witness box, turns his back toward the jury, and looks over his right shoulder. "His hands were somewhere in front of him. I couldn't see them. He was looking like this."

I notice the jury has not shown emotional reactions in response to dramatic displays or contentious testimonies.

Their objective manner remains the same toward Officer Smith as he sits down.

Kelly asks, "Did that have any particular significance to you?"

"He looked at me in a confrontational way. We're trained to look for what's called a thousand-yard stare, [which] is basically a cold stare looking right through you."

"What did you do at that point?"

"I couldn't see his hands. The way he was staring at me caused me concern. I drew my firearm off my right hip and pointed it at him."

Smith demonstrates how he held his firearm, the right hand extended with the left hand clasping the gun for stability.

"What did you do next?" Kelly asks.

"Things were happening very fast. I started immediately yelling, 'Show me your hands, show me your hands,' while pointing the firearm at him. I started to approach him. I wanted to get both of us out of the middle of the road."

"Do you know how many times you said that to Mr. Reid?"

"Several. It was like a broken record."

Kelly asks, "Did he ever show you his hands while he was in the center of the road?"

"No," Smith states, shaking his head.

"How about traffic?"

"I was focused on him, not traffic."

While motorists were stopped in both directions witnessing someone pointing a gun at someone else, Smith approached the suspect. He quickly repositioned by pulling his firearm back toward his chest while keeping his left hand extended to grab Franklyn's right shoulder.

"Explain why you changed your position," Kelly says.

"We are trained at the academy to keep distance between whoever you are in contact with and the gun, as far as possible."

"Did you get him off the road?"

"Yes, I did. I wanted to get both of us out of the road. That is the worst place to put someone in custody. It puts myself, the suspect, and the public in danger."

"Did you say anything to him as you were proceeding from the center to the shoulder line?"

"I'm still yelling, 'Show me your hands. Show me your hands. Show me your hands.'"

"Did he?"

"No," Smith answers while shaking his head again.

"What happened when you got onto the shoulder of Route 202?"

"As I'm pulling him off the roadway, he resisted...He didn't flail with his arms or try to punch me. He pulled away as if he wanted to go in another direction."

"He didn't strike you?"

"No, he did not."

"Did he kick you?"

"No."

"What happened next?"

"I got him up onto the grassy area, and then we ended up on the embankment."

All eyes are focused on him as he explains his version of events.

Kelly asks, "What occurred next?"

"I wanted to lay him out on his stomach, pull his hands behind his back, and arrest him. So, as I'm yelling, 'Show me your hands, show me your hands,' I'm yelling, 'Get on the ground. Get on the ground. Get on the ground.'"

"Did he?"

"No. He wouldn't go down willingly, so I had to try to force him down onto his knees."

"Did you succeed?"

"No, I did not."

"What happened?"

"At some point, I don't recall exactly when, I switched my grip from his right shoulder area to his left shoulder area, grabbing his clothes," Smith explains.

"What did you attempt to do in that hold?"

"I tried to force him down with all my force, to the ground, like pushing on his shoulder to get him onto his knees."

"Did he go to his knees on what I'll call the first attempt?"

"No. I pushed him down again and his knees buckled. He struggled but then pushed his way, very hard, back up toward me, bent his knees and stood up straight."

"Were you surprised?"

"Yes. Very," Smith says.

"Why?"

"Here I am, a police officer holding a firearm at this guy. He is not showing me his hands, and I'm becoming more and more scared. I don't know what this guy is thinking. I'm telling him to get on the ground, and I have to physically try to force him down to the ground, and he is not going. I couldn't make any sense of it. And it was scaring the crap out of me, for lack of a better term."

"What happened next?"

"I tried again to force him down onto his knees. This time I was able to force him onto his knees."

"Then what happened?"

"I tried to force him toward the embankment. I pushed him forward. His hands came out and hit the ground. He pushed off with his hands and sprung back up into a kneeling position."

Sounding repetitive, Kelly asks, "Then what happened?"

"I believe he was still on his knees, lying on his right shoulder area, possibly even the side of his head."

Kelly asks his same question.

"His hands are underneath him somewhere in his midsection. I can see the back of his arms and shoulders. They are starting to move very quickly. He is searching either for a gun or a knife is what I believed, at that time."

The officer demonstrates the movement by taking to the floor, facing Judge Gill's direction, and begins to move his back and arms, stating he could not see Franklyn's hands.

While he returns to the witness box, Kelly asks, "Why not holster your weapon?"

"It would have been suicidal on my part. I can't see the hands. The hands kill, plain and simple. He could very easily pull a concealed weapon, turn around, and stab or shoot me. That would be absolutely ludicrous to do, at this point," Smith says.

"What happens next?"

"His hands are moving quickly. I'm still yelling, 'Show me your hands, show me your hands.' Now I'm thinking: this is going bad. I'm really scared. I can't see his hands. What's he doing? He is not responding to any of my commands. He's just run through two lanes of traffic. My previous knowledge of him is all coming into play. I'm like, what is he doing? Just show me your hands. And he moved very suddenly up toward me, and I believe he starts to twist toward the left with his left arm coming out."

"What did you do when you saw that?"

"I was scared to death when he made that classic move, that very sudden move toward me. I thought, Oh, shit, I'm dead."

All eyes are locked on a now stoned-face Smith as he continues.

"I thought of my mother, my father, my sister, and how much I was going to miss them and how much I loved them."

If any moment exists to display raw emotions and potentially melt the hearts of many, this is it. But no emotions or remorse surface, just seemingly empty words.

I can't believe I just heard an officer of the law say how he was feeling while pointing a gun at someone's back. I'm sure Franklyn wasn't thinking about how much he was going to miss his family; that would have been suicidal. He may have had his issues with the law, fighting an uphill battle at times, even spending a few years behind bars, but losing his marbles with a deadly weapon in his back? I guess we shall never know what he was thinking.

Kelly continues, "Did you believe he had obtained a weapon and was about to use it on you?"

"Absolutely."

"What did you do?"

"I fired my gun once."

"Where did you fire it?"

"The available center mass. That means the largest central portion of the body that is available to you, at that time."

Kelly moves to discredit Dr. Carver's conclusion regarding a contact wound. "Do you recall the barrel of your firearm being close to the back of Mr. Reid."

"I wasn't concerned with the distance of my firearm, at that point. I was concerned with saving my own life," Smith admits.

"What happened?"

"He fell to the ground. He wasn't moving. I couldn't believe what just happened to me. I turned to look for Detective Shortt, to see if he was around."

"Did you see him?"

"Yes. He was basically behind me. I had to look a hundred and eighty degrees."

"Did you say anything?"

"Get me an ambulance."

"What happened, thereafter?"

"I recall Detective Jordan getting there very quickly, starting first aid and CPR. He yelled for me to go get rubber gloves out of the trunk of his car. I remember that task being very hard. I think it took me a longer period of time than normal. I think I might have brought the gloves back to him...but I remember Detective Jordan rolling Franklyn Reid over from his stomach to his back."

"See anything at that time?"

"I recall seeing a red item underneath him."

From my seat behind him in the courtroom, I have a bird's eye view of Connelly's every movement or profiled facial expression. Well, something in Smith's last response triggers an interesting reaction from him: he quickly jars his head to look at and then lean in toward Assistant State Attorney Robin Lipsky's right ear. Anticipation for the cross-examination sets in.

Kelly resumes with, "You mentioned earlier, in the Sunoco station, that Mr. Reid was carrying—I think you described it as a jacket or sweatshirt?"

"That's correct."

With that, court adjourns for thirty minutes.

* * *

After it reconvenes, Kelly takes aim at other eyewitnesses.

"Mr. James DeMaria testified that he observed Mr. Reid resting on his elbows, with his knees bent. Was Mr. Reid ever in that position?"

"Never," Smith says.

"Mrs. Gail Meehan testified that when Mr. Reid was on his stomach, you were behind him. You had your left foot approximately in the center of his back and, with your left hand, you had Mr. Reid's two hands behind his back. Did you ever do that?"

"Never," Smith repeats forcefully.

Moving on, Kelly asks, "When you were in the gas station parking lot, did Mr. Reid say anything to you?"

"Not a word."

"When you pursued him along the shoulder of Route 202, did he say anything to you?"

"No, he did not."

"When you came into contact with him in the center of Route 202, did he say anything to you?"

"No, he did not," Smith repeats.

"When you took him from the center of Route 202, did he say anything to you?"

"No, he did not."

"Did that have any significance to you?"

"I thought it was kind of eerie. I felt he would have said something to me, either: you got me, I give up, screw you, or some expletives but he was very, very quiet, and that was just eerie to me."

Kelly, who prefers to stand still on the floor, repeats his most important point. He asks, "In terms of your decision to fire your weapon, would you explain what led up to your decision?"

Connelly interrupts. "Objection, Your Honor. Asked and answered."

Judge Gill rules, "I will allow it."

"Based on my knowledge of Franklyn Reid, the fact that I engaged in a foot pursuit, he ran into traffic, he was making very irrational moves—it was at that moment he made that very sudden movement up toward me and I could not see his hands. Out of fear for my life. I believed he had obtained a weapon, and he was turning to stab, shoot, and kill me. That is why I fired my gun."

Those words trigger a familiar, intense emotion. I'm back in the hollow tunnel, staring into space as my eyes water and body warms. I assume that I'm not alone in this spaced-out bottomless well of emotions. My parents' hearts also ache, as do Smith's family's. They feel for Scott; we feel for Franklyn. It's the unintended consequence that has linked both families together, no matter the type of justice either of us seeks.

* * *

Connelly assumes the floor for what's sure to be a blistering cross-examination.

"Officer Smith, just so it is clear, when you pulled that trigger that morning, you intended to kill Franklyn Reid, did you not?"

"I intended to stop the threat," Smith says.

Connelly rephrases. "You had your handgun pressed up against his back, and pulled the trigger, your intent was to kill Franklyn Reid, correct?"

"Officers are trained to stop a threat, and a person will die with a bullet in the center mass."

I am stunned. And glancing around, that is the emotion displayed upon most faces in my immediate vicinity.

Many have speculated, myself included, that this was an accidental shooting.

Connelly asks, "That gun didn't go off by accident?"

Smith affirms with vigor, "Absolutely not."

My dad looks on with a blank stare, unsure what to think at this moment. For nearly two years, he found slight comfort that his eldest son may have died accidentally. Suddenly, his belief crashes down after Smith categorically denies that. He further wrestles with the notion that a sympathetic jury will find Smith not guilty.

Connelly revisits the Use of Force Continuum by referencing training at the academy, which instructs one to start at the lowest level of force when confronting someone.

"You can very quickly go from a compliant person to somebody that is about to hurt you, assault you, kill you. It's a fluid model. You don't have to exhaust all five steps before you get to the top," Smith says.

Earlier in the trial, Attorney Kelly had produced a drawing depicting Franklyn sitting on the ground with his knees bent as observed by Mr. DeMaria. Connelly asks, "What would you consider that in this force continuum?"

"Compliant or passive resistance."

"In that situation, you do not use deadly force, correct?"

"That's correct."

Connelly moves to the top of the model—deadly force— and reminds Smith of the alternative method he told Mr. Kelly.

He asks, "That Heckler & Koch is a pretty solid weapon, correct?"

"Yes, it is."

"When Franklyn Reid was kneeling down in front of you, how far was the butt of your gun from Franklyn Reid's head?"

"A foot, approximately, I'm not really sure."

"You never struck Franklyn Reid in the head with the butt of your gun, did you?"

"At the academy we're not trained to hit anybody over the head with our firearm, ever," Smith states.

"But you can? You are there to save lives; you are not there to kill, and if it takes whacking somebody in the head with a gun or a nightstick or another hard object, that is all right, correct?"

"We're not trained to whack anybody, especially with a firearm in any circumstance."

Connelly repeats, "No circumstance, whatsoever, even—"

Smith interrupts Connelly in mid-sentence. "Hit somebody over the head with a firearm? No."

Unfazed, Connelly revisits the arrest procedures Smith discussed with Kelly. He sets the stage.

"Your ultimate goal that morning was to get Mr. Reid in handcuffs?"

"Absolutely."

Connelly meticulously goes through the process Smith learned at the police academy before circling back to the ultimate goal.

He asks, "How do you do that to handcuff?"

"You have the suspect on his stomach, hands spread like

an airplane, palms up. At this point, if you have a firearm drawn or any other weapon, now it should be safe to holster it, because he is looking away and you can see there are no weapons. You say 'Raise your hand toward the sound of my voice.' They reach back toward the sound of your voice, and you grab ahold of their hands as soon as it is safe to do so."

"What is the purpose of kneeling on the suspect's back?"

"To control him."

"You are trained to put a knee in the back, because you want to try to control the man on the ground, correct?"

"Once you see the hands are free," Smith states.

Regarding Mrs. Meehan's testimony, Connelly says, "She saw Franklyn Reid on the ground, you over him, straddling him with your left foot on his back, and both his hands in your left hand. That is not far off from the scenario you are taught at the police academy?"

"In that situation, it's totally different," Smith insists.

"Your testimony to this jury at this point is that you never had control of Franklyn Reid's hands?"

"That is correct. I never saw them."

Connelly poses another scenario as seen through the eyes of Mr. DeMaria and depicted in the drawing. He sets the stage, his voice elevating.

"You had your gun pointed at him yelling, 'Franklyn, get on the ground,' and Franklyn sat on the ground. Isn't that true?"

"No, that's not true!"

Undeterred, Connelly continues. "In your passive resistance training, you went over to him, grabbed his shoulder, rolled him onto his stomach so you could get his hands behind his back and handcuff him. That is exactly what happened, didn't it, Officer Smith?"

"Mr. Connelly, you weren't there!"

"Yes or no?"

"You weren't there. I was!"

Connelly retells the scenario, now demanding a yes or no in a tense exchange. Smith is clearly flustered, unwilling to provide a concrete response, as the prosecutor seeks Judge Gill's intervention.

Judge Gill speaks. "Answer the question, please, sir."

"No, sir!" Smith says to Connelly's question.

My heart is racing, listening and seeing the dramatic moment unfold. I can feel the temperature rising. Whether it's Smith on the hot seat or the courtroom warming up, I can't tell. Whatever the cause, there's no break to institute solutions such as opening the windows or turning on the air conditioner. Connelly doesn't appear ready to pause from this pivotal moment as he directs the witness to October 16, 1998.

Connelly offers two warrants for identification purposes—the first issued by the department for four counts of threatening. He wants to know if Smith attempted to serve that warrant but Kelly quickly objects and requests his client see the underlying affidavit, which includes a signature and date.

It appears Smith knows where Connelly is going with this series of questioning, as he's hesitant to provide clear responses.

Unrelenting, Connelly asks again, "Is this the warrant you were going to arrest Mr. Reid on?"

All eyes and ears shift toward Smith.

"I believe this warrant was issued afterward."

"Well, what warrant were you going to arrest Mr. Reid on?"

The officer recalls other charges but is unsure. "I believe they were for threatening and possibly breach of peace."

"You told Mr. Kelly you went to his house specifically on October 16 to arrest him on warrants for threatening, failure to appear, and breach of peace. Breach of peace is the underlying charge in this warrant, isn't that true?"

"I believe it was, to the best of my knowledge."

Satisfied, Connelly instructs Smith to look at the paper in his hand and tell the court the date a judge signed the first warrant. He is forced to say, "10-26-98."

Connelly reiterates, "October 26, 1998. So, you would agree with me, Officer Smith, this warrant was not in existence on October 16, 1998?"

Smith acknowledges that to be true.

Connelly turns to the second warrant and points out that a judge signed it on November 2, 1998. "This warrant wasn't in existence on October 16, either, isn't that true, Officer Smith?"

"That's correct."

Now, it's understandable why Connelly had such a sharp reaction earlier when the date didn't make sense.

Moments before Smith engaged in the foot pursuit, he says there was no dialogue with Shortt other than, "Get as close as possible; it looks like he's going to run."

"I made the decision for myself to get out of the car," Smith says.

Connelly interjects, "The decisions you make in life, Officer Smith, you have to live with them."

"That's correct."

"It was your decision to chase Franklyn Reid and to capture him single-handedly?"

"My job was to arrest him, plain and simple."

"You didn't want to wait for Detective Shortt to catch up with you?"

"I was chasing a suspect. I didn't have time to sit and wait. He would have been gone."

Quick-witted, Connelly digs deeper. "Where would he have gone?"

"I have no idea."

"Do you know where Franklyn lived?"

"I know where his parents live."

"Well, that is the same house you went to look for him when you were supposedly serving these nonexistent warrants, correct?"

"That is correct," Smith says softly.

In a boisterous tone that echoes throughout the courtroom, Connelly adds, "That is three-tenths of a mile from where you killed him."

Smith appears like he could use a break, but Connelly is not going to relinquish another pivotal moment. Smith expressed to Kelly how scared he was moments before pulling the trigger.

"Officer Smith, the reason you shot him was because

you were in fear of your life. You thought, in his hands, he had a weapon, either a gun or knife?"

"That's correct."

Connelly asks, in roaring volume, "Did you ever bend down and check to see if he had a gun or knife in his possession?"

Kelly immediately interrupts. "Your Honor, I would ask that my client be treated like a human being and not be screamed at!"

Judge Gill speaks. "The question is allowable; the volume is not."

"I don't recall doing that. No, sir," Smith says.

Connelly states in a stern, sincere tone, "You told the jury that visions of your life were flashing in front of your face. Franklyn was going to reach up and either shoot or stab you. Yet after you shoot him, as a police officer, you did not even bend down to look to see if your life-and-death decision was the correct one?"

Smith ponders this a few seconds.

"No, I did not, Mr. Connelly. I was scared out of my mind, at that point. I didn't know what the heck just happened. I was just happy to be alive, at that point."

"You didn't know what happened? You just killed a man. You told the jury you killed him because you thought your life was in danger, and you didn't know what happened?"

"I knew," Smith says with another awkward few seconds' pause. "I couldn't believe what had happened to me. I never thought in my whole career I would ever have to make a decision to shoot, and in self-defense," Smith adds.

Connelly points out, "I have never heard you once say, 'I couldn't believe what just happened to Franklyn Reid,' because you didn't care what happened, right?"

"Of course, I cared what happened to Franklyn Reid."

"Did you ever ask anybody to check the hospital to see if he was alive or dead?"

"I did not."

Connelly has given Smith numerous opportunities to display sincere emotion and show sympathy in front of the jury; that clearly seems to be lacking.

Kelly had introduced Smith's three-and-a-half-page affidavit which he produced on December 31, 1998, with Attorney Allingham. Connelly reintroduces and digs deeper.

"You were never interviewed by the Connecticut State Police regarding this, were you?" Connelly asks.

"No, I was not."

"You were never interviewed by the state attorney's office regarding this incident?"

"No, I was not."

"The only version of events that you've ever given regarding this incident was a statement or an affidavit that was compiled in your attorney's office?"

"Yes."

"What were the mechanics of it?"

"I told Attorney Tom Allingham what had happened on a couple different occasions. He drafted the document, then I spent several hours going over it, making corrections, and we made several revisions."

The prosecutor emphasizes the importance of Smith's

statement that he dictated within forty-eight hours after the incident.

"You knew this was going to be reviewed by the Connecticut State Police to see whether or not charges should be brought in this case?"

"Absolutely," Smith says.

"So, you wanted to be as concise and as articulate as you possibly could when you drafted this statement?"

"Be as precise, at that time, as I possibly could, yes."

Connelly has set the stage again and revisits why Kelly walked back a response from Smith.

"How many times do you mention the red jacket?" Connelly asks.

Smith skims through the statement he carries. "I believe there was one time, sir."

"That is when you first saw him at the Sunoco station?"

"That's correct."

"There is nothing in that statement about any red object, or red jacket, or red ball, or red dot being under Mr. Reid when he was rolled over?"

"That is correct."

"The reason you told us today that you saw this red object underneath him is because you subsequently learned, after you gave that statement, that there was a two-and-three-quarter-inch blade folding knife found in Mr. Reid's pocket?"

"That's correct."

Connelly takes further aim at what is potentially the defense's core evidence, the jacket. "Nowhere in your statement do you ever say that while you were chasing Mr. Reid, that Mr. Reid had that jacket in his hands?"

"No, I did not."

"Nowhere in your statement do you say that Mr. Reid had that jacket in his possession when you had him on his knees forcing him to the ground?"

"I did not say that in my statement," Smith admits.

The prosecutor implicitly challenges Smith's response to Kelly that Franklyn was running *very fast* and leaves it for the jury to decide. He asks, "You said you are six foot two, a hundred ninety pounds?"

"Approximately, yes."

"You heard Dr. Carver testify that Franklyn Reid was five foot four, a hundred twenty-nine pounds. You doubt that?"

"No, I do not."

"He had baggy clothing on, kind of hanging low on his waist?"

"They looked baggy, I don't—specifically know if they were hanging low."

Connelly points to an exhibit. "He had these big black boots on, correct?"

"I don't specifically remember him wearing black boots," Smith states.

"But you have seen the boots introduced in evidence?"

"Yes, I have."

"He also had a pair of sweatpants on, underneath those baggy blue jeans?"

"I have since learned that, yes."

"He had three shirts on—one a big, heavy, almost like a sweatshirt type, the Air Tech one?"

"Yes."

"So, he was pretty weighed down in clothes, wasn't he?"

"I wouldn't define it as weighed down, but he had several layers on, yes."

"Did you ever tell Franklyn, if you don't show me your hands, I'm going to shoot you?"

"I did not do that," Smith says.

"You never warned him verbally, that you were going to shoot him?"

"I didn't have time, sir."

"You kept yelling at him. How difficult is it to say, show me your hands or I'll shoot you?"

"At that time, I'm yelling show me your hands. He makes a sudden movement. I have no time."

Connelly presses further, "Officer Smith, you never warned him you were going to shoot him, did you?"

"No, I did not."

"I have nothing further," Connelly says.

Kelly has been anxiously waiting to retake the floor and appears fired up. Repetitive statements such as, "Objection, Your Honor, those are leading questions, and this is his witness," are voiced by Connelly, and subsequently followed by, "You can't lead, Mr. Kelly," from Judge Gill. Sparks fly between the Irish lawyers, but the Irish judge keeps order, and Smith is in the crossfire.

Kelly asks, "In dealing with someone like Franklyn Reid,

did it make any difference to you that he had stabbed a police officer versus a non-police officer?"

"The most important thing was that he stabbed somebody, injuring him very severely."

Kelly elaborates. "What happened was that Mr. Reid went to stab the young lady and the man stood in the way."

Connelly flies out of his chair. "Objection!"

Kelly fires back without Judge Gill's ruling. "Mr. Connelly has opened the door trying to get the jury to think it's an accidental stabbing. You don't go to prison for accidental stabbings."

Judge Gill intervenes. "Come on, Mr. Kelly. Off the soapbox. We went astray here, ladies and gentlemen. We are going to come back now to being lawyers asking lawyer questions."

Kelly rephrases. "With reference to the stabbing, without going into details, were you told that injuries were sustained by the person who was stabbed?"

"Yes."

Kelly's last cross-examination question focuses on Franklyn's hands.

Smith states, "I had no reason to shoot Mr. Reid. It was not until he made that sudden movement and I thought he was going to shoot or stab me is when I felt my life was in danger. That is why I fired."

Connelly takes the floor once more. "You want this jury to believe that Mr. Reid was on his knees, facing up the embankment, with your left hand on his left shoulder, trying to force him on the ground. He puts his hands in front when you saw his hands, correct?"

"Very briefly," Smith says.

"Was there anything in his hands, at that time?"

"I don't believe so, no," Smith admits.

"Mr. Reid just popped back up, like a jack-in-the box?"

"Toward me and started to turn, yes."

Connelly repeats in a profound tone, "Just popped right back up off his knees, and with your hand pushing him down, he just popped up?"

"I wasn't watching his knees," Smith says, concluding his long-awaited testimony.

Court adjourns for the day. Both families exit the courtroom separately into a barrage of cameras and reporters asking for reactions. No words are shared. Smith may be happy his part is over but the defense continues.

ACT V SCENE IV

DEFENSE'S EXPERT

The next day, Mr. Emanuel Kapelsohn, the defense's main expert witness, testifies. Kapelsohn provides firearms and tactics training to law enforcement and security officers, teaching them how knives and other edged weapons can be held, concealed, and the amount of time it may take a suspect to attack with one.

Kelly begins his questioning with Smith's Heckler & Koch nine-millimeter semi-automatic pistol. He aims to debunk Mr. Edward McPhillip's conclusion that the handgun can only discharge in one order.

Kapelsohn disagrees. He demonstrates with Smith's actual firearm.

"The gun is designed purposely so that you could fire it either by squeezing the cocking lever first, which I'm going to do now, then pulling the trigger. You could pull the trigger first, which I'm doing now, and then squeeze the cocking lever, and when I do so, you are going to see the firing pin come out the rear of the gun and then go forward like it just did. You can do both of them simultaneously. That click you just heard was the firing pin going forward to fire the gun. It's designed in that way not to be sequence-critical, so that an officer under stress doesn't have to do things in just the right sequence to make the gun fire. He could do it in any of those three ways and the gun will fire."

"Have you tested that particular firearm in terms of the weight it would take to pull the trigger?" Kelly asks.

"With a cocking lever compressed, it takes between four-and-three quarters and five pounds of force on the trigger to fire this gun. The cocking lever on this gun takes about eighteen or nineteen pounds of force to compress it to where the gun can be fired."

Officer Smith testified Franklyn was either going to shoot or stab him. Kapelsohn provides another demonstration with the knife found in Franklyn's jacket. He stands up, grips the knife, and pulls open the blade with one hand while grasping the handle with his other hand.

"This is called a lock blade knife, and that snap you hear is the blade locking open. The knife blade has this little piece of metal, which is called an opening stud, and it's provided specifically so that the user can brace his or her thumb against it and open the knife easily with one hand. It could also be opened by simply gripping the blade in the fingers (he uses his thumb and index finger) and flicking the knife downward, so that momentum opens the body of the knife."

Sitting down, Kapelsohn adds, "The partially serrated

and straight blade is called a tanto, the same tip on a Japanese samurai sword. The tip will not break if used in slashing, thrusting, or stabbing motions."

Kelly seeks a demonstration. "If you can just stand up again for a moment, and could you demonstrate, based on your training and experience, the various ways you can hold this knife and use it?"

"I object!" says Connelly.

"Overruled."

Kapelsohn illustrates his knowledge. "The knife can be held in what's called a fencing grip. When you go to stab, it would be both safer for the user and more effective to brace the butt of the knife into the heel of the hand."

The courtroom is treated to other stabbing motions, such as ice pick grip (hand clasped around the handle), advancing windmill (blocking the person's arm and stabbing downward), and backhanded (gripping the handle with knuckles facing upward and stabbing in a backward motion).

"A knife can be concealed in a pocket, waistband, sock, underwear, or around the neck for easy accessibility," Kapelsohn states.

He goes on to elaborate on police procedures which Smith discussed during his testimony. "Officers are taught things about positions and proximity. If we're dealing with a person known to carry weapons, or we're arresting the person for a crime that involves violence, officers are taught to maximize their distance from the suspect to the greatest extent they can. We try to get the suspect turned away from us, prone out on the ground or in some cases hands against a wall, feet back, or bent over the hood of a car. Officers always want to be able to see the suspect's hands."

Kelly asks, "What's the importance of that?"

"Hands are what people use to hold or wield weapons. Officers want to see the palms of the person's hands. If a suspect has hands turned away from you, in their pockets, or under an article of clothing, that is a special danger. We teach the officer to try to get the suspect to show his hands before the officer edges in to close proximity with the suspect. Officers are taught to try to use backup whenever they can. If you have a situation that will permit it, you should wait, ideally, until you have other officers there. The more officers that are there, decreases the likelihood of the suspect trying to resist or fight. The other side of the coin, it would be very dangerous for the officer to approach close to this suspect without having his gun out. Because if the suspect has a weapon (and) the officer's gun is holstered, the officer is behind the reaction time curve.

"So, the ideal situation is for a backup officer to stand at a distance with his gun out and pointed at the suspect, and the officer who is going to apply the handcuffs can holster his gun and then come close for the purpose of handcuffing and searching the suspect. That way we have the suspect covered at gunpoint, but not by the person who is close to him. All these things I just described are in ideal circumstances where backup is right there when you need it, where the suspect will comply. In other words, when you say, 'Show me your hands,' he does it."

Kelly follows up. "You mentioned reaction cycle. Would you explain that?"

"Yes. When an officer encounters a suspect in close proximity, training and common sense plays an important role in either diffusing or escalating a situation. The officer may react to something the suspect is doing. When the suspect takes that action, the officer must first perceive it, see it, and distinguish that from an innocent movement. In other words, the suspect may just be nervous, shrugging his shoulders, or maybe reaching for his identification. We can't have the officer use deadly force at any innocent movement of the suspect, so the officer has to not only perceive the movement but has to judge that this is a life-threatening movement, consistent with an attack. Then, after seeing that and making that decision, a nerve impulse has to go down the arm to cause the finger to pull the trigger. Whether it's an edged weapon or firearm we're dealing with, the suspect's action has an advantage. The officer's already behind the eight ball because he's waiting to see the attack and react to the attack."

I'm trying to discern what I've heard thus far. Smith and Chief Sweeney testified that training protocols were followed, yet Kapelsohn is discussing standard procedures which essentially conflicted with what transpired that December day.

* * *

Connelly cross-examines Kapelsohn. "Do you own that knife?"

"One similar to it, but without the serrated edge—"

Connelly interrupts. "What do you use the knife for?"

Kelly cuts in. "Your Honor, might he have the courtesy of finishing his answer?"

Before Judge Gill can rule, Kapelsohn speaks up. "The one that I carry without the serrated edge or tanto point, I use for a variety of work tasks—opening boxes, cutting string, sharpening and cutting. It's also available as a weapon."

"On a daily basis, would you carry pocketknives?" Connelly asks.

"Yes, I carry two knives."

"That is not unusual, a lot of people carry pocketknives, correct?"

"That is correct."

Connelly shifts his cross-examining to Smith's Heckler & Koch. Although the witness eloquently explained its operation with a demonstration, Connelly focuses on usage by New Jersey State Police.

"What's the experience they have with accidental discharge?" Connelly asks.

My dad's ears perk up after hearing those two words.

"There have been a number, as there have been in any large police agency using any kind of handguns—"

Connelly interrupts again. "Isn't it true that the New Jersey State Police have an inordinate amount of accidental discharges with this gun by state troopers because of how the gun fires?"

"Will you let me answer?" Kapelsohn hollers.

"Answer yes or no," demands Connelly.

"I can't answer yes or no, but I can answer it."

"You can't answer yes or no?"

"But I can answer it," the witness repeats.

"I'm not here to argue with you, Mr. Kapelsohn. Tell us the experience, if you know, about accidental discharges with this gun by New Jersey State Police," Connelly insists.

"New Jersey State Police, like any other agency that size, have had a number of accidental discharges over the years, but have continued to use that gun because they find it satisfactory."

Connelly provides a history lesson about the danger of that particular handgun and a suitable response to his own question. In part, while holstering their guns, New Jersey state troopers have shot themselves in the leg and foot because of the safety mechanism.

Kapelsohn confirms this.

Connelly asks, "Do you know New Milford Police is the only department that uses it in Connecticut?"

"That doesn't surprise me. It's an extremely expensive gun."

My dad's belief in an accidental discharge resurfaces. He feels conflicted on who to believe—the officer or statistics?

"Mr. Kapelsohn, tell us again, as you did to Mr. Kelly, what intentional action you have to do to fire that gun."

"In the context of this case, it requires two things: the squeezing of the cocking lever and the pulling of the trigger.

This can be done in that order, the reverse order, or both together."

Connelly reiterates to the jury that two distinct actions are required without completely agreeing with Mr. Kapelsohn.

While examining the pocketknife, Connelly reminds the witness about his previous demonstration of opening it with one hand. Mr. Kapelsohn says it can be done by flicking it.

Connelly eyes an opportunity. "Well, here, flick it. Being an expert with this knife, flick that knife as hard as you can."

The witness is hesitant to try, prompting Connelly to say, "Because you can't, Mr. Kapelsohn."

Determined to prove Connelly wrong, he takes the knife, holds the blade, and flicks it open.

Connelly asks, "If you hold it by the blade, and flick it like that, aren't you going to cut your fingers?"

Although Kapelsohn avoids cutting himself, Connelly seizes the moment and loudly attempts to nullify the expert testimony.

"Would you attempt to open that knife, while you were kneeling on the ground, with a man who is at least ten inches taller than you, at least sixty pounds heavier than you, having this gun (Smith's pistol), pressed up against your back, holding you with his left hand on your right shoulder, pinned down like this? (He demonstrates with an imaginary person on the ground.) Would you try to open a knife in that situation?"

Kelly interjects, "I don't object to the text of the question, again, if the witness could not be yelled at!"

Connelly rebuts, "I'm not yelling at him."

Judge Gill rules, "Litchfield volume, again, Mr. Connelly."

Toning it down, Connelly asks, "That scenario with less volume?"

"I have opened it that way, in that position, last night in my motel room."

"Who was the person who was ten inches taller than you with a gun in your back when you were doing that?"

"I don't know if he is ten inches taller than me, but it was Scott Smith."

Connelly looks surprised. "Scott Smith? And with a gun pointed in your back?"

"No, it was a plastic gun."

"It wasn't outside, after a chase down the street for about a hundred yards?"

"We didn't run down the street."

"It wasn't a chase where Officer Smith pointed that gun in your face and said, 'Show me your hands,' right?"

Kelly objects, "There has been no such testimony."

Judge Gill rules, "I'll allow it. It's cross-examination."

"Officer Smith didn't point a gun in my face in the motel room, no," Kapelsohn says.

Connelly moves forward with a demonstration related to police training. He extends both hands high in the air. "Let's say you are the police officer, and you say to me, 'Show me your hands,' and I do this. Have I complied?"

"With that order, yes."

Connelly puts both hands down and asks, "Why do you want to keep the distance?"

"You want the distance to maximize your safety and make it harder for the suspect to get to you."

"You said it's dangerous for an officer to approach a suspect especially if he feels the suspect is a violent person, correct?"

"Yes, officers are taught that sometimes they have to approach a suspect. Maybe he refuses to show his hands or to get on the ground, and that is dangerous. So they should avoid it if they can, but sometimes they have to do it."

"And especially, to avoid it, wait for a backup?"

"If it's feasible to wait for backup," Kapelsohn says.

Connelly reads a series of statements from the publication, *Officer's Safety, Use of Force, Arrest Mechanics*, authored by Reginald Allard, Jr., such as: don't push a bad position; use time and tactical communication; avoid creating a self-imposed danger zone; coordinate the contact/cover officer response to threat; develop a master plan that fluidly adjusts to threat level; do not accept vulnerability casually. Kapelsohn agrees with it all as Connelly transitions to the treatment of an arrestee.

He poses an eyewitness scenario. "A police officer has the suspect laid out on the ground, belly down. What he wants to do is handcuff him. He is straddling him, one leg on the left side, and one leg on the right side. He has the suspect's two hands behind his back, holding them in one hand. At some point in time, he has his foot on the suspect's back; his Heckler & Koch in his right hand pressed up between the shoulder blades of the man on the ground. In that situation, do you train police officers to fire the gun?"

Without hesitation, Kapelsohn replies, "In that situation, I train officers to fire their gun if they perceive the suspect is doing something which is an immediate threat of death or serious bodily harm to them or some other person."

I don't know where it comes from in the audience, but a gasp echoes in the courtroom.

In a loud perplexed tone, Connelly asks, "With his hands behind his back?"

Kelly interrupts, "Excuse me, Your Honor."

Judge Gill speaks, "Hold on, hold on. I think we've come to the conclusion of this area of questioning."

Connelly agrees. "We have, Your Honor. I have no further questions."

Kelly takes the floor. Maybe the squeaky chairs, benches, or Connelly's voluminous overtures are still ringing in the courtroom, because Kelly asks, "Might I examine without noise, Your Honor?"

Judge Gill's eyebrows raise, and he looks directly at Kelly. "Without—I didn't hear any noise."

I can't help cracking a quick smirk along with others in the audience.

Kelly poses a scenario reflecting Officer Smith's account. "You are in a position where you are on your knees, on an embankment, and your hands are clutched in front of you. Are you able, in that position, to obtain a knife that you had concealed and get to the person holding the gun on you before he fired?"

"Yes, I was able to open an actual knife with one hand. I

deflected the gun and cut the person five or six times—what I would consider to be disabling and lethal blows."

Connelly takes the floor once more. "How about if the man is over on the side of the road, the police officer is standing on the double lines in the middle of traffic, he is pointing the gun at the suspect, and the suspect is standing with his hands up like this (holding up both hands). What should the police officer do next?"

"Depending on the traffic danger, the officer may continue where he is, if he feels it safe enough to stand there and command that suspect."

"Traffic is now stopped because people driving by have seen what's going on. What should the officer do next, tell him to get on the ground?"

"The officer should stay where he is, if it's safe, make suggested commands to have the person turn away, get down on the ground, arms out, palms up, don't move."

"What if the person gets to the ground and sits instead?"

"It's a dangerous position and the officer will need to force him by laying hands on him."

"After forcing a person to his stomach and his hands are behind him, if you have that gun in your hand, you should put it away, correct?"

"At the point where you are going to handcuff, you need to put the gun away."

Connelly is clearly summarizing the incident step-by-step based on eyewitness accounts.

Mr. Kapelsohn asserts it is permissible for an officer to put a knee on certain parts of the back.

"If you can't get your knee in the back, the next best thing is your foot, right?"

"I think this is a bad move, because it's very precarious for an officer to put his foot on a suspect who is not completely under control."

Kelly is aware Connelly's last point mirrors a portion of Mrs. Meehan's testimony. He takes the floor.

"Do you know any training technique where a police officer is taught—when he is attempting to arrest someone who is lying on his stomach on the ground—to step on the person's back and at the same time grab both of the suspects hands in one of the officer's hands, and then in the other hand have a firearm?"

"No, this is contrary to all arrest procedures and tactics that I'm aware of in Connecticut or any place else in the country," Kapelsohn asserts.

Smith looks on, pleased that this testimony supplements his self-defense claim. The jury heard a tremendous amount of information which they will soon deliberate on to weed out inconsistency from consistency, but Kelly is not done yet.

The defense wants to further convince the jury that Franklyn's character caused the officer to act in self-defense. Assistant State Attorney Guy Wolf testifies that in his opinion, Franklyn was a violent person. Kelly recalls Detective Shortt to the stand; he testifies Franklyn could be a violent person.

After listening to character assassinations one after the other, the defense's message to the jury is Franklyn's violent past, which Smith had heard about, stuck out in the officer's mind seconds before he delivered the fatal shot. Smith believes he acted in accordance with his training and on prior knowledge, with emotions playing the largest role.

After three days of testimony, the defense finally rests, bringing to close the trial's evidentiary phase.

* * *

At this point, it's also customary for the defense to make another request for acquittal.

Kelly argues, "No crime has been committed when Smith's self-defense actions were completely justifiable based on the discovery of a pocketknife in Reid's jacket and his penchant for violence. The charges against my client should be dismissed."

Connelly asserts, "Smith's own words have strengthened the prosecution's case as being in direct conflict with eyewitnesses and the evidence when looked at objectively."

The hands of justice, or injustice, can clear Smith of all charges by throwing the trial into the arena of acquittals. A jury would essentially have their abilities to render a verdict removed.

Once again Judge Gill rules in opposition to the defense. "The Motion for Judgment of Acquittal is denied as the court finds the evidence presented could reasonably permit a finding of guilty."

ACT V SCENE V

___

CLOSING ARGUMENTS

The historic trial is nearing the end as closing arguments will be the lawyers' final remarks before the jury. The stakes are high, and the outcome could set a precedent for future encounters. Not a single empty audience seat can be found. The families, NAACP dignitaries, lawyers, police officers, media, and supporters alike squeeze together, shoulder to shoulder. For today, we are one, as we await Connelly and Kelly's highly anticipated grand finale.

Throughout the proceedings, it was apparent from watching their faces, that numerous clouds of emotion floated across the minds of the courtroom attendees—uncertainty, curiosity, confusion, and bewilderment. I sense new clouds may materialize during the attorneys' remarks.

Looking relaxed, Kelly begins. "Your Honor, if I could put something on the record?"

Judge Gill asks, "Would you like to do so now?"

"Yes, Your Honor. Yesterday, I was given the opportunity to use one of the rooms in the courthouse to discuss with my client and his family the issue of lesser included offenses...After that consultation, we are not asking the court to charge the jury on any lesser degrees of homicide, and it's my understanding the court intends to do so. I will take my objection at the appropriate time."

"Very well," Judge Gill says.

The attorney's "something" is duly noted. It may be nothing or it could be everything. The future holds that answer.

Judge Gill explains today's proceedings.

"Ladies and gentlemen, we are about to start the argument phase of the case, and I'm going to give my usual warning that I give in every single case, which is to caution them [Attorneys Connelly and Kelly], to keep their arguments based upon the facts. To refrain from using overly loud voices and emotional appeals to the jury. We'll start that process right now with Mr. Connelly."

The prosecutor, who also looks relaxed, takes the floor and positions himself in front of the jury box.

"The charge here is murder...The definition of murder in Connecticut General Statutes 53a-54 subsection (a) simply says that 'A person is guilty of murder when, with intent to cause the death of another person, he causes the death of that person.' And for a murder to be proven, the state must prove that beyond a reasonable doubt.

"Officer Smith claims he acted in self-defense. The state has the burden. It has to show that the defendant did *not* act in self-defense, or his conduct was unreasonable. He wasn't justified in shooting Franklyn Reid in the back.

"When you first came here as a juror, one of the things you were told is when you become a juror, you leave all your biases, all your prejudices, all yourself, the preconceived ideas of what the law should be; you don't bring that into the jury box with you. The one thing you do bring into the jury box is your common sense.

"What you're going to have to determine is what happened, whether or not when Franklyn Reid was shot to death by the defendant, the defendant was justified in doing that. How do you decide that? Well, you are going to have to decide that by the testimony you heard in this courtroom, and also from all those exhibits that have been introduced as full exhibits."

With the formality established, Connelly reveals his final strategy. He stands near Smith's firearm and proceeds to reconstruct the scene, frame by frame.

"If you recall when I was questioning the defendant on the witness stand, I got to the point where I tried to demonstrate to him what the truck driver, Jim DeMaria, saw...When he looked over to the side, he said he saw the black man sitting on the ground, and I said, 'Officer Smith, isn't that what occurred when you had this gun pointed at Mr. Reid?' He shot back at me and said, 'Mr. Connelly, you weren't there.'

"He is right. I wasn't there. You know who was there? Daniel Merton, Abu Nassir, William Eayrs, Jim DeMaria, Gail Meehan, and Leon Angelovich.

Connelly also mentions Diane Swanson and Christopher Gardner, the two defense witnesses.

"You know who also was there? Detective Shortt. You've heard all of their testimonies, and to believe the scenario that Officer Smith told you as to what happened, to believe *him*, you are going to have to disbelieve all of those people I just mentioned. Not one of those individuals confirmed what Officer Smith said, not one of them. You are not only going to have to disbelieve all those people, but you are going to have to disbelieve the physical evidence in this case that does not support Officer Smith's side of the story. It just doesn't. Every one of them viewed the interaction between Smith and Reid, bottom line being they thought it was all over. Reid had surrendered.

"What interest would those people have to come into this courtroom and tell you anything but what they honestly and truly saw? They have no interest. They are not connected to the New Milford Police Department. They don't know the Reid family. They don't know the Smith family. These are just every day, ordinary people who, I guess, some would say, were just in the wrong spot at the wrong time. They no more wanted to be here in court and testifying; they had no motive to lie; they had no motive to mislead you. And what does everyone say? It was all over. All over."

Signifying Reid had surrendered, Connelly demonstrates "hands up" as testified by eyewitnesses. Connelly then moves on to Detective Shortt's testimony.

"Think about this. This is common sense. Detective

Shortt, in his statement, had three options. He could have told State Police what he actually saw. But if he did that, his partner, his coworker, his brother police officer, was going to be in big trouble. His second option was to lie. I don't think Detective Shortt is that stupid. He is not going to write a totally false statement, where later he would face criminal penalties...So, what's the third option? 'I didn't see anything.' Do you really believe that Detective Shortt didn't see anything, especially when he sat on that chair (Connelly points to the witness box) and said Franklyn Reid was a violent man? Here, a seasoned detective is going to let a guy—in the detective bureau *a week and a half*—run off after this violent man, and not pay attention to what was going on? Does that make sense? The whole chase lasted about a hundred feet (at most), from where he (Smith) parked the car."

The prosecutor's blistering rebuke of Shortt continues as he reads the detective's words, "I was more concerned about setting the parking brake, so I looked away." Connelly adds, "You don't have to look down to set the parking brake."

I am captivated, listening to Mr. Connelly. His passionate, compelling summary of the trial feels like a coming-to-realization moment.

Officer Smith looks perplexed as Connelly tells the jury, "If what happened is the version that Officer Smith gave you, you and I know it's just common sense that Detective Shortt would have been riveted on that action.

"After hearing a gunshot, Detective Shortt sees Mr. Reid

lying on the ground with a bullet wound in him, his partner standing over him with a gun, and he doesn't say to him, 'Smitty, what the hell happened?' You know why he did not say that? Because he saw what happened."

In what I can describe as another moment of awakening for some in the courtroom, Connelly tackles the department's belief about my brother. Referring to the dispatch tapes, the prosecutor reminds the jury, "Cramer thought it was a white male who drove past him. When he was given Franklyn's name and address, it didn't click in the seventeen-year veteran's head. If Franklyn Reid was so dangerous, then why doesn't Sergeant Cramer even know who he was? If everybody in the New Milford Police Department was warned about him, don't you think Sergeant Cramer would have known who he was?

"Does he say, when he hears it's Franklyn Reid, 'Men, we know who this guy is. He may be armed and dangerous. He is the guy we discussed on roll call, so be careful out there.' What does he do? He laughs, 'Ha, ha, ha, ha,' when he finds out it's Franklyn Reid. Does he give chase? Sergeant Cramer decides to stay with the car. He is leading from the rear. That is how dangerous this guy is."

Connelly transitions to the defense's focal point, the pocketknife. "The knife is what is called a red herring. Nobody, nobody, nobody, sees Mr. Reid with the jacket over on the grassy area. Everybody says his hands are up. Nobody sees a jacket. The jacket is on the ground. It was dropped. That makes sense.

"Smith, in his statement to lawyers two days later, only

mentions the jacket once...when he saw Reid carrying it in the Sunoco parking lot. He told Mr. Kelly (while testifying) that when the body was turned over, he saw a red object there. I asked him about that. It is nowhere in his statement, that is an afterthought. Why is it an afterthought? Because nobody knew the knife was in the jacket. The State Police— Detective Sabetta—found the knife, not the New Milford Police Department. Scott Smith didn't know the knife was in the jacket for a long time later...after he pulled the trigger. But now the knife becomes important. It isn't important."

Connelly's time on the floor is almost up. He recapitulates eyewitness accounts and reminds the jury of common sense. I can feel my eyes watering as Connelly transitions to rights and I listen to an impactful closing argument.

"When you compare Officer Smith and Mr. Reid—Officer Smith is a policeman, he is protecting us, he is there to be our friend...Franklyn Reid, on the other hand, is a violent guy. He's been to jail. He's got a felony conviction and therefore when you compare—you know, please. Franklyn Reid was a human being.

"Police officers have the same rights as every one of you. They don't have any greater rights...You know who else had the same rights as you and me in this case? Franklyn Reid.

"Franklyn Reid may have been a lot of things. They want you to believe he was a bad guy; he was violent. I didn't hear *one* witness come up on this stand and say Franklyn Reid was stupid. Franklyn Reid saw the gun. Franklyn Reid was lying on the ground. He had to feel the gun pressed into his back. Nobody said he was suicidal. Do you think Franklyn

Reid or anyone else would have made any move when that gun is pressed in his back, with a boot on his back, his hands behind his back? Do you think he *could* have made a move? I guess Mr. Kapelsohn said, 'It's okay to shoot somebody in that circumstance.'

"Officer Smith let his emotions take over, and because of that, Franklyn Reid is dead. It's not pleasant, it's not nice. The law applies equally to all of us. The law applies to police officers as it applies to engineers, mechanics, doctors, and lawyers. No man in this country is above the law. Just because you put a badge on doesn't mean you are above the law. When we give you that gun, when we give you that badge, you also have to accept responsibility. Officer Smith is not above the law. *No* police officer is above the law. As difficult as it may seem to be, believe me, I work with police officers every day."

In a stunning show of heartfelt emotions, I see Connelly crying as he concludes.

"Objection, Your Honor. Immaterial, irrelevant, and prejudicial," Kelly says.

"I haven't heard anything so far. Overruled," Judge Gill rules.

I feel a flood of emotions—pride for police officers, hope in a voice for injustice and a sense that together as one nation, we can truly crush the barriers of inequality, and work to resolve divisive issues that tear communities and people apart. The path to trusting one another hasn't completely disappeared. We've temporarily detoured to mistrust. Together though, we can find our way back for the sake of our future.

Judge Gill gives the courtroom a quick break.

Twenty minutes later, Mr. Kelly kicks off by taking a swipe at Connelly. He stands in front of the jury. "Ladies and gentlemen, I hope you don't mind listening to me once more, but I would like to think what I have to say is important. I would prefer you rely on reason and logic, and not histrionics and emotions. So if I am low-key, it's me. It doesn't mean I don't take the case seriously. I don't want to play on your emotions; I want you to use your reason and logic.

"When we first began to interview each of you to sit on this case, each of you assured my client you could be fair and impartial; there would be no baggage brought into the courtroom, to listen to our defense. And we took you at your word. That is why all of you are here.

"Franklyn Reid, a man who had been in trouble with the law, convicted of assault, and seriously stabbed someone, having gone to prison for that, having come out, having been placed on probation, was considered by the people in the system that are forced to deal with him—police, probation, prosecutors—as a violent person."

Kelly casts doubt with inconsistencies in eyewitness testimonies. "This is Mr. DeMaria's version of things: Franklyn Reid is sitting like he is at a day at the beach, not a care in the world, not worried about being caught by police, not worried about going back to prison. Just sitting there having a good time. Gail Meehan is directly behind him, says, 'Oh, no, that is not the way it was.' By some magic or osmosis, Franklyn Reid, who had been pursued and uncooperative, apparently just voluntarily, quickly rolled over and assumed the position."

His emotion revs up as he continues to discredit Mrs. Meehan as she approached the commotion. "She is looking right. She is looking left. Remember she sees Dave Shortt's car screech to a halt. She looks right again, and she sees what could only be described as a bizarre position. Remember, she couldn't even demonstrate it to you; Mr. Connelly had to demonstrate it for you."

Kelly takes two steps toward the jury box. "Now, let's compare Mrs. Meehan's testimony with Mr. Angelovich. I'm not going to call any witness a liar. That is not my job. But different people have different vantage points and saw different things. You can't put Mrs. Meehan's testimony and Mr. Angelovich's testimony together and come out with a result that makes sense."

The attorney's searing criticism of eyewitness accounts appears to draw a line with Smith's version of events. The jury's eyes are locked on Mr. Kelly, listening, without displaying any emotion. He transitions to Smith's boots and reiterates that Mr. Zercie's results did not satisfy the prosecution, so they decided to seek Mr. Bodziak, a private consultant.

"There is no footwear impression on the back of Franklyn Reid's shirt," Kelly says as he refers to a crucial eyewitness. "That should make you stop and think, as it relates to reasonable doubt. To accept the state's theory, you have to accept the testimony of Gail Meehan, placing Scott Smith in that position. I submit to you, if he is in this absurd position, he would have fallen over. He is six-two. They are partially on an embankment."

Kelly is casting doubt over every aspect and piece of evidence presented during the trial by Mr. Connelly. He goes for the jugular of the prosecution's case.

"The scenario the state asks you to accept is as follows: six-feet-two inches tall, Scott Smith, a police officer, well-trained, comes into contact with a convicted felon, Franklyn Reid. Spends thirty-five, thirty-six, thirty-seven seconds trying to capture him to bring him to court. And then in the last couple seconds, all of a sudden, changes his mind and says, 'I'm going to shoot you, and I'm going to do it in a place where anybody on Route 202 is going to be able to see it, and I'm going to do it completely unjustifiably, and then I'm going to come into court and con the jury and claim self-defense.' That is the state's theory.

"Self-defense is a complete bar to any conviction for any crime. Every citizen in this country has the right to defend themselves, to defend that which is most precious to them, their own lives. That right of self-defense is no less applicable to any police officer, including Scott Smith. He did not have to wait until Franklyn Reid turned around with a weapon, he didn't know if it was a gun or knife—in this case it happened to be a knife—and get stabbed or slashed before he could defend himself.

"He gave Franklyn every possibility to surrender. All he had to do was say, 'The chase is over. You got me. I have evaded court. I have evaded the police. And I have evaded everything for three months. I don't mind going back to prison. It's no big deal.'

"The state will have you believe Franklyn Reid made no effort in attempting to escape from Scott Smith. He made no move, whatsoever, to do that. When he was at the side of the road, you are told Scott Smith's emotions changed." Kelly pauses for a few seconds. "His (Franklyn's) did, from being a convicted felon to doing anything he could to escape.

"Franklyn Reid was resisting Scott Smith's efforts to take him into custody, bring him to a police station, and later to court.

"Recklessly, Franklyn attempted to get to his knife and he failed. Because he failed and didn't injure Scott Smith, the state wants you to convict Scott Smith of murder."

Kelly walks toward the pocketknife in evidence and points. "This is not a figment of anyone's imagination. This is real, as every other physical piece of evidence in this case. He has a knife; he's not showing his hands; he's got them in front of him fumbling. He's trying to get that knife in the jacket.

"Remember the knife. The jacket wasn't planted. Mr. Connelly suggests to you that Franklyn Reid dropped that jacket while being pursued. Someone had to plant the jacket there."

Kelly steps closer to the jury box. "You're Franklyn Reid. You have been arrested. You know the ropes. Where the hell is Pam? Jesus, where is she? I've got to buy me some time. How do I buy time? Want me to go over to the side of the road? I'll go on the side of the road. Down on my knees? No, I'm not going down on my knees. He pushes back up.

"What do you think happens when he pushes up? The gun that Scott Smith is holding is now in relation to Franklyn Reid's back, close. What kind of person who isn't reckless, namely Franklyn Reid, with a known police officer, wouldn't surrender?"

If a stranger, unfamiliar with the case, walked into the courtroom during Mr. Kelly's presentation, I'm sure they would believe Franklyn was the vilest and most dangerous villain who ever walked the streets. His worthless, pitiful life paled in comparison to the good ole' squeaky-clean Officer Smith.

"I want to thank you for your attention. I hope you keep your word that you, during your deliberation and verdict, will ensure that my client gets a fair trial; you conclude that his claim of self-defense is not a fabrication; it was based on what he confronted that day. He didn't have to be perfect. He didn't have to be right. He just had to be reasonable. And based on everything he saw that day, utilizing his training, when he saw those movements on the part of Franklyn Reid, he knew what was happening. He knew what was going to come next. And I suppose you might not even have been here if Scott Smith had waited one second and permitted Franklyn Reid to turn around, and then saw the knife. Maybe he would have been lucky."

Kelly's closing arguments end, but Connelly has a final rebuttal.

"Ladies and gentlemen, let me make one thing perfectly clear...I never said that anybody planted that knife or anybody planted the jacket. Remember Michael Gabriel? He is the first one there along with Detective Jordan. Mr. Gabriel doesn't see any jacket. Who needs the jacket? They need the jacket near Scott Smith because that is all they have—that knife. So, who do they call? A friend in need is a friend, indeed. Let's call in Mr. Silvernail. You saw him on the witness stand. I'm not even going to talk to you about his testimony, because I am not going to insult your intelligence. The knife is nonsense. He wasn't reaching for a knife. Even Smith says he only saw the jacket at the Sunoco station."

If words hurt, that's as impactful as they can be. In what I can describe as a ripping-the-band-aid-off story, Connelly informs the jury that Officer Wheeler's incident report regarding the knife was dated December 29, 1998. The day Franklyn died.

Connelly sums up. "You have just shot somebody. The reason you shot him is because you thought that person was reaching for a weapon, right? That is the argument here. The thing you are going to do is look to see if, indeed, you made the right decision: if Mr. Reid was reaching for a weapon; if Mr. Reid had a weapon in his waistband; if Mr. Reid had a weapon in his hand? They never even looked to see if Scott Smith made the right decision. Never. And that is beyond belief. The reason they didn't look is because they knew there was no weapon there."

Connelly brings up what the courtroom heard from Smith. "I couldn't believe what happened to *me*. I couldn't believe what happened to *me*," he says, repeating it multiple times. "Didn't care what happened to Franklyn Reid; me, me, me. Totally self-absorbed, *me*, I'm in trouble now," echoes loudly from Connelly's lips.

"You know, this whole thing Mr. Kelly objected to earlier—when I was talking about Reid being a human being and he had a life, too, and they are going to try to paint him as a violent person, and therefore he has got a..." Connelly pauses for a few seconds. "Lord, he has been in jail, and therefore he is a non-person. He is a non-face. Let's demonize him. Mr. Reid is the enemy. Let's make a demon out of him, so when he is dead, who cares?

"People run from the police all the time, and you know something, running from the police doesn't carry the death penalty. Failing to appear in court doesn't carry the death penalty. Because you spent time in jail doesn't mean the next time you run from the police the penalty is death. This is America. This isn't El Salvador, Nicaragua, Cuba, China."

Suddenly, Kelly jumps out of his chair. "I object."

Undeterred, Connelly continues. "This is America."

"This is not proper, judge," Kelly argues.

"It's argument," Connelly rebuts.

Judge Gill intercedes, "I know it's argument, but just tone it down a bit, please."

Doing as asked, Connelly takes a few steps toward the jury box. "I'm going to tell you one thing. The state is not looking for a conviction at any cost. What I am asking you to do is the right thing...It would be easy and it would be popular in a lot of quarters for you to go in that jury room and say: Franklyn Reid, a violent, bad guy. So what, he's dead? Scott Smith, a young police officer; ah, you know, be much easier to say not guilty and walk out of here. The popular thing for the time being is not necessarily the right thing. You, as jurors, you have to do the right thing because that is when justice is served. That is what the state of Connecticut, what the people, are looking for in this case. Justice. Justice. It takes courage."

How refreshing those words sound. A man that has had a challenging time prosecuting one of his own.

Connelly concludes, "You know, Abraham Lincoln once said, just before the Civil War, they asked him about slavery, and Lincoln said, 'When good people sit back and let wrong be done, that is the first step on a community road to ruination.' When good people sit back and let wrong happen, that is when we're all in trouble. This is the jury system. This is the best criminal justice system in the entire world. This system has worked for over two hundred years. This is what distinguishes us from the other countries. So, all I ask is that you summon up the courage to do the right thing, because when you do that, justice will prevail."

Judge Gill dismisses the jury for lunch.

After the jury exits, Kelly requests to address the court.

"It's always [been] my belief the rules that govern final argument, the fact that Your Honor called us up to the bench and said to me, 'Don't argue the effect a verdict in this case could have on other police officers.' Foreign countries are not part of this case, reference to emotion, and Lincoln, is not part of this case; expressing a personal opinion about the guilt or innocence of my client is improper. Your Honor knows that. I move for mistrial; repeated prosecutorial misconduct during final argument."

Judge Gill rules, "The motion for a mistrial is denied."

ACT V SCENE VI

JURY INSTRUCTIONS

The battle has simmered, signifying the end is approaching. Connelly and Kelly have nothing further to add; their moments have passed. Now the floor belongs to Judge Gill. Counsel delivered convincing arguments spiced with testy exchanges, but they are lauded for their skills and zeal which allowed the trial to proceed smoothly and finish in a suitable time. Justice and exoneration had excellent representation.

The jury is uniquely positioned to have heard the case in its entirety and will soon comb through the evidence, asking for any clarification before rendering a unanimous verdict. They pay rapt attention to Judge Gill's instructions.

"It is my duty to state to you the rules of the law involved in the decision of this case, and it is your duty to find the facts. You alone are responsible for determining the facts. It is your exclusive province to deal with the evidence and determine what the real facts were, and to reach the final conclusion as to whether the accused is guilty or not guilty."

Being an audience member, a familiar word such as "verdict," must be based solely on evidence seen and testimonies heard within the walls of the courtroom. Weighing the credibility of any witness resides only with the jurors. They may believe all, none, or part of their testimonies. Judge Gill offers a few considerations for finding the facts.

"What was the witness's manner while testifying? Did the witness have an interest in the outcome of this case or any bias or prejudice concerning any party or any matter involved in the case? How reasonable was the witness's testimony considered in light of all the evidence in the case and was the witness's testimony contradicted by the testimonies of other witnesses or by other evidence?"

They are reminded not to decide the case between the lawyers' brilliancies but rather, between the state of Connecticut versus Scott Smith, who is presumed to be innocent until proven guilty. Both expect fair and just treatment. The information containing the charge is not evidence but merely a formal manner of accusing someone of a crime. If something in the evidence or lack thereof casts reasonable doubt, Smith must be given the benefit of that doubt and be found not guilty. He claimed self-defense which states in part, according to the law, a police officer "is justified in using deadly physical force upon another person" when the officer "reasonably believes such to be necessary to defend himself from imminent use of deadly physical force" by that person. Smith didn't have to prove his innocence or self-defense claim; that burden clearly rests with the state. If Connelly failed to disprove Smith's claim, he must be found not guilty.

The information: John A. Connelly, State's Attorney for the Judicial District of Waterbury, accuses and charges Scott Smith of New Milford, Connecticut with the crime of Murder, in violation of Connecticut Statutes Section 53a-54a section (a), in that on December 29, 1998, at approximately 11:20 a.m., at or near the intersection of Route 202 and Park Lane West, in the Town of New Milford, Connecticut, the said Scott Smith with intent to cause the death of Franklyn Reid, caused the death of Franklyn Reid by shooting him in the back with a handgun.

Judge Gill explains that if the state has proven both elements beyond a reasonable doubt, the unanimous verdict must be guilty. If not, they should consider the included lesser offenses to murder: if Smith intended to cause serious physical injury to Franklyn but caused death with his handgun, he must be guilty of First Degree Manslaughter with a Firearm. If Smith engaged in conduct that created a risk of death and caused the death by means of a handgun, he acted recklessly which demonstrated apathy for human life. He must be found guilty of First Degree Reckless Manslaughter with a Firearm.

Judge Gill reiterates that if the state proved beyond a reasonable doubt all elements of either lesser offense, the verdict must be guilty. He concludes his meticulous instructions to the jurors with a reminder of their oath and duty to accept the law as given by the court.

Smith looks on, knowing his fate now rests with these twelve people.

ACT V SCENE VII

—————

THE VERDICT

Three alternate jurors are thanked and graciously excused while the twelve regulars begin deliberation. Judge Gill retires to his chambers to await the verdict. A sheriff's deputy posted at the door patiently waits for that most important knock.

The suspense is gripping. As anxiety builds, butterflies seem to have free rein in my stomach. They jab and roll before delivering that sinking feeling. Nausea kicks in as my thoughts run wild wondering what the verdict will be. Why am I sweating profusely in winter? I'm not sick. I don't want to puke in front of all these people. I need to stay calm. That's imperative!

But it seems like people are looking at me. I need to get out of there, run as fast as I can, and leave everything behind. Maybe my heart will explode, I'll collapse, and this nightmare trial will be over. Damn these thoughts. Damn this feeling. I'm losing control. Bottled-up emotions are seeping out at the wrong time. I don't want to be feeling this way. I breathe deeply to get it back together.

While waiting, my family, our entourage, and Smith's people leave the courtroom to dine out. Luckily enough, Litchfield has a few places that offer variety and precludes opposing sides from accidentally eating together.

Strangely though, I wouldn't mind sitting a short distance across from Officer Smith. Maybe our eyes could meet, lock in a stare down, not for intimidation, but to see our plight. A difficult situation has entwined us in the court of law. Connelly and Kelly impressed the jury on our behalves so victory could be determined. I'm fully aware that neither of us are winners. A Reid will define a Smith and vice-a-versa. That's the real game, my friend! How do we accept it and move forward with our lives? Our connection can never be broken, even after death do us part. Sounds like a union we didn't ask for, but it's there. With tears rolling down my cheeks, I wish our eyes could meet and deliver this unspoken message. Instead, we've played the avoidance game, walking inches from each other. Who knows if in that split second, our energy could find friendship and have this discussion?

While we dine, the jury debates. Quick deliberation could hand Smith a favorable verdict. The longer they take, a decision may swing in Franklyn's direction. In either scenario, all eyes are on the pendulum.

* * *

Back at the courthouse, a knock activates pandemonium, sending a skeleton crew of reporters stationed around the door scrambling. Has the jury reached a verdict hours after closing arguments? If so, statistically, Smith may be vindicated. Anticipation spikes while the sun sets over Litchfield Hills. The sheriff opens the door and accepts a note. Whispers and jitters are giving butterflies a field day but confirmation is necessary before spreading news. That piece of paper which holds answers is meant for only one pair of eyes: Judge Gill's. He accepts the note in his chamber. Minutes later...

It's a false alarm. Calmness returns courtside, anticipation ascends. Many wonder what was written in that note. It may shed important clues on which area the jury is focusing on and which direction the scale may be tilting toward.

No verdict echoes on the nightly news yet. Pundits add their two cents since the trial has garnered major coverage. The public does not know the specifics contained in the note, but rumors are swirling regarding testimonies to be reread.

Court reconvenes the following morning. Judge Gill announces that the jury has requested eight testimonies to be read aloud: Dan Merton, James DeMaria, William Eayrs, Abu Nassir, Gail Meehan, Leon Angelovich, and defense witnesses Diane Swanson, and Christopher Gardner.

Purely speculation, but a direction may be in focus based on those names.

Once again, Smith's only option is to sit and listen to what strangers allegedly witnessed, how their recollections mesh. His testimony is not asked for. Even Detective Shortt's testimony doesn't make their list. But Smith's demeanor doesn't change. He remains stoic.

Every juror—seven men and five women—are completely enthralled as they listen to the witness testimonies read aloud. They avoid looking at any supporters, knowing a head swerve could result in eye contact. Audience members are looking for signs, something, anything, to determine the reason for the jurors' request, but they remain emotionless.

An hour and a half into listening to four testimonies, Judge Gill breaks for twenty minutes. It feels like a theater intermission. Long restroom lines and people grabbing drinks as they prepare for the second half. This time around, two and a half hours pass, completing the day's reading.

Fresh in their thoughts, deliberation resumes at 2:00 p.m.

At 4:55 p.m., the sheriff's deputy delivers a note from Judge Gill to the jury. Five minutes later, the deputy brings a note to the judge. He skims it and instructs the deputy to reconvene court. Minutes later, Judge Gill updates the courtroom while the jury is summoned.

"What's happening here is that I sent them [the jury] a note and gave two options. One, if they felt they needed to continue deliberation, we would let them do so, or they could go home and come back first thing Monday morning. Their response was that they will continue until 7 o'clock tonight...I'm going to bring them back in and chat with them for a minute."

The jury looks focused, without any sign of tiredness, as they take their seats. Judge Gill addresses them.

"Ladies and gentlemen, you have my note, and I have your response. We don't know where you are, what you're doing; so, if you're close to a decision, one way or the other, that is fine. If you are still in the deliberative process and you feel as though you need more time to resolve whatever issues you are trying to resolve, and that would amount to several more hours, then we would probably gamble and have you come back Monday morning, real early, and start again."

The jury huddles back in their room and discusses options while the courtroom occupants stay put. I suspect those jurors want a conclusion before the weekend but do not want a rush decision.

Minutes later, Judge Gill is the recipient of another note. Information flows quickly; court is called into session. Late Friday afternoon, a verdict will not be reached. Court is adjourned after Judge Gill's usual jury spiel.

"Don't discuss the case, or allow anyone to discuss it with you. Friends, family, no one whatsoever. Should your eyes or ears inadvertently come across anything that is in the print media, on the airwaves, the television, or even on the computer; you have to divert your eyes and ears elsewhere. It's imperative, now that we are getting very close to the end of the case."

* * *

On Monday morning, a bizarre silence leads many into court. Shunned reporters respect "no comment," as many feel today is verdict day. I fantasize that Franklyn may have gathered with friends on the other side, sporting his favorite suit, looking down from above. He and Smith are preparing for one final face-off.

For those of us still living, it is a sad situation all around. We learned "how" this incident happened, as revealed through the trial. The "why" is fate's twisted lesson to people: make a change. If a clear and present danger does not exist, an outcome should not be determined by a gun. If an assailant clearly intends harm or death, the officer's gun or *non-lethal* weapon can determine that outcome. We've seen countless examples where excessive force contributes to a growing divide among people. I believe law enforcement can resolve this issue and avert future tragedies, starting with modified training at academies. Inaction produces no solutions.

It's noon, and midday broadcast news reminds their viewers that a verdict is imminent. Somehow everyone senses time is winding down.

The jury requests a twenty-minute break at 12:40 p.m., after deliberating for three and a half hours. In terms of statistics, probability is at an all-time high that the next knock will be the most important.

The wait allows pondering whether a terrible chapter in many lives will end with closure today. However, decisions by final arbiters are often questioned, thus avoiding the finish line by veering toward a court of appeal. Automatically filing such papers is becoming the new norm. Even when no basis exists for an appeal, some will create artificial scenarios to discredit a jury or blame the trial judge. I wonder what tomorrow will bring if, in fact, a verdict is delivered today? Smith desperately wants the criminal trial to end with exoneration; if not, an appeal is most certain.

Knock. The sound sends reporters to standby with their respective networks. The sheriff's deputy answers and accepts a note. He quickens his pace to Judge Gill's chamber.

Most spectators hang around the courtroom. Then the deputy announces, "Court is ready to be called into session."

Carrying that note, a standing room welcomes Judge Gill. At 3:36 p.m., court reconvenes.

"Good afternoon, ladies and gentlemen. The jury has indicated that they have reached a verdict."

Some reporters in the gallery want their network to deliver breaking news. In TV Land, regularly scheduled programs are interrupted.

My stomach is knotted while Judge Gill forewarns spectators to be respectful, calm, and refrain from any emotional outbursts. After the verdict, no one is permitted to leave until all jurors have returned back to the deliberating room.

"You may bring in the jury," announces Judge Gill.

The sheriff's deputy replies, "Very well!"

I hadn't noticed how long it took the jurors to walk in and take their seats until now. Maybe their final act requires an embrace, knowing lives will change. Whispers cease and even squeaky wooden chairs seem to heed Judge Gill's warning. A hush falls over the courtroom. In a perfectly formed line, the jury enters, their heads and eyes locked straight forward as if marching. There is no emotion or twitch to acknowledge a room full of people. Any deviation would most certainly result in eye contact.

I, along with everyone else, study their body language. Maybe one or two will let their guard down, but that's only wishful thinking.

Judge Gill observes them looking solemn. He asks them to stand as both counsels agree all members are present. The clerk assumes control and asks the foreperson to identify herself.

"Ladies and gentlemen of the jury, in the case of the state of Connecticut v. Scott Smith, have you agreed upon your verdict?" the clerk asks.

I feel a chill, as if Franklyn has abandoned his friends on the other side and dashed into court after hearing, *"We have."* Where he's standing, I don't know, but a guess is by Smith's side.

"Will the defendant, Scott Smith, please rise and face the jury," the clerk says.

The officer stands, buttons his jacket, and clasps his hands together in front.

What a powerful scene: the jurors and accuser upright; all eyes connected, quite possibly for the first and only time during the entire trial. And I believe honor and respect serves a unique purpose when looking someone in the eyes before casting judgment.

We are witnessing an extraordinary moment as Smith gently bites his lower lip, his teeth showing. Coincidently, he wore the same black suit, blue shirt, and yellow tie, from his first court appearance. Attorney Kelly joins him.

I reach for my brother Dwight's hand to my right, my father's hand to my left. He reaches for my mother's hand which creates a chain reaction. Holding hands sweeps through spectators, most noticeably, Smith's family across from us. They, too, are locked on the jury, their eyes pleading innocence for their son.

Positive and negative energy has intertwined, perfectly balanced in the space before the announcement. Obviously, one side will experience disappointment and negative energy.

The moment of truth arrives. The clerk requests the verdict.

"The Substitute Information charges the defendant with the crime of Murder, in violation of General Statute Section 53a-54a subsection (a). Is the defendant guilty or not guilty?"

Anticipation has pinnacled. The foreperson answers, *"Not Guilty."*

Our hands squeeze as body temperatures increase. My dad's eyes close with the belief Smith is about to walk free. He takes a deep breath and opens his eyes. Smith appears mighty relieved clearing the greatest obstacle life has thrown at him thus far. His lower lip releases. His facial expression says thank you. Dwight wipes away a tear. Judge Gill shudders a bit at the "not guilty" verdict.

Energy bounces back and forth, an intense emotional reaction. Somehow it remains inside all of us. No joyous outburst is heard in the courtroom. Smith's family looks relieved, knowing their son or brother escaped the law's most severe punishment. Smith's colleagues appear pleased.

The clerk continues.

"As to the lesser included offense of Manslaughter in the First Degree with a Firearm (intentional), in violation of General Statute Section 53a-55 subsection (a), is the defendant guilty or not guilty?"

The foreperson answers, "*Guilty.*"

Our hand grip tightens, body temperatures ease, my eyes glisten and release a tear. Smith's demeanor, relaxed seconds ago, shifts. His lips quiver and display a frown, his head bows. Judge Gill sighs in relief, knowing he is face-to-face with true American justice. Police officers in the audience appear stunned and confused. Smith lifts his head for one more charge.

The clerk reads.

"As to the lesser included offense of Manslaughter in the First Degree with a Firearm (reckless), in violation of General Statute Section 53-55 subsection (a) (3), is the defendant guilty or not guilty?"

Smith cleared one hurdle. Franklyn obstructed the second. The final is up for grabs.

"*Not Guilty.*"

Smith looks toward the ceiling, takes a deep breath knowing two obstacles are cleared. Seconds later, he faces the jury again.

Connecticut's Practice Book allows either side to poll a jury after a verdict is rendered. Attorney Kelly utilizes that right. The clerk calls each juror by name and asks, *"Is the verdict announced by your foreperson your verdict?"* Twelve yeses are recorded, sending Connecticut's landmark trial into an ominous phase.

The families now must live with split decisions; neither can claim victory. The one guilty verdict out of three means Officer Smith faces between five and forty years in prison. Smith has to live with his decision. But Franklyn's death may serve as a reminder that we, the people, can create change in law enforcement and communities, to seek common ground, to learn from each other, and to tear down barriers for the betterment of all.

Perhaps no jury in Connecticut has had such a difficult case, Judge Gill tells the jury, congratulating them for their courage.

A juror bows her head and wipes tears from her eyes. My mom closes her eyes and mouths a silent prayer. Supporters pat her shoulders. Dad nods his head a few times toward the jury, a silent thank you. Pam, who once told reporters she wants to see justice, experiences elation. Smith shakes Kelly's hand slowly as Judge Gill orders the Department of Adult Probation to prepare a pre-sentencing investigation (PSI) regarding the officer's background. Imposition of sentence is scheduled for May 5, 2000.

The gavel sounds. The jurors vacate their box. Silence is lifted, and spectators are free to leave. Sweaty palms unlock, breaking the physical connections but the emotional impact remains. Quiet tones deliver congratulations and sympathies. Disappointment clings to Smith who embraces his family while surrounded by brothers in blue, some openly weeping. A sheriff's deputy provides a box of tissues, placing it on an empty chair for their convenience.

Smith remains free on $250,000 bond. Outside the court, he walks calmly through a sea of reporters and cameras toward a black car that whisks him away. He makes no comment.

Connelly shows no emotion. His victory is not sweet. Fairness guided by principles and rather than political aspirations weathered a firestorm. Everyone will not agree with Connelly's pursuit, even though in the past he exonerated three police officers of any criminal wrongdoing after reviewing their cases. (Connecticut utilizes the State Attorney's Office to determine charges.) An officer in Smith's entourage stares Connelly down with contempt, disgusted by his actions, but Connelly pays no attention while exiting the courtroom. Outside, he reiterates that this is a joyless victory for him. Sadness fills his comments.

"It was a difficult case for everyone. I took it because it was my job. I work with cops every day. It's not a case of winning or losing. It's a case based on a set of facts."

Those words resonate now more than ever. This case was not about race...a white officer killing a black man. It was about corroborated facts, evidence, and right versus wrong.

The same court steps we once stood upon as enablers of injustice, now give my mother a platform to thank Connelly's team, Judge Gill, clergies, State Police, eyewitnesses, and supporters across our beautiful country. Courage displayed by strangers, connected by one incident which lasted forty-one seconds, proves people can make a difference.

"Thanks, a trillion times a trillion, trillion to the jury for your courage," she reads from prepared remarks.

For many, Franklyn is the new face of justice. For others, Smith is law enforcement's dangerous precedent.

Reverend Kimber, president of the Greater New Haven Clergy Association, attended the trial regularly. He thanks Judge Gill and Connelly for their handling of the case.

Speaking with reporters, he says, "We went there expecting justice would be done and it was done. The system worked in his case."

While news breaks in TV Land and reporters vie for interviews, Judge Gill, accompanied by law clerk Ryan McKinstry, has a post-trial meeting with the jurors. Soon they will be free to give interviews and provide insight into their decisions. Collectively, the jurors have a favorable impression of the judicial system. The only black juror says his faith was not completely restored in the system, but he feels good about the process that occurred. They praise the attorneys' professionalism, Judge Gill's control, and various court personnel they interacted with. Most importantly, they are quite confident in their decision and are glad the case is over.

The veil protecting their identity is lifted. Some jurors

speak with reporters outside the courtroom. People are curious to know their thoughts, to know which of the witnesses the jurors thought had credibility.

"We reached a decision based on evidence and instructions given to us by Judge Gill," juror Tanya states. She found Smith's self-defense claim unbelievable and his testimony unemotional, "like he was reading from a script." She adds, "The witnesses had nothing to gain. They happened to see something that day. There were too many of them. Scott Smith did not support what the eyewitnesses had seen."

"We believed the testimony of the eyewitnesses, and the physical evidence did not support Officer Smith's contention that he acted in self-defense," juror Allen says. "If you have all the framework in the film that seems to follow a sequence, and then you hit a blip in one of the frames that doesn't fit anything, you have to make a decision to credit it or discredit it. That's what we did with Smith."

Why the lesser conviction? The jury determined Smith didn't wake up the morning of December 29 and decide he was going to kill someone. Why should he suffer the worst penalty?

Forewoman Mary, whose name was pulled from a cup to lead the jurors, gave Smith the benefit of the doubt although she believed he made a wrong decision. "What stuck out was the way the gun was in [Reid's] back and the evidence that showed it. He said he feared for his life and intended to kill him. I don't think he is a cold-blooded murderer, but I think he could have done what he needed to do in a different way." She added, "We looked at all the forensic evidence and the statements from eight eyewitnesses who had no stake in this at all. They just happened to be driving by or filling their car up with gas, and that's what really made the difference. Their testimony clearly showed that Mr. Reid was already apprehended, had surrendered with his hands in the air, then was down on the ground when he was shot."

March 13, 2000, history recorded Connecticut's landmark verdict as a way forward which could end with years behind bars. I sense muted tongues have waited long enough. In the melee of boundless comments, community citizens react. Some call the verdict a travesty of justice; others say our jury system performed as expected. A poll shows reactions evenly divided among respondents. I hope the mixed reaction is temporary and both sides can unite for the sake of vanquishing division sparked by emotions. It's a long shot. We have to see beyond the immediate impact. Maybe a healing process is underway.

Counselors again visit the New Milford Police Department as Mayor Peitler issues a statement.

"At a personal level, we are disappointed and saddened for Scott Smith and his family. The ramification of this decision is significant and is not limited to the confines of the New Milford Police Department or the community it serves. It is my belief the decision will have far-reaching and significant effects on law enforcement officers throughout the state."

Some officers, law professors, and defense attorneys

agree with Peitler's perspective. Nicholas Pastore, founder of the Criminal Justice Policy and former New Haven Police Chief offers another.

"This was an example of egregiously bad police work. This verdict was a just decision that will prove good for society and good for police work." Mr. Pastore believes the verdict will force police departments to reexamine their deadly force policies. Commenting on Franklyn's position when Smith had him under control, he said, "This case falls under the umbrella of a government-sanctioned execution. This is the type of police work we're used to hearing about in the Third World."

His words may sound harsh but to many who agree, that is reality.

Hoping for unity isn't an absurd idea. While rummaging through newspaper articles, an editorial in the *Litchfield Times* echoes my feelings.

> As a community, we must stand united under the law. Those of us who feel loss and vindication for the Reids and those who feel pain and compassion for the Smiths must come together. We must support our police department which has served us well in the past and which has pledged to continue to serve us well in the present despite its members' disappointment and sadness with the jury's decision. It is at these times that the fabric of our society is tested. Let New Milford be a model for communities throughout the state and the nation that are struggling to understand similar situations.

Let all of us have compassion for all parties affected by that cold December day.

Optimism is a shining a light we can't see today. The future waits for us to open our eyes and start a new era of unity. Unfortunately, darker days wait over the horizon first.

ACT VI SCENE I

———

A TIMELY FISHING
EXPEDITION

Hours after the verdict, I drive to South Beach, Florida to join college friends for spring break. The 1,230-mile trip seems daunting and perhaps ill-advised since I haven't slept. Luckily, I'm not entirely alone. My brother Dwight decided to hit the road for Atlanta, Georgia. I drive behind him for approximately seven hundred miles before parting ways with a honk and a wave. The thought of Franklyn setting a precedent in Connecticut travels with me. Maybe this case can become an example for future encounters with law enforcement and minorities. But if I don't pull over at the next rest area and sleep for a few hours, my future and potentially others' may be jeopardized. Twenty-six hours later, at 3:00 a.m., I arrive.

ABC News Channel 8 and NBC Connecticut Channel 30 score sit-down interviews with the jury forewoman Mary as she once again publicly defends the guilty verdict. "A lot of people said I did the right thing. I know I did the right thing, and the other eleven people on the jury know we all did the right thing," she tells Channel 8's Leon Collins.

The news stations take measures to protect her identity. NBC shows a dark shadow while Channel 8 displays Mary's back. Her voice is not disguised in either interview.

Days later, Kelly files a motion to reverse the verdict, claiming the evidence *"did not permit the jury to find the defendant guilty beyond a reasonable doubt."* Connelly files an objection stating there was an *"abundance"* of evidence which supported the jury's decision.

A few days after that, acting Police Chief McCormack terminates Smith's employment. If his conviction is overturned, he will be reinstated. A year prior, McCormack supported the decision by the former chief (Sweeney) to lift Smith's suspension, allowing him to return to administrative duties. "We operate under the premise that people are innocent until proven guilty," McCormack said back then.

Linda Kleinschmidt, a local radio personality in Middletown, Connecticut, hosts a program called Police on Patrol. Early on, she had sought involvement in Smith's case. A connection flourished with the defense which provided an access pass to Kelly and possibly ensured firsthand accounts of legal proceedings.

Kleinschmidt knew Mary as an acquaintance and perhaps recognized her voice from television interviews. She initiates contact with Mary days after the trial is over.

Apparently, Mary is having second thoughts regarding

the verdict. Feeling coerced, intimidated, and scared, she remained silent during the deliberative process. Initially, on the charge of Manslaughter with a Firearm, nine jurors voted conviction, three favored acquittal. Mary was in the bottom three.

Linda believes Mary's concerns warrant further investigation and agrees to be an intermediary between her and Kelly.

Mary believes she can convince the other two dissenters who also favored acquittal to join their team. First, she contacts Juror C and tells her about Linda Kleinschmidt's volunteered services. Convinced, the three meet at Friendly's, a fast food restaurant, to discuss a game plan. Kleinschmidt organizes a meeting with Kelly.

Kleinschmidt waits outside Kelly's office while she talks with both jurors. Kelly jumps onboard, but they also need Juror K. Mary contacts Juror K and convinces him to meet with Kelly under the guise of discussing their original vote. Kleinschmidt again waits outside Kelly's office while he speaks with the three jurors.

On April 5, 2000, several media outlets report that three jurors in the Franklyn Reid murder trial—two women and one man—are claiming misconduct impaired their deliberations. They claim one juror displayed an honorable sheriff's badge and another juror discussed his military experience. This, they claimed, was meant to be intimidating.

The timing of this potentially blockbuster news makes skeptics wonder: why now? Reporters contact Mary and the other two jurors, only to hear "no further comments."

The next day, Kelly and Connelly have a meeting with Judge Gill in chambers to discuss sentencing.

Afterward, reporters crowd Kelly for comments. "The meeting had been planned for weeks and it was purely coincidental," he says.

A reporter shouts, "Did you meet with the three jurors?"

Kelly declines to comment but says, "I am researching case law on juror misconduct."

Reporters surround Connelly, who confirms the lawyers did not discuss the recent claims with Judge Gill.

Yet the question is raised: could allegations of juror misconduct void Smith's conviction for manslaughter?

* * *

On April 13, one day after what would have been Franklyn's twenty-ninth birthday, Kelly announces he will file a formal complaint of jury misconduct. He is making sure his desire for Judge Gill to reverse the verdict will be dealt with.

Connelly reacts by stating the obvious: "If a juror was concerned about the proceedings and how they occurred, one would think they would bring it to the attention of Judge Gill and not the defense attorney."

While the defense's intentions are clear, my family chooses to stay out of the spotlight.

In 1999, Reverend Cornell Lewis, an activist, contacted my parents after seeing the one-sided protests in favor of Officer Smith. He organized rallies on behalf of my family. His steadfast pursuit for equal representation created a groundswell of new supporters which shaped public perception.

On April 16, Reverend Lewis organizes a reception at the Phillips Metropolitan CME Church in Hartford, Connecticut, to honor my family. New Perspective, a community group, sponsors the event. The theme is *courage*. Throughout the evening, beautiful messages are delivered to a crowd of more than seventy people.

"I want the Reids to know, many people admire your perseverance, and you can count on support from religious groups and organizations such as the Urban League of Greater Hartford and the NAACP," Cornell says. "We're not going to stand by and let something that was done legally be overturned. In America, people of color lose all the time in court."

City Councilwoman Elizabeth Horton-Sheff echoes similar sentiments. "Not only do we share and celebrate your strength; we share your pain. Because when we lost Franklyn, we lost yet another black man whose potential was not realized."

Those kind words overwhelm my parents. Flanked by my father, my mother speaks. "We have faith in the justice system and are not concerned that the defense is seeking to have the manslaughter conviction overturned. We're here to see justice is done, to the end." The reception marks the first public comments from my mother regarding jury misconduct.

Kelly files his motion on April 20, claiming nine improper occurrences during deliberation, fuel for his request for a new trial.

Contrary to Judge Gill's instructions, the jury never reached a unanimous verdict on the murder charge before discussing and voting on the manslaughter charge.

Before entering deliberation, one juror stated to another juror he had made up his mind that Smith was guilty of murder. He further stated that other jurors may not agree but he will convince them to vote for manslaughter.

One juror displayed a badge, stating he had law enforcement experience and the manner in which Franklyn died was improper based on police training.

One or more jurors said they had served in the military and had been in combat. Smith's shooting of Franklyn was like being in combat and was not justified.

One juror stated he had shot and killed a deer, and the deer's legs were positioned in a certain way. He compared that position to Franklyn's position.

One or more jurors brought notes into deliberation.

Several jurors had asked that Smith's testimony be reread. The others refused to submit that request to Judge Gill.

One juror drove by the scene, observed flowers, and wanted to determine the proximity of the Sunoco gas station and how close a state's witness was to the scene.

One juror, referred to as "Rambo," caused other jurors to feel fearful and intimidated them into voting for manslaughter.

Connelly submits a twenty-one-page document, rebutting each claim. The only element that distinguishes murder from manslaughter is *intent* to kill or cause serious harm. By virtue of returning a not guilty verdict on murder, jurors had to have voted on eliminating the most detrimental charge. Although a member decided on murder from the onset of deliberation, it is not prejudicial against Smith; it just reinforces that all of the evidence was carefully discussed before agreeing on a lesser charge.

"An inquiry as to what was discussed and whether there was an agreement invades the sanctity and integrity of the jury deliberations," Connelly states.

Statements from jurors familiar with law enforcement, with military experience, and who had used a firearm to kill a deer, were merely friendly reminders. The defense knew their backgrounds from the extensive questioning the jurors endured during the jury selection process. Smith believed they would be sympathetic to his cause and greenlighted their selections.

Connelly writes, "The three claims dealing with the various disclosures of life experience by the jurors, individually and collectively, are inconsequential and do not require extensive inquiry to determine their frivolous nature. The claims put forth in the defendant's offer of proof are currently unsubstantiated and not attributable to any source, let alone one of reliability."

Connelly contends it's impossible to conclude that the existence of notes or driving past the scene located along a busy highway, created an improper verdict.

As for claims of intimidation and denied requests for documents to be reread, Connelly reiterates the sanctity of the deliberation process in which jurors voice opinions.

But most importantly, he says, Smith elected a trial by jury. Connelly calls it "absurd" to now suggest Smith was "deprived of constitutional protection because some members of the jury had stronger opinions than others." A new trial, he said, should be denied.

Judge Gill must address both motions before sentencing and determine their validity and rule upon them if necessary. He conducts in-chamber interviews with each of the twelve jurors on May 3.

Linda Kleinschmidt shows up at the Litchfield Courthouse and reveals herself to the media as Mary's acquaintance. She presents herself at the clerk's office and asks where to report, ready to testify though she was not subpoenaed. Confusion arises until her role is finally established as simply a spectator. Aside from moral support, she makes herself available for media interviews, to discuss private conversations she had with the three jurors.

My parents also attend the hearing and wait patiently inside the courtroom along with Smith's family and a handful of supporters from both sides. My parents have no idea who Linda Kleinschmidt is. I decide to stay at college and prepare for final exams.

Three allegations warrant investigation: the unauthorized crime scene visit, notes by jurors, and displaying of a badge. Judge Gill tosses out the remaining six as a "fishing expedition" that seek "in violation of our law, to enter into the general mental processes of the jurors."

The remaining three, however, merit investigation. Smith, both counsels, a court reporter, and a clerk are allowed into Judge Gill's chambers and pay close attention to how the process will unfold.

Mary's interview provides insights about Linda Kleinschmidt's involvement. Mary can't recall Linda's last name, though they claim to be friends. Judge Gill conducts the questioning.

Judge Gill: "What was your motivation, then, to make contact with Mr. Kelly?"

Mary: "Because I felt that I made the wrong decision, and I should have just stuck to what I thought in the beginning."

Judge Gill: "Okay. Our law provides, specifically, that what you just said is inadmissible. Okay? Jurors don't make two decisions, one on the jury day and one a week later or even a day later, you see?"

Mary: "My mind was made up when I was there [on verdict day]."

Judge Gill: "Okay. Well, that is what I thought I heard you say on TV."

Judge Gill's observation of Mary prompts a mild concern about her credibility. Her demeanor appears distraught, alternately guarded, and emotional. He needs to monitor her throughout the day.

The judge explores Juror K's reluctance to come forward, to understand if he was persuaded by others to join the group. When he talked to Mary about meeting with Kelly, he wasn't sure what he could contribute, but he was willing to meet with the attorney. He says he was not sure why Kleinschmidt was at the meeting.

Judge Gill: "Would you have gone to Mr. Kelly without being asked by the foreperson [Mary]?"

Juror K: "No."

The day's inquiry ends as Judge Gill addresses the jury one last time. Mary continues exhibiting noticeable signs that are hard to overlook. She avoids eye contact with Judge Gill. She's bent over, in a head down position, occupying two chairs. She appears covered, protective and, under the circumstances, socially detached. Judge Gill promises a ruling in a few days. He instructs the jury not to speak with reporters or anyone else about the case or hearing.

Connelly meets my parents and provides a quick update. Outside, a reporter asks my mother her thoughts.

"I believe it's hogwash for the defense to bring these motions," she says.

A reporter asks Kelly, "With Judge Gill taking only three of the nine [complaints of misconduct], what does that do?"

"Well, it shortened the hearing, that's number one; and number two, maybe poses another appellate issue."

Connelly sees it differently as reporters hustle toward him as he leaves the court. "This jury decided a tough case. They came up with a fair and impartial verdict."

Some media outlets entertain Kleinschmidt's availability to flavor their nightly broadcast. She discusses conversations she had with the jurors. She tells NBC 30 News that Mary was "just going through the motions," and Juror C and K "felt they made a mistake even before they left the court."

Lynn Jolicoeur from Fox 61 News has a walking

interview with Kleinschmidt who reiterates that the jury forewoman, an acquaintance, shared concerns with her two days after the verdict.

"I advised her and the two other jurors to go to Smith's attorney," she says.

Lynn asks, "Why didn't they bring this stuff up during the trial?"

"Once again, it was, as I was told by them, the fear."

* * *

Later that evening, News Channel 8 Erin Cox reports.

"Linda Kleinschmidt, a radio talk show host, claims three jurors told her they were pressured. She recounts the forewoman's story of other jurors telling her not to screw it up when she read the guilty verdict."

Viewers hear Kleinschmidt's voice from an earlier interview say, "Which would answer the question as to when she was polled individually, why she didn't say something then. She still had this perceived threat."

"The judge is also considering an interview the jury forewoman gave to News Channel 8, after the verdict. In it, she told us the decision was unanimous," Erin adds.

Mary's interview from more than a month ago is replayed. Mary is saying, "A lot of people said I did the right thing, and I think, you know, it's just, I know I did the right thing and the other eleven people on the jury, we all did the right thing."

But Linda has an explanation. "She was just going

through the motions at the time—as well as the other two jurors who already felt they made a mistake, even before they left the court."

"The Reid family is confident the verdict will stand," Erin reports.

My mom's interview outside the courthouse backs up Erin's statement. "It's very lucrative for three of them to come out and say something contrary now, and I believe we're not going to reach a point where we have a new trial."

"The judge will issue his decision by Monday," Erin concludes.

While I receive daily updates from my parents, I distinctly recall a cohesive jury holding the mantle of fairness; it did not appear deceitful. Firsthand accounts typically trump Monday morning quarterbacking, especially since Linda never graced the courtroom throughout the trial.

* * *

On May 8, Judge Gill rules. He shares his opinion on the close-knit jury who were together almost eight hours a day for several weeks. Each morning about 9:00 a.m., they gathered at the rear of St. Anthony's church, located a short distance from the courthouse. They were met by two sheriff's deputies, scanned by a metal detector, and brought to the basement of the church to have coffee together. That essentially became their waiting area until summoned by the court. They always moved as a group, having lunch and breaks together. They were observed displaying tremendous respect toward each other.

Judge Gill says he has never spoken with a jury that was more confident in its verdict. "There was absolutely no indication of dissent or of any emotional strain. Every juror was totally composed after the verdict was rendered."

Conspicuously, two of the investigated misconduct claims were committed by dissenters. Juror C had made the unauthorized crime scene visit. Although her admitted act could constitute misconduct after the court cautioned against visits, Judge Gill states five reasons why it was not prejudicial against Smith:

She never informed any of the other jurors.

She wanted to determine if a witness could observe Franklyn and Smith from a location inside the gas station but she simply drove by without stopping.

The crime scene was hardly a mystery. The jury saw a videotape of the entire scene from every conceivable angle and numerous photographs and charts containing measurements as to distances between all locations.

She heard eyewitness accounts twice in which Kelly had them approximate distances from various points within the courtroom.

Mary had spoken honestly and accurately about the civilian

witnesses during her Channel 8 interview. "There is no way that these people would just make it up. I mean, because like I said, they were just people driving by, you know, doing their daily thing, and came forward; and what he [Smith] said, to me, it just seemed like it just didn't match. Nothing, you know, matched."

Juror K had brought notes into deliberation that he had typed overnight with questions he wanted to ask fellow members. Another juror did the same on a smaller scale. Judge Gill rules that this is not jury misconduct by any recognizable legal standard.

The displaying of a badge essentially draws a line in the sand. Considered most serious, Juror M's purported connection to law enforcement is reviewed. During jury selection, the court learned he is a corporate executive with a large corporation. While living in Indianapolis, Indiana, he actively volunteered with children and youth. As a result of his good citizenship, he received an "honorary" sheriff's badge from the sheriff of that area. Judge Gill and both attorneys discussed that award and inquired if it would have any impact on his ability to serve as a juror. All parties had agreed he would be fair and impartial; both sides accepted him.

During a routine magnetic scan at the church, Juror M placed his belongings in a basket. The badge was displayed after his wallet opened which caught another juror's eyes. In answer to that person's curiosity about whether he was in law enforcement, Juror M had said, *"No, I'm not a cop."* On subsequent scans, he ensured that his wallet was face down.

After the unanimous verdict was reached, the jurors held a roundup discussion in which each gave their opinion on the case. Juror M's law enforcement connections resurfaced. He explained to the group that while he understood Smith's position, he could not be sympathetic because, as they were instructed, they had to base their decisions on evidence and statements presented to them.

Judge Gill reviewed the matter in his in-chamber interview with Juror M.

Judge Gill: "The only time anybody could see it was at the church, coming through the metal detector?"

Juror M: "Yes."

Judge Gill: "And the second time after the unanimously reached verdict?"

Juror M: "Yes."

Judge Gill: "And no times in between?"

Juror M: "Absolutely not."

Judge Gill: "Okay. Did you at any time show your badge to any juror in an attempt to influence that juror's vote?"

Juror M: "Absolutely not."

After interviewing the jurors, Judge Gill finds there is no basis for the claim of misconduct. While the three dissenters agreed with each other, their nine colleagues sharply disagreed with them. On each of the pivotal issues, Judge Gill finds credibility rests with the nine jurors.

He rules: based upon the court's finding of facts, its observation and the law, the defendant's motion for a new trial is denied.

Connelly comments with reporters outside his office.

"The juror who brought this to the attention of the media in the first place was probably misguided by one of the defendant's supporters."

A perfectly timed maneuver to secure an unprecedented campaign victory fell short under the rule of law. But one matter continued to cause anxiety in my family: what would Officer Smith's sentence be?

ACT VI SCENE II

SENTENCING

The stage is set. The props haven't changed and the cast has virtually remained the same—judge, counsel, defendant, court personnel, and the families. The obvious members not in attendance are the twelve men and women responsible for this scene.

Out of respect for their excused absences, their seats remain empty as a symbolic gesture. Selected, they saw, they heard, they deliberated, and they voted unanimously. That is the role of our jury system.

New faces join old faces to occupy available spectator seats. The same rule applies as before: admission is free but first come, first served. The overflow crowd bunches together outside the courtroom doors wanting to be a part of history.

Quite fitting, both families are front and center occupying their same seats. We have, once again, found ourselves in that hollow tunnel, connected since December 29, 1998, by an act that intertwined our individual paths. Both mothers will soon take center stage in honor of their respective sons. Where once we sought justice or exoneration, we now seek fairness or leniency as we're all at the mercy of the court. We have witnessed numerous climactic moments; I'm sure their words will reverberate with dignity.

I drove back from college the night before to join my parents and supporters to see closure in this criminal trial. I am fully aware the defense may explore all available options to keep Smith away from prison but displaying human decency toward one side is equally important as any fulfillment I may experience.

Each counsel has a final opportunity to address the court before Judge Gill imposes the sentence. Kelly leads by motioning for another acquittal under the premise that Smith's self-defense claim was based on the evidence presented to the jury, and it was not disproven beyond a reasonable doubt by the prosecution.

Connelly simply states the motion should be denied.

For the third time, Judge Gill denies the motion.

After a brief back and forth between the lawyers, we arrive at the reason we're in court today: an appropriate sentence for Smith. Connelly is not asking for the maximum of forty years or the five-year minimum. He leaves that decision to a fair-minded judge. Kelly asks for the absolute minimum.

Before Judge Gill hands down the sentence, it is time for the Family Impact Statements. My mother speaks first. Keeping it simple, she echoes Connelly's sentiments regarding how fair Judge Gill has been to both sides. "Connecticut is proud of you, and all those in the judiciary arena are proud of you."

My mother speaks about her son. "When Franklyn Reid was born, we adored, cherished, and loved him. Franklyn was a kind and loving son to his parents, brothers, children, and others who knew him well. Franklyn was supportive of Wayne…He did not get the chance to see his children grow… He was robbed of his dreams."

Typically, the victim's family would ask that the maximum sentence be imposed. My mother punts the decision to Judge Gill. "Your Honor, we trust your judgment and know you will impose a sentence that fits this heinous crime."

Personally, I don't believe tens of years behind bars is in Smith's future.

Next, Mrs. Smith speaks. "Scott has brought his father, sister, and I, great joy, love, and pride. He worked hard in school, excelled in sports, and has had many friends and is considerate of all. Scott also has an amazing sense of awareness of his surroundings and great attention to detail. As a student, Scott worked hard to achieve his goals, first to go to college, then to become a police officer. But I am most proud of the man he has become. The adjectives that best describe him are: kind, loyal, dependable, trustworthy, honest, responsible, and considerate. Since that night, Scott has spent many sleepless nights reliving the event. Knowing what happened and knowing Franklyn vowed never to return to prison, the conclusion he reaches every night is the same. He did what he had to do at the moment.

"If Scott is sent to prison, I fear he will either be killed or abused because he personifies all that is good and all that is disdained by prisoners." Mrs. Smith doesn't ask for the minimum; she simply does not mention the sentence at all.

Putting myself in her shoes, as I've watched my brother sentenced before, it's challenging to suggest any amount of time behind bars. I certainly don't envy her at this moment because I know her plight. It's no secret, prison life is rough.

Both mothers are proud of their sons. Everyone's path in life differs, which makes us individuals. No one is immune from problems, questionable circumstances, or a fall from grace. That is who we are, human beings, capable of doing great things and not so great things.

Officer Smith had testified in his own defense, hoping his words would bring about absolute vindication, but a split verdict vanquished that hope. The proceeding minutes will dictate his future, but this pivotal moment will not pass without Smith's closing remarks.

"On December 29, 1998, I went to work as I had for approximately the prior two years. I went to aid a brother police officer in which I encountered Mr. Reid. I attempted to take him into custody. He resisted my efforts to arrest him. During that period of time, I sincerely believe he was attempting to gain access to a weapon and he was about to kill me. I shot him before he was able to do that, and my attorney has said everything else that I wish to say."

I can't help recalling Connelly's opening remarks. "The one thing, Your Honor, that strikes me during the whole course of this case and in reading the PSI (pre-sentence investigation) is that the defendant has not shown the least bit of remorse for what he did."

But I also remember Kelly's countering remarks that Smith had experienced stress throughout this case. "To picture him as someone who is cold-hearted and emotionless is not an accurate picture of the man I know. He is someone who is guarded in his feelings. That's who he is. He is someone who outwardly doesn't show a lot of emotion. That's how he is. But if anyone thinks that he took comfort or pleasure in the events that occurred on December 29, 1998, or thereafter, they're sadly mistaken."

My prevailing thoughts highlight the facts: a *forty-one-second* public incident cast self-defense against right versus wrong, resulting in a sad situation for all involved. Judge Gill has certainly been mindful of the facts. He has reviewed over one hundred exhibits, heard numerous technical motions and legal arguments from each counsel and ruled accordingly. Judge Gill listened to and observed forty-five witnesses who testified. At times, when a circus-like atmosphere occurred beyond the courthouse, he paid attention. When emotions, articles, and rallies beyond his control captivated the public, he paid attention. Though police-involved shootings are trigger points for high emotions and controversy, Judge Gill stepped forward and presided over a trial which lasted nine days. I believe that fairness will distinguish him in Connecticut's landmark trial.

Judge Gill tells those present that sentencing doesn't get easier with experience even though he has sentenced thousands of people since sitting on the bench. "This case is, by far, the most difficult one I've been called to perform."

Being the father of three children (two being boys, the age of Franklyn and Scott), Judge Gill reminds the court that any conscientious person, as he is, can clearly see the tragic picture both families are enduring. He's looking at the trial through the eyes of a parent *and* a judge.

"Both sets of parents here are decent, hardworking people. Both sets of parents have worked hard at parenting, an extremely challenging task. Both sets of these parents have produced children of college-level abilities; Franklyn's younger brother, Wayne, is about to graduate from college. One set of parents, we know, had a troubled son and the other set of parents has a son now in trouble. One set of parents has a son who's deceased, and the other set has a son heading to prison. There are no winners here. There is no sentence that atones for a life, equals a life, or in reality makes the loss of a life more acceptable, under any circumstances. None whatsoever."

Before getting to sentencing, he addresses a few concerns seen through the lens of understanding the greater issues outside his courtroom. As a like-minded person who feels unbiased in my relationships with other people who are different from each other, I feel proud hearing him bring up these issues.

"I am frankly appalled at the misinformation about this case that has been accepted as truth by some members of our public...The jury's verdict was based upon the facts as they found them to be. Their decision had nothing to do with philosophy, politics, or popularity.

"Those with a genuine concern over racial prejudice in America should not raise the flag of victory because of this case. On the other hand, the flag of respect for the vast majority of police officers should not be lowered either."

The judge tackles police concerns, speaking with experience, since his father was the president of the New Haven Board of Police Commissioners for sixteen years.

"This court does not believe the prophets of doom, which unfortunately include some police officials, that this case somehow represents a public belief that officers will now endanger their lives by failing to use deadly force in appropriate situations to save their lives or the lives of others. Or on the other hand, walk away in the face of a dangerous criminal activity lest they be wrongly charged with a crime. That ill-thought-out alarmism is not only incorrect but misleading to the public as well. In fact, clearer thinking and more experienced police leadership has thankfully and thoughtfully debunked both of those erroneous and inflammatory notions."

Judge Gill's words solidify my understanding that even the best trained of our police officers have legitimate fears in our violent and dangerous country.

"Few of us here would want to be in the shoes of a police officer in America. Our police do not need less training, less community support, or less understanding. They need more training, more community support, and more understanding. Those who believe the policeman is always wrong in such confrontational situations are susceptible to the same errors and the same perils of a closed mind as those who believe the policeman is always right."

He reiterates an essential point that some people tend to ignore or are unaware of: police thoroughly and fairly investigated this case themselves.

"Because of our laws, it was investigated by the Connecticut State Police. They competently gathered physical evidence, went to extraordinary lengths to find and interview eyewitnesses. They prepared a twenty-two-page affidavit, and the Connecticut State Police applied for the arrest warrant for Scott Smith."

Judge Gill continues to speak and his words reflect my own feelings that racism did not rear its ugly head during this trial. He is a man whose first job was as a neighborhood lawyer in New Haven, Connecticut's inner city, where 100 percent of his clients were poor and 90 percent were minorities. He spent three years representing convicted defendants in Somer's prison. Judge Gill understands the thirst for racial justice but as he has said, *"This case is not the drink that will quench that thirst."* Both sides in this case had witnesses who were black and white.

I applaud his belief we can move away from skin color references and replace them with right versus wrong.

"You know, the Statue of Justice is always depicted as being blindfolded. It is important that she be blindfolded, so that she will weigh the evidence on the scales of justice without regard to race, age, or the sex of those seeking justice. I can assure you that the jury in this case was absolutely colorblind, and weighed the facts as they were presented to them. I am confident this jury did not view Scott Smith's actions as racist in any way and neither do I."

I couldn't agree more with Judge Gill, as he speaks highly of the New Milford Police Department. There are many wonderful and respected people in that department who are doing terrific things for the community. They may have been thrust into the spotlight and experienced low morale, but they have weathered the storm. It's vital that a community torn apart after a tragic event mend for the sake of unity.

"The best advice for the Town of New Milford comes from one of your citizens, a local historian, an African-American woman (Fran Smith). She said, 'In time, with truth and love, the wound will heal.' I earnestly implore all of you here to heed her sage advice, because regardless of what sentence is imposed or appeals taken, whatever—*the need for all of us to heal is painfully obvious.*"

Deliberating upon the sentence to impose took into consideration a breadth of knowledge and information. In addition to presiding over the trial, Judge Gill had read letters submitted in support of Smith and the pre-sentence investigation report, which included a seven-page letter Franklyn had written to Judge Walsh a month before his death.

Judge Gill explains that there are two types of sentencing a court can impose. The first is a flat sentence with a defined number of years. For example, the minimum five years or maximum forty years. The second type is a split sentence, such as forty years suspended after serving twenty years. A person would then leave prison and go on probation.

"The probation officer who prepared Scott Smith's presentence report recommends to the court a split sentence. The court agrees with that recommendation. The probation officer also recommends, based on the likelihood that Scott Smith will succeed on probation, that there be a minimal term of probation. The court also agrees with that recommendation."

Judge Gill has agonized over the precise number of years to impose. He has examined his own conscience and listened to the eloquent pleas of both mothers. He's leaning toward the lower end and reiterates that, by no means, does that devalue the life of Franklyn. At the same time, a convicted police officer would be placed in protective custody, which means serving time in a cell by himself for twenty-three hours a day.

"Like Franklyn, who made mistakes in his life which he honestly and sincerely admitted, I have another young man here, Scott Smith, who has made a serious mistake in his life. Scott Smith will never ever commit another crime.

"The court is going to impose the following sentence on Mr. Smith."

The former officer voluntarily stands for potentially the final time in this criminal case and looks directly at Judge Gill.

"Scott Smith, on the charge of intentional manslaughter in the first degree with a firearm, I sentence you to the custody of the Commissioner of Corrections for a term of twelve years, which sentence shall be suspended after you've served six years, five of which are non-suspendible and non-reducible. You are, thereafter, placed upon probation for a period of two years."

Smith has no immediate choice but to accept his punishment.

And so it was, the first officer in Connecticut charged with murder on January 19, 1999, found guilty of a lesser charge on March 13, 2000, is officially sentenced on May 11, 2000. The clerk gives Smith a series of documents, one which includes a Notice of Right to Appeal the Judgment of Conviction. Kelly will waste no time in submitting that form and the defendant's Motion for Bail pending the appeal.

The final gavel sounds as Judge Gill rules. "The court is going to set an appeal bond in the amount of $250,000 cash or surety. That ends our proceedings. We'll have a recess."

The silent courtroom watches the sheriff's deputy approach Smith. He stands up, turns around, and places his hands behind him. *Click, click, click* reverberates through the courtroom. A somber sight for anyone who has a heart, and trust me, everyone witnessing handcuffs placed on Smith has a heart. But Smith's time in handcuffs is short-lived, lasting only until his bail is processed.

* * *

Soon after, outside the courthouse, Smith breaks his media silence while a few supporters chant, *"Appeal! Appeal!*

Appeal!" Others in the group sing a religious-themed jingle. *"He's got Sccccccott Smith, in his hands! He's got Sccccccott Smith, in his hands!"*

"I appreciate the support. I've got overwhelming support, and I thank everybody out there," Smith tells reporters.

His father's disdain for the trial is clearly visible as he steps past reporters. "Politics," he mouths.

Kelly tells reporters, "Scott should not have been arrested or prosecuted. He acted properly in self-defense as law permitted."

Connelly tells reporters something different. "I think the community has viewed this shooting as number one, legally improper, and also morally and ethically improper."

Reverend Kimber, president of the Greater New Haven Clergy Association, offers his own assessment of proceedings. "I think that history has been made in this state, and this state will no longer tolerate the abuse of a firearm by a police officer."

During sentencing, Smith's demeanor catches the eyes of onlookers and reporters.

"I think one of the most, ahhh, disappointing things in this case is that, ahhh, Scott Smith never showed any remorse about shooting Franklyn Reid," Kimber adds.

It certainly feels like we've arrived at the end. Regrettably, another tumultuous period is yet to come.

ACT VI SCENE III

———

JUROR REFLECTIONS

Three more jurors break their silence for the first time, commenting freely on a series of questions in subsequent interviews.

They reflect on which evidence was most persuasive. Juror W states, "The boot in the back. The fact that he [Reid] was face down. The fact that he [Smith] had a gun in his back. That was probably a determining factor given the stance he [Smith] took."

Juror H seconds the gun pressed into Reid's back and the transcript between dispatch and Detective Shortt. "He was so sure that Reid was under control."

And Juror V adds, "The physical evidence—his shirt, wounds on his body, the evidence that was on his shirt, the footprint. The gun being pushed into his back, with abrasions from the barrel of the gun. That was vividly portrayed by the prosecutor, John Connelly."

While evidence was compelling, the eyewitnesses traveling along Route 202 were the most persuasive element, according to Juror V. Similarly, Juror W believes, "The oil truck driver and the couple. It was such a visible point that I felt that these eyewitnesses were, in fact, seeing what they were talking about seeing. They were credible. The overall fact is that these people were witnessing it from the side of the highway. And it all took place not eight feet off the highway. They had a good view. They were credible."

Likewise, Juror H thinks, "The woman who had been coming from the bank. Her husband was driving, and she was the passenger. She seemed very sure of what she had seen and was able to present it very clearly. She had seen Scott Smith with his foot on Franklyn Reid's back and his [Reid's]hands behind him."

In terms of expert testimonies, Dr. Carver and Mr. Bodziak receive high marks for persuasiveness, while Juror W feels Mr. Kapelsohn was weak for the defense.

Counsel receives mixed reviews as Juror H says, "Connelly and Kelly were so like night and day. They really were direct opposites. Kelly was just so soft-spoken. I don't think he ever raised his voice. And Connelly was very dramatic. You didn't pay too much attention to that, though, because the witnesses and the evidence became more important. In spite of his approach and manner of presenting stuff, Connelly seemed to have more evidence. I think Kelly did the best he could with what he had to work with. They had the scene, trying to show how Franklyn Reid could have pulled the knife out. That seemed like grasping at straws."

Juror V thinks each counsel was prepared but had a hard

time believing Smith feared for his life given the circumstances. Yet Juror W thinks Kelly didn't present as strong a case as he could have. "I felt the legal firm had erred. They led him into a defense instead of looking at the facts of what might have been stronger for his client. If he had said it was an accident, knowing that the weapon had a tendency to misfire, there would have been more doubt within the jury pool. By not taking that stance and saying it was self-defense, when it clearly couldn't have been, it didn't make sense."

Judge Gill scores impressively high praise in how he managed the trial and himself. Juror W elaborates: "I think Judge Gill tried to be very thorough, and I think he did an excellent job. I don't think he could have foreseen these jurors called for misconduct when they were talking with the radio lady and bringing in that they didn't feel he was guilty after they said he was guilty. We were unanimous, and it was hard work getting there. We weren't unanimous in our early deliberations. There were three who thought they were pushed. And they weren't pushed; they were just shown the facts of the case. The facts all pointed to our decision."

Juror H keeps his appraisal of the judge simple. "I was impressed that he didn't let race become an issue. It just wasn't an issue. He kept decorum in the courtroom, he was eminently fair."

Equally positive, Juror V states his opinion of Judge Gill. "There were a few instances where things started to get a little out of control; he just cut that out. A few times there was sarcasm or perhaps a little levity, and he cut that out. I think there was a give and take with the prosecutor and the defense, but he cut that out. I was impressed with his demeanor on the bench. He was in control the entire time. I was impressed with his professionalism."

Juror reflections should signal a curtain call, but another emotionally charged roller-coaster is yet to be experienced.

ACT VI SCENE IV

——

THE DAGGER

The notion that justice ascended the steps and delivered a conviction that carried a jail sentence suggests the legal system worked in this case.

While Smith remains free on bond, his mother employs the mighty pen, soliciting donations to cover legal costs. In view of how the incident occurred, her letter deviates from what was revealed during the trial. Nevertheless, she summarizes: "Scott and the other officer found Reid at a gas station. My son left his police car and began chasing Reid on foot. Scott shouted at Reid to stop—but Reid kept running. Fearing Reid might have a weapon, Scott pulled his service weapon out of his holster. Finally, he caught up with Reid, grabbed his shoulder and pulled him out of the road into the grassy area on the side. Over and over, Scott yelled at Reid to show him his hands. But Reid just kept on struggling and refused Scott's repeated commands. Then— while still hiding his hands—Reid suddenly made a move toward Scott! If Reid had a gun or knife, it would take only a split-second for him to stab or shoot Scott. Fearing for his life, Scott fired once from his service weapon—just like he had been taught at the service academy. Scott was devastated—but when investigating officers found a knife in Reid's jacket, he knew he'd done the right thing. And so did his fellow officers in the New Milford Police Department. But prosecutors for the state of Connecticut didn't agree. They charged Scott with murder. My friend, it was just awful."

Her words find their intended audience just as my mother's letters did prior to the incident. One commonality in their plea: both families experienced financial crisis. "We were barely able to pay for Scott's legal bills in the original trial. An appeal could drain every penny we have," Mrs. Smith writes.

But appeal they did. In April 2001, Kelly submits a seventy-page document to the second highest court in Connecticut, the Appellate Court. In it, he details a list of issues on why Smith did not receive a fair trial and concludes with:

"For all the foregoing reasons, this Court should reverse the defendant's conviction and remand the case to the trial court for a new trial."

Shortly after the shooting, my family had retained Koskoff Koskoff & Bieder to manage a potential civil lawsuit. While the court reviews the appeal, attorney Richard Bieder and his team ramp up their investigation.

Life continues as time heals most wounds. Although my mother experienced her darkest hour after learning her son had passed, she refuses to believe or accept that conclusion—even after sitting through the trial. For years, she looks through windows, beyond the trees, over mountains, and into space, hoping that her son will miraculously reappear. Then, one late summer afternoon in 2001, she sits alone on the back deck, gazing through the bountiful trees. Mesmerized, her son dwells in her thoughts. *He's hungry, tired, and weak from his journey. First, I will give him water and then food.*

Suddenly an angel appears to her as tears roll down her cheek. "I know you're looking for him. He's gone and he's not coming back. Move forward with life," the spiritual figure says before vanishing.

That moment, she realizes it is time to let go.

After graduating from college in May 2000, I begin my career in New York City, moving to Jersey City, New Jersey. Each morning, I commute on the PATH train into the ground level of the World Trade Center, arriving at 8:45 a.m.

On September 11, I decide to leave my apartment five minutes early. I arrive at the World Trade Center at 8:40 a.m., ascend the long escalator, exit the building, and jump on the Number 4 subway to Grand Central Station. I arrive at work and my coworkers are crowded around the television. My eyes bulge, mouth drops open, and tears form.

"I was just there!" I say to my colleagues.

We stare in shock as the North Tower burns. Time appears frozen. Suddenly, a second plane crashes into the South Tower. Gasps and sounds of horror consume our area.

Fear sets in as rumors swirl that the United Nations may be a target—our office is in the vicinity. We stay put, watching the news before embarking on a long, emotional journey home.

After hours waiting in line, I board the ferry for the short trip across the Hudson River toward Hoboken, New Jersey. As we pass the skyline, smoke rises where two towers once stood. My heart aches as tears roll down my cheeks, unable to fathom this incredible tragedy. I recall that my first interview after graduation was with Morgan Stanley on the seventy-fourth floor in the North Tower. After arriving home, I call my parents.

"Mom, I am safe," I say.

"We were worried sick because we couldn't get in contact with you," she says.

The horrific events of September 11 change our world and many lives in a dramatic way. I move back to Connecticut in November 2001 to be closer to my family and commute into the city for work. The thought of Smith being free on bond seems to take a backseat since our country is in the midst of a national tragedy, but I feel his day is on the horizon.

* * *

On October 18, 2002, my cell phone rings while I'm at work. My mother informs me that news stations are reporting stunning information. I take a deep breath. I will leave work immediately.

ACT VI SCENE V

THE APPELLATE COURT

Sprinting up 42nd Street toward Grand Central Station, I am vibrating with anxiety, uncertainty, anger, and frustration. What follows is the process that causes the blind bearer of justice to lose her footing and drop her scale.

The appellate court reviews the case between April 2001 and October 2002. Naturally, in a highly sensitive case such as this, with the evidence seemingly overwhelming (as the cover shows), the defense is obliged to throw everything it has to block a most certain conviction. They throw the proverbial kitchen sink at the court. It almost reaches the absurdity level.

During the trial, Kelly had offered four videotapes of police training into evidence. Judge Gill rejected all four. Here are explanations to help you understand why:

The first is titled *Deadly Force*. In it, there are scores of face-to-face confrontations between police and citizens. All from a distance, unlike Smith's up close and personal.

And unlike my brother's situation, the citizens in the video are visibly armed with pistols, knives, or blunt instruments such as bricks.

The second, *Miami Firefight*, depicts a Western style shoot-out between eight FBI agents and two armed-bank robbers. Two FBI agents and the two robbers are slain. The robbers had previously killed two citizens and wounded several others.

The third is *Ultimate Survivor*. For credibility purposes, it is narrated by William Shatner of Star Trek fame! It tells the stories of four police officers in jeopardy. See if you find anything in their situations comparable to Scott Smith's.

Officer Tuthill: This officer is shot point-blank in his face while in his car writing a report. The shooter believes he was ordered by the president of the United States to shoot a police officer.

US Marshall: A US Marshall is transporting a federal prisoner to a medical appointment when he attempts to escape. Two persons approach him, one with his revolver drawn. The US Marshall is able to draw his own revolver and kills both persons.

Officer Mike Buckingham: A drunk driver causes this officer to crash into a tree whereupon it bursts into flames. The officer survives.

Officer Steve Chaney: This officer and his partner respond to an attempted burglary complaint. In the house, they encounter the perpetrator who was lying in wait for his former love interest. Upon seeing the police officers, the perpetrator shouts, "Why don't you just kill me? You got me." The perpetrator then grabs Officer Chaney's pistol and a struggle ensues, during which the perpetrator and Officer Chaney's partner are killed. Later in his career, Officer Chaney shoots and kills another perpetrator who comes out of a bar, faces him, and pulls a gun on him.

Surviving Edged Weapons, the last video, begins by depicting a caveman reenactment scene, then deals with what it calls the "knife culture." It points out that most knifings involve domestic disturbance calls. It spends significant time spotlighting edged weapons used by emotionally disturbed persons (termed EDP's). It also covers swords, beer bottles to the head, and screwdrivers (the second most prevalent edged weapon used, according to the video). The video also dwells on prison "shanks" (homemade knives) and presents knife scenes ala Bruce Lee, and provides officers' defensive tips for such situations.

The hope of the defense is that police training might somehow legitimatize Scott Smith's actions. Unfortunately, the appellate court falls for this argument lock, stock, and barrel.

What must be resolved by the appellate court is whether Scott Smith "was justified in using deadly force under the relevant self-defense statute." That statute reads that deadly force is justified only when:

1. "He reasonably believes such force to be necessary."
2. "To defend himself...from the use or imminent use of deadly physical force."

The appellate court notes in its decision:

> On the basis of the evidence and the reasonable and logical inferences to be drawn therefrom, and construing the evidence in a light most favorable to sustaining the jury's verdict of guilty, we conclude that the cumulative effect of the evidence was sufficient to support the jury's conclusion that the state had met its burden of disproving the defense of justification.

The appellate court not only finds that there was enough evidence for the jury to find Smith guilty beyond a reasonable doubt, but also that the jury had sufficient evidence to conclude that the state had met its burden of disproving Smith's defense of justification. Shouldn't that be the end of the case? The jury agreed. The trial judge agreed and the appellate court agreed.

But the appellate court decides to go beyond the evidence presented at the trial into "maybe land" and address a mountain of unimportant, repetitive, irrelevant, and seriously questionable evidence offered by the defense. The defense's appeal to the appellate court contained reports from two additional expert witnesses on the issue of police use of force, and a third—Kapelsohn—who has no police experience.

During the trial, Judge Gill ruled the jury needed only one expert to say the earth is round, not three. In other words, it's like having three psychiatrists testify that someone is insane. In court parlance, Judge Gill excluded "cumulative" evidence, which is a trial judge's job.

In appeal, Kelly argues, "The expert witnesses' testimony concerning the police training they provide and which the defendant received would have assisted the jury in analyzing the defendant's state of mind and his course of conduct from the time he first encountered Franklyn Reid and attempted to arrest him, until approximately forty seconds later, when he fired a single shot which killed Reid. The court's exclusion of their testimony violated the defendant's constitutional right to present to the jury his version of the facts."

On October 18, 2002, the appellate court releases their decision:

"We cannot conclude that the exclusion of the expert testimony regarding the defendant's training in the use of deadly force was harmless beyond a reasonable doubt. The defendant, therefore, is entitled to a new trial, and we remand the case to the trial court for that purpose."

* * *

The appellate court reverses the jury's verdict and Judge Gill's rulings solely on its belief that Judge Gill should have allowed not one, but three experts to testify as to Smith's and all other police training. However, even in the appellate court's decision, it notes that each of the three defense witnesses would testify as to "police use of force."

The following additional facts and procedural history are necessary for our resolution of the defendant's claim. The defendant sought to introduce the testimony of three expert witnesses. One of those witnesses, Reginald F. Allard, Jr., had been an instructor at the Connecticut Police Academy for approximately sixteen years. Allard instructed the defendant at the police academy, both in the classroom and in practical skills. The defendant also offered the expert testimony of David M. Grossi, Sr., a former police officer and an instructor on police use of force and a lecturer on police use of force issues; and Emanuel Kapelsohn, who is certified by the Federal Bureau of Investigation (FBI) as a police firearm's instructor, and who lectures on weapons and police use of force issues. Essentially, the defendant offered the testimony of those witnesses to allow the jury to evaluate the defendant's conduct against that of a reasonable police officer.

Note again that all three witnesses would testify to the exact same issue, "the police use of force." The jury had heard about this issue in great detail from defense witness Emanuel Kapelsohn and from Smith's own extensive testimony about police use of force.

A reasonable analysis of the case shows that this balloon of a defense is totally deflated, and that the actual printed words of three defense experts work more for the prosecution than the defense.

* * *

Prior to the appellate court's ruling, the civil case was in full swing. Our private attorneys researched police training (the basis of the civil suit) thoroughly; conducted several depositions from Officer Smith (on two occasions), my parents, eyewitnesses, Chief Sweeney, Detective Shortt, Detective Jordan, Mayor Peitler, Reginald Allard, and a host of others. They contacted Dr. James Fyfe to evaluate this case in detail. Dr. Fyfe has testified over five hundred times in thirty-four states and consulted on over ten thousand police-involved incidents. He reviewed numerous documents ranging from depositions, trial transcripts, police training materials, *all three* of the defense expert witness testimonies, and the New Milford Police Department Deadly Force Policy. His professional court testimony résumé is as long as the appellate court's decision.

Dr. Fyfe provided his report to our private attorneys on April 7, 2002, more than six months before the reversal. In it, he identified several inconsistencies, unresolved questions, and improbabilities in Smith and Shortt's accounts.

Dr. Fyfe writes, "These should have been apparent to any reasonable and competent police investigator or administrator and should have created great doubt that this incident occurred as described by Officer Smith."

Here is what this fair, unbiased, and educated man had to say about this case:

1. Officer Smith claimed that, even though he feared that Reid was armed and that Reid was giving him "a hundred-yard stare" which he was told "could be a sign of, you know, that an attack is imminent," Smith approached to within an arm's reach of Reid because he was trained to do so. Dr. Fyfe: *I know of no training*

that suggests that this method of approach is appropriate, and any training that did so would be grossly improper.

Who would you believe?

2. Several uninvolved witnesses (William Eayrs, Christopher Gardner, Abu Nassir, Diane Swanson) testified at Officer Smith's criminal trial that they saw Officer Smith pointing his gun at Mr. Reid, who had his hands raised in the air. Officer Smith denies that this ever happened.

Who would you believe?

3. Another uninvolved passerby witness, Gail Meehan, testified at Officer Smith's trial that she saw a black man lying face down on the ground while a white man held his arms, that the white man had his foot on the black man's back, and the white man held something in his hand. This was consistent with the report of William Bodziak, of the FBI, and the testimony of Kenneth Zercie, of Connecticut Police, both of whom reported finding apparent traces of footprints on the back of Mr. Reid's clothing. Officer Smith denies that this ever happened.

Who would you believe?

4. Another uninvolved witness, James DeMaria, testified that he saw Mr. Reid lying on his back, resting on his

elbows with his knees bent. Officer Smith denies that this ever happened.

Who would you believe?

5. Officer Smith claims that he was standing and that Mr. Reid was on his knees and moving about quickly. Yet, the forensic analyses of his trousers, conducted by Dr. Virginia Maxwell of the State Police, found no evidence of dirt or vegetation on the knees.

Who would you believe?

6. Officer Smith testified he held his gun relatively high when he shot Mr. Reid. But the only gunshot residue found on Officer Smith's clothing was on the lower left leg of his trousers. This is inconsistent with Smith's account, but it *is* consistent with the testimony of Mr. Nassir and Ms. Swanson that they saw Smith pressing an object into Reid's back while straddling Reid on the ground. It also is consistent with Mrs. Meehan's testimony that she saw Smith standing over the prone Reid with his left leg on Reid's back.

Who would you believe?

7. The police claim that they found a knife in the pocket of a jacket that Mr. Reid had been carrying. Officer Smith suggests that Reid must have been searching for the

knife while Smith held him restrained. But none of the witnesses who testified that Reid had his hands in the air indicated that Reid was holding a jacket in his hands. Nor, in fact, does Officer Smith indicate that Reid was holding the jacket in his hands. (The knife was two and a half inches long; my pinky finger is larger.)

8. Officer Smith testified that he was trained never to hit anybody in the head with a gun. Dr. Fyfe: "If asked, I would testify that this training is improper and that, if there were no other way to save an officer's life, an officer should not refrain from hitting someone in the head with a gun."

Who would you believe?

9. Officer Smith indicates that, after the shooting, he did not look for the weapon he had assumed Reid was trying to obtain. Dr. Fyfe: "If asked, I would testify that, in the ten thousand or more police shootings I have reviewed, I recall none in which the shooting officer did not immediately attempt to locate and seize any weapons that might be on the scene. I would testify also that officers are trained to do this to assure that the threat against which they have used their weapons has truly ended."

Who would you believe?

Dr. Fyfe had even more damaging opinions based upon facts—even setting aside inconsistencies—and accepting the police accounts at face value.

Fyfe notes: In his expert report for Officer Smith's criminal defense, David Grossi wrote, "One of the justifications for shooting Mr. Reid was that Officer Smith was alone when he confronted Mr. Reid."

This is a wrong-headed analysis. Officer Smith was alone only because Shortt let him chase Reid alone, and without a police radio to summon help. This was a violation of one of the fundamental police principles: always back up your partner. In this case, Shortt failed to do this and set up a situation in which the inexperienced Smith was stuck alone with Reid.

Fyfe goes on to state, Officer Smith indicates that he drew his gun and approached to within an arm's reach of Mr. Reid because he was trained to do so, and because he felt that this was the best way of subduing Mr. Reid. Then, he indicates, he tried to force Reid to the ground so that he could handcuff him.

Officer Smith committed a gross violation of generally accepted police custom and practice when he tried to subdue Reid alone. This improper conduct was a direct and proximate cause of the wrongful shooting and death of Mr. Reid. The training provided by the NMPD that allowed this to occur was grossly inadequate. All the reasons that Smith gives for approaching Mr. Reid, however, are reasons to keep a safe distance from him and to wait for assistance before attempting to handcuff him. Especially when assistance is as near as Smith had reason to believe Shortt was, they should remain at a safe distance, holding their guns on suspects, while waiting for assistance.

Dr. Fyfe adds: This standard is defined in two books published by *Calibre Press*, the organization for which Mr. Grasso wrote his report in the criminal case against Officer Smith. One advises officers that, when dealing with any suspects:

> You should consider a distance around you of at least three feet as your "safety zone." Closer than that, the danger that you will be struck or that an attempt will be made to grab your gun is vastly multiplied...Don't permit anyone to move in closer than thirty-six inches or try to touch you.

This shooting was inappropriate because it was the end result of self-imposed jeopardy. By the most charitable reading, Smith eliminated what Mr. Grossi calls the reactionary gap by approaching to within an arm's reach of Mr. Reid. Having done this, he was too ready to misinterpret Mr. Reid's movements as a threat to his safety, and wound up shooting him in the back when he purportedly saw Mr. Reid reaching for a weapon that, if it was, in fact, anywhere near Mr. Reid, was closed and in a jacket pocket not within arm's reach when Reid was shot.

Officer Smith committed a gross violation of generally accepted police custom and practice when he shot Mr. Reid, and this conduct was a direct and proximate cause of the wrongful shooting and death of Mr. Reid. The more realistic reading of what happened in this situation is this: Smith stood too close to Mr. Reid, holding a gun on him, and shouting for Reid to show his hands. When Reid responded to these commands by trying to pull his hands out from under his body, Smith shot and killed him."

Dr. Fyfe concludes: This improper action was caused by the improper supervision and training of Officer Smith by the New Milford Police Department.

The most relevant part of Smith's testimony on this point reads as follows:

Q. Did you believe he had obtained a weapon and was about to use it on you?

A. Absolutely.

Q. What did you do?

A. I fired my gun one time.

The conclusion by Dr. Fyfe was that Scott Smith had not only inadequate training but absolutely no training as a plainclothes detective. *The record is replete with evidence of other supervisory and training deficiencies. When Officer Smith became a police officer, he attended a sixteen-week training program. Such programs, however, are designed to prepare officers for duty in uniformed patrol, the entry-level police task. Regardless of the quality of this training, therefore, it was not sufficient to prepare him for the duty he was performing on the day he shot and killed Mr. Reid. On that day, he was in his second week of duty as a detective (investigator). In this position, he worked in plain clothes rather than in uniform, in an unmarked car that had been seized from a criminal rather than in a marked patrol car. In this investigative position, he carried only a gun and handcuffs, rather than the baton and pepper spray he had been taught to use as a patrol officer. When he shot Mr. Reid, he was not carrying a portable radio or a bullet-resistant vest, both of which are standard equipment for patrol officers in almost all jurisdictions. These are all substantial differences from the patrol work for which Officer Smith was trained.*

∗ ∗ ∗

Let me summarize the testimony of the actual and potential defense witnesses that the appellate court would have wanted this jury to hear.

Emmanuel Kapelsohn testified: "Officers are taught to try to maximize their distance from the suspect until they can get the suspect, if he will comply, into what's called a position of control by the officer. Officers are taught to use backup, meaning a fellow officer or officers, whomever they can. If you have a situation that warrants it, you should, ideally, wait until you have another officer there."

How many feet away was Detective Shortt? *What do you think?*

David M. Gross, Sr., who did not testify, is a former police officer and instructor on police use of force. (His company produced two of those enlightening videos.) He wrote that one of the justifications for shooting my brother was that Smith was alone when he confronted him. Recall, Fyfe calls this is a "wrong-headed analysis." Smith was alone due to his own bad choice.

Reginald F. Allard, Jr., the third expert the defense wished to hear from, was an instructor at the Connecticut State Police Academy for sixteen years. He instructed

Smith in practical police skills. According to his written statement, "There was no specific plainclothes training at the State Police Academy."

The appellate court, by maximizing its dedication to justice and fairness for a totally untrained, uniformed policeman in his first role as a plainclothes pre-detective, actually minimized its common sense and the rulings of an experienced criminal trial judge who had presided over many more serious cases than they had. They decided to become the jury. However, they did not see, hear, or feel, the reality of this trial. How can they be right and the twelve diverse citizens who saw, listened to, and lived the entire trial, following accepted directions on the law, be wrong?

The end result was not justice, but injustice. Perhaps they thought a new trial would let them off the conscience hook. What family wants to go through this horror show twice? Did justice take a holiday?

While sitting on the Metro North train, leaving New York City after hearing the shocking news, I stare through the window at the zipping trees. *Would a second trial deliver the same outcome? What if Smith walks free or what if he's found guilty of murder? Would my boss be as lenient as my college professors if I needed to miss work for a second trial? I'm sure he would be*, I think, trying to convince myself. *I suspect Smith is gleeful about this decision.*

I arrive home and my parents are sitting around the dining table looking disappointed and angry. We embrace but this time feels different, unlike the first time I arrived home after my brother's death. No tears are shed, no one reaches for an alcoholic beverage.

"The media came by the house earlier today and asked for comments," my mother says. "Your father and I prepared a statement which I read aloud."

She hands me the statement.

"We are very upset by the decision. However, we believe, as we have since Franklyn was killed, that justice will ultimately prevail in this case. Our understanding of the decision is that the evidence supports the conviction."

"Very nice," I say.

Later that evening, *Conviction Overturned* leads all the nightly news programs. My mother is broadcast reading her statement from our front yard with Dad standing by her side. Reporters had also secured comments from Connelly and Kelly.

"Even if there is a new trial, the outcome would be the same," Connelly comments from his office. "I don't think one other expert witness or two other expert witnesses or a half a dozen other expert witnesses would have swayed this jury in favor of Mr. Smith."

Kelly disagrees. "He [Smith] is not a criminal. He should not have been convicted. His conviction was a travesty of justice."

Smith's family and supporters are overjoyed by the decision while my family's supporters see a familiar pattern.

James Griffin, Connecticut's NAACP president, tells reporters that the reversal means one thing. "It just goes to show why there is such a mistrust in the justice system, especially when it comes to black people."

Mr. Griffin, Reverend Cornell Lewis (our staunch family supporter and activist), and others mobilize, calling for justice.

ACT VI SCENE VI

———

CALLING FOR JUSTICE

One day before the reversal becomes official, October 21, 2002, my parents, Cornell Lewis, Mr. Griffin, a small group of supporters, and I gather on the steps of the appellate courthouse in Hartford. Armed with a microphone and speaker, we stand in solidarity while State Police and the media look on. Our plea: reconsider your decision. If not, we're asking Connecticut's Supreme Court to take up the case. Supporters respectfully and peacefully express their thoughts.

"Target practice on men of color is not acceptable," Lewis says.

"We want justice; we want justice," my mother exclaims.

Former Hartford Mayor Carrie Saxon Perry shows up to support a fellow mother suffering. She embraces my mother on the steps.

"She's going through all of this again. So, you know, sometimes you just hold hands," Mayor Saxon Perry tells a reporter.

Another reporter asks for my comments about the reversal.

"There's no police training that says when a man is face down on the ground, both hands behind his back—and the cop had his hands behind him—to shoot him in the back."

I think that what fueled my passion for justice was reading Smith's deposition that he gave to our lawyers in 2001. When asked, "If you had to engage in this confrontation all over again, would you have done anything different?" His answer, "No."

Cornell Lewis sums up with another reporter. "So even though the language is technical and they let Scott Smith off for now, still, we feel there is no justice for black men or men of color that get shot in the back in America by a white policeman."

The next day, the reversal is official but we vow to continue peaceful rallies.

Days later, Cornell Lewis and others visit our home to plan our next move. My dad, the main cook in our family, feels discussions can't bear fruit on empty stomachs. He prepares curry goat, jerk chicken, and rice and peas. The finger-licking food is a hit as Cornell Lewis attests.

"Dwight, you should invite us every weekend for your cooking. Hahahaha!"

"You're always welcome," Dad says with a smile.

While sitting around the dining table, Cornell asks my parents, "Would you like to hold a rally in New Milford?"

"Absolutely," my dad says.

"Okay, I will organize the logistics."

To publicize the event, Cornell's team distributes flyers that read in part: "Pilgrimage for Justice! Saturday, November 2, 2002. March from the home of Franklyn Reid to the spot where he was killed by Officer Scott Smith in December 1998."

On a sunny but chilly day, a handful of supporters, family, and friends, show up at the house ready to march. Armed with a megaphone, Cornell leads the chant. "Justice for Franklyn Reid. Justice!"

"Justice for Franklyn Reid. Justice!" echoes during the fourteen-hundred-foot march to the scene. Ten minutes later, we position ourselves on the embankment while some stand along the sidewalk on Route 202 holding signs. Traffic flows freely as numerous vehicles honk. Supporters take turns with the megaphone.

In a passionate moment, I feel the urge to reenact the "position."

"Daddy, I'm going to lie on the ground, and you play the role of Smith?"

"Okay, son," he says.

I lie face down, head up on the embankment and put both hands behind my back. My dad places a foot on my back, grabs my hands and points his right finger into my back, like a gun.

"This is how Franklyn Reid met his death," Cornell says over the megaphone.

While that image replays on the news, I tell my parents, "We must keep the pressure on."

Ten days later, on November 12, 2002, Connelly files

an appeal with the Connecticut Supreme Court to review the appellate court's decision. In it, he writes, "There has been enormous public attention and involvement by both the law enforcement community and the public at large. Further review by Connecticut's highest court of the legal questions presented would serve the salutary purpose of ensuring public trust and confidence in the integrity of judicial proceedings."

My family and supporters are pleased that Connelly is taking the next step, but Kelly disagrees.

"I will ask the Supreme Court to reject Connelly's appeal," he tells a reporter. "In my view, there is nothing to review."

Unsure when the high court may rule, Cornell plans another rally, this time for December 29, 2002, to coincide with the fourth anniversary of Franklyn's death. Once again flyers are widely distributed. The reenactment Dad and I did at the previous rally is the image displayed on the flyer that announces: *Justice for Franklyn Reid*.

Days before the rally, the Connecticut Supreme Court refuses to review the case and remands it for a new trial, essentially upholding the appellate court's decision.

"I can't believe the setbacks we're experiencing," I say to my parents.

With emotions running high, the police department fears anger may instigate violence. Chief McCormack and the mayor's office take precautionary measures. They request a contingent from State Police in case a bunch of minorities decide to terrorize their quiet community.

On a cold rally day, a van load of supporters from Hartford and surrounding areas barrels toward New Milford. Cornell Lewis organizes members from the black community, Puerto Rican Nationalists, Quakers, and others, to protest peacefully.

Unlike the previous march, Cornell notices something peculiar—State Police line the highway leading toward New Milford. As they drive through town, patrol and undercover cars greet them at every street corner as they approach our home. It appears the department prepared well, at any cost.

At our house, vehicles park along the street as if there is a neighborhood block party. Supporters and the media stand together on our front lawn. Some were fortunate to find space inside.

Cornell directs a supporter to distribute white T-shirts imprinted with *Justice for Franklyn Reid* in large black letters on the front.

"There is heavy police presence out there," Cornell says, from inside the house. "They must be expecting the worst."

"I saw police in riot gear and a patty wagon," a supporter says.

They are also at Center Cemetery, the graveyard," a local resident says.

"Okay, I guess we have their attention," Cornell says.

Suddenly, someone rushes in from outside.

"Cornell, there are people in the street we don't recognize."

"Okay, let me take a look," he says.

Cornell weaves through the crowd as I follow behind.

Maybe they could be family or friends. We look through the front door.

"I don't recognize them," I say.

Cornell focuses on the group as if he's seen them before. "Those are Scott Smith supporters."

"Really? How do you know that?"

"I never forget faces," Cornell says. "They are the same folks who accosted me at a protest outside Litchfield's courthouse during the pretrial. I'm going to get to the bottom of this."

Cornell walks toward them as I and others observe. Maybe they're here to infiltrate and send word back to the department?

A few minutes later, Cornell returns.

"They said, two years ago, they believed Scott Smith after the shooting. As the trial progressed, they changed their minds. They are here to march and support the Reid family. I could have beaten them down verbally but we need people in the fight to lead a movement. I accept their sincerity but I don't fully trust them yet or have forgotten about the things they said."

I glance at the clock and realize we're falling about thirty minutes behind the scheduled start time of 3:00 p.m. I imagine the department must be wondering what the heck is taking so long. Nevertheless, the rally kicks off toward the scene on Route 202.

Bunching together, my parents lock arms with people in front, signifying unity. I scan the amazing crowd of about one hundred diverse, young, old, familiar, and unfamiliar faces chanting, "We want Justice for Franklyn Reid. Justice!" The Puerto Rican Nationalists incorporate Spanish. "Justice! Justicia! Justice! Justicia!"

We arrive at the site, assemble along the embankment, and occupy both sides of Route 202. Respectfully, supporters avoid blocking traffic. Once again, motorists show support or dismay by honking their horns. We listen while some call out the question, "What do we want?" "Justice!" the crowd answers.

An hour later, we march back to the house, pile in vehicles, ready to visit another venue. I ride with Cornell and supporters in a church van along with my parents. We turn into the cemetery and follow the road toward my brother's grave. I see police cars parked on side roads as the cemetery is designed like a maze—only one way in and the same way out. Some supporters skipped the march toward the scene on Route 202 and wait in the cemetery as the crowd swells to a hundred and fifty or more.

I am in awe. I imagine Franklyn observing from somewhere and saying in his Jamaican dialect, "All dis fi me?"

Supporters speak and chant while law enforcement looks on. The crowd's energy is electrifying. Again, I lie face down in front of my brother's grave. Dad and I reenact the "position" to camera lights and repetitive *click, click, clicks.*

As the sun sets and dusk descends, Cornell chats with other organizers about revisiting the scene along Route 202 once more. They alert officers who offer to provide an escort. We exit the cemetery and turn right onto Route 202.

"Change of plans," Cornell says. "We will be turning

into the police driveway. Park along the side and march toward the station to exercise an act of civil disobedience. Other vans are aware of our intentions. We have reserved funds in case they arrest a few of us, which I anticipate they will do."

Suddenly, a surge of adrenaline rushes through my body coupled with a bit of nervousness.

Cornell had informed our driver not to be the lead van so that the intended action is not obvious. I look ahead while the escort and a few vehicles pass the station. As our van approaches the entrance, I grip the seat. We take a sharp left up the driveway. I look through the back window and three or four vans follow suit. The police escort in the rear, caught off guard, quickly activates their siren lights, commandeering the other lane, and speeds toward the driveway. Reporters turn on cameras as people exit vehicles. Almost immediately, law enforcement stands down. Presumably, Chief McCormack issued an order.

"Justice for Franklyn Reid, Justice!" reverberates loudly as we march toward the station's entrance.

"How do you think this helps your son's cause?" a reporter asks my mother.

Surrounded by cameras, she replies, "It's helping Franklyn Reid, and it's helping all the rest of the people in Connecticut who were shot down by police officers."

We stand near the entrance doors, chanting, looking inside. Most lights inside the building are turned off; some officers observe the crowd from outside.

"Do not arrest Minister Lewis. Repeat. Do not arrest

Minister Lewis," Cornell hears from an officer's radio who's standing nearby.

Cornell leads a few people up to the doors, which are locked. They sit. Josh (another staunch supporter) motions me to join them.

Instantly, cold feet freeze me in place. Unsure if the situation will escalate out of control. *Don't be afraid, Wayne,* I tell myself. *This is for your brother.* Seconds later, I join my compadres. Mom and Dad stand near me. I glance inside the station and see Officer Young recording with a camcorder. I turn and look at the supporters chanting and the cameras capturing this extraordinary moment.

"Justice! Justicia! Justice! Justicia! Justice for Franklyn Reid!"

Many minutes later, we stand. "We'll be back! We'll be back! We'll be back!" echoes through the megaphone while banging on the front doors.

While law enforcement was overly prepared and perhaps expected the worst, the rally ends peacefully. No property is defaced, damaged, or arrests made. Our conduct has been steadfast since the shooting. Express emotions in a dignified manner. It doesn't matter on which side of justice we stand. We are in this together.

Afterward, outside the station, Chief McCormack tells a reporter, "I am very pleased that we handled the safety aspect, both for the folks that were participating in this event—which we were very concerned about—as well as the motoring public."

Later that night, after supporters leave, Mom, Dad, and I, reminisce about the day while watching the news.

"What will 2003 bring?" I say.

"I don't know," Mom says. "Today was a good day. I am thankful and grateful for Reverend Lewis and all our supporters."

"Likewise," I say.

While Smith remains free on bond, Cornell Lewis and the NAACP keep the story relevant through organized media events and rallies in 2003. His continued support, grass roots movements, and guidance are beyond appreciated. Without a doubt, he molds public perception toward facts.

On May 20, 2003, my parents, Smith's family, and others, revisit a familiar setting. Both families are back in court, occupying the same seats they once did more than three years ago. Reports of a plea deal swirl before the hearing as today will dictate tomorrow. The long-drawn-out criminal trial could officially end, or the road toward a second trial begins. Connelly pulls my parents aside.

"How are you both holding up?"

"We're hanging in there," Dad says.

"Thank you for everything you're doing," Mom adds.

"Absolutely," Connelly says with a nod. "The state is prepared to offer Smith a chance to avoid a second trial if he pleads guilty to second-degree manslaughter. It carries a maximum ten years in prison, but the state will offer a suspended five years and two years' probation. What are your thoughts?"

"So, he wouldn't spend time in prison?" Mom asks.

"That's correct, Mrs. Reid. But the plea comes with a felony conviction which would prevent Smith from becoming a police officer again."

"Okay. We will go along with it," Mom says, knowing there aren't any winners in these types of cases.

Connelly discusses this with the defense in another room. Minutes later, he approaches my parents. "Smith rejected the offer and is opting for a second trial because he wants to serve as a police officer again."

Smith believes he will be fully exonerated. If he accepts the plea, it would dash any hope of him continuing his dream.

Outside the courthouse, reporters shout questions at Smith, who walks past them silently. Minutes later, those same journalists ask my mother her thoughts on Smith rejecting the offer.

"Smith is under the delusion he will be a police officer again. I don't see who would employ him," she says.

Next, the reporters surround Connelly for comments. "I think the offer that we made was fair to all the people involved. I did that after consulting with the Reid family."

Over the next ten months, Connelly and Kelly prepare for trial while keeping all options open. The overwhelming support Smith experienced after the shooting has dwindled over the years and perhaps financial support as well. A second trial could potentially bankrupt his family. Then he would still face civil litigation. Both attorneys hammer out another plea offer.

On March 23, 2004, I join Mom, Dad, the Smith family, and supporters in court for another hearing. Jury selection for a second trial is scheduled for March 29. This case has been a magnet for the media since day one. They, too, are present.

Judge Robert C. Brunetti replaces Judge Gill on the bench. Connelly pulls my family and attorney Richard Bieder (our civil lawyer) aside.

"I have always been upfront and honest with you folks. Mr. Kelly and I have had discussions about a possible deal his client would accept. Smith does not want to face another trial," Connelly says.

"How do you feel about going to trial, attorney?" my mother asks.

"As you know, Smith could get a sympathetic jury or be found guilty again. Everybody would be rolling the dice. But I am prepared to prosecute him again," Connelly says.

"Thank you, attorney," my dad says.

"If Smith pleads guilty to criminally negligent homicide, the state would offer him one-year jail time, suspended, and two years' probation."

"He gets two years' probation, and I get a dead son," Mom hollers.

A few seconds of silence...

"This is a good offer, Mrs. Reid. Smith would admit what he did," Connelly says.

"I agree with attorney Connelly; a second trial is unpredictable," I say.

"Okay," Mom says. "I would like to add a stipulation

that Smith can never become a police officer again in the United States."

"I will discuss this with Mr. Kelly," Connelly says.

Connelly hurries toward the judge's chamber.

Many minutes later, Connelly reemerges along with Kelly and Smith. He looks in our direction and nods in the affirmative as court is called into session.

After a brief formality, Judge Brunetti reviews Smith's written *nolo contendere* plea. "The court finds that it's in order."

The judge looks at the prosecutor. "Facts, Mr. Connelly."

Connelly stands. "The facts of this case are as follows. And I take these facts primarily from the appellate court decision..."

Over the next few minutes, Connelly summarizes the entire case based on the state's version as a packed court-room listens.

"Mr. Smith, I have to ask you a few questions before I can accept your plea," Judge Brunetti says.

Smith stands and provides answers before getting to the charge.

"The statute simply says a person is guilty of criminally negligent homicide, when, with criminal negligence, he causes the death of another person. Is that what was explained to you?" Judge Brunetti asks.

"Yes, Your Honor," Smith says.

"The maximum penalty here is one year to serve or a $2,000 fine or both. It's what's called a Class A Misde-meanor. Do you understand that?"

"Yes, Your Honor," Smith repeats.

"You have entered a plea of what's called *nolo contendere*, which means you choose not to contest the matter. You don't agree with them; you don't disagree with them. Is that correct?"

"That's correct," Smith says.

"Has anybody promised you anything other than the plea agreement?"

Before Smith answers, Judge Brunetti turns to Connelly. "You didn't state, but I understand, it is one year suspended, two years' probation. Is that correct?"

"That's correct, Your Honor. It's an agreed-upon recommendation. Also, Mr. Smith has signed a document, and I will read it for the record. It says:

'I, Scott Smith, have pled *Nolo Contendere* to the crime of Criminally Negligent Homicide in violation of Connecticut General Statutes & 53a-58 in the above-captioned case [CR-99-97546], and having been found guilty of said crime, as part of my plea agreement, do hereby agree that I will not now, nor ever during my lifetime, seek or accept employment or reemployment as a sworn law enforcement officer in the State of Connecticut or any other state within the United States.'"

Mom shudders hearing her stipulation.

Judge Brunetti asks, "Mr. Smith, you signed this document freely and voluntarily?"

"Yes, I did."

"All right. Now you heard Mr. Connelly state certain

facts in this case. Are those facts upon which you are pleading *nolo contendere*?"

"Yes, they are," Smith says.

"The plea is accepted, and the finding of guilty may be entered."

For years, I've believed, along with my family and many others, that nervousness gripped Smith and he accidentally pulled the trigger. I've observed Smith, and like my brother, he is a good human being. Hate did not course through the family's journey in court, it was just an unfortunate situation.

At the conclusion of the families' connection in the criminal case, *how this incident occurred* was answered through the presentation of facts, evidence, and eyewitnesses during the trial. Perhaps a long trial could have been avoided if Smith received better advice immediately after the shooting by acknowledging his gun discharged by accident. Presumably, those individuals thought the state attorney's office would justify Smith's action and exonerate him.

The civil suit, which lasted more than three years, had to wait until the criminal case was finalized. In December 2004, the town settled for $1.6 million dollars.

Why this incident occurred may still elude us. Perhaps my brother's life was cut short so his story can serve a greater purpose—to lead people toward a path of *unity*.

ACT VI SCENE VII

———

JUDGE GILL VS. THE APPELLATE COURT

WRITTEN BY JUDGE CHARLES D. GILL

These post-trial thoughts could have been offered as an epilogue—which usually means the end or conclusion of the topic. For the families involved in this drama there may never be a complete ending. Tragic memories are difficult to completely erase. However, the universal care, respect, and love, of Wayne Reid toward everyone should be a beacon of hope for all of us. He has proven with this drama that humanism is more powerful than racism. Through this entire drama, hatred has never made an appearance. Knowing him over the many years of our efforts, creating this book from a real-life script have made me not only an admirer and best friend, but I've witnessed how Wayne is a man for whom the word "unity" has true meaning. My remarks are a tribute to this national hero on the American stage for the prevention of unnecessary police killings. Keep in mind, we have the highest regard for those thousands of police officers, sheriff's deputies, and troopers, who protect citizens daily 24/7. Thank them, thank God!

Judges are like umpires. Umpires don't make the rules. They apply them. The role of an umpire and a judge is critical. They make sure everybody plays by the rules. But it is a limited role. Nobody ever went to a ballgame to see the umpire.

—JOHN ROBERTS, CHIEF JUSTICE OF THE
UNITED STATES SUPREME COURT

Being a judge must be one of the most difficult jobs in a democracy. In my thirty-five years as a superior court judge in Connecticut, I have been through hundreds of emotional meat grinders where rules are of little comfort. Imagine being the umpire when you have physically and sexually abused children as victims in front of you. Or family violence cases, illegal drug sales, burglaries, assaults, murders, rapes. Family love turned to hatred. The best intentions for children becoming secondary to adult egos in divorce. Thousands of other heart-tugging situations that leave families of the victim and the criminally accused weeping in front of you.

Judge Alexandra DePentima introduced me to *this* drama when she assigned me to be the trial judge. Obviously, cases involving a killing by young white police officers of young black men are not exactly cases that we, as judges, line up to hear. I have presided over a dozen murder cases—including one that was the subject of the best-selling nonfiction book, *Catspaw* by Louis Nizer—but none like this. This one seemed to have unusual aspects to it from the beginning. All three of the legal participants had prior dealings with each other in court. I, as a judge, and John Connelly and John (Jack) Kelly (a former prosecutor) as prosecutors in front of me.

The opening scene was challenging. Uniformed police officers flooded the front of the courthouse. None of them knew the facts. The police officers who really knew the facts had signed an arrest warrant application and had it approved by a state's attorney and subsequently by a superior court judge.

Trying to keep the selected jurors from having their objectivity destroyed by the demonstrations, I had them assemble each morning a block away at St. Anthony's Church. (Father Robert Tucker was the obliging pastor.) The marshals would check each juror by hand detector wands and escort them across the street, down an alley, and into the rear of the courthouse, free from cameras and demonstrators.

So the trial began. You have read the testimony and the arguments. Your twelve citizen jurors heard the entire case. I need not comment extensively on the testimony. However, there are a few observations that may break precedent by a trial judge in such a case. I do not recite them to denigrate or harm anyone, including my colleagues on the appellate court for whom I have the highest respect, but even they are sometimes reversed by the Connecticut Supreme Court.

Many of the protesting police were solidly off base, including their outrageous attacks on State's Attorney Connelly calling him "Judas." Extremely ignorant and immature behavior. Connelly was probably the most pro-cop state's attorney ever in Connecticut. At the end of his argument to the jury, at the end of the case, his final words—to the effect that he revered police—actually had him in tears as he returned to his chair. I do not believe that Attorney Kelly saw the tears or heard Connelly's trembling voice. I did and so did the Reids and the jury.

The entire courtroom each day was like a wake. The family of the young deceased sat stage right. Smith's loving family stage left. Facial expressions were quite revealing. I observed both families every day. Their grief was quite evident and heart-wrenching. Neither side could believe that this was happening, but it was. I thought, perhaps, no matter what I or we did, there would never be closure.

Now is the part of the trial that is the most distressing to me. The testimony of Scott Smith himself. After hearing hundreds of police testify in front of me, it totally befuddled me. His approach was unbelievable. Was he coached by police pals who took advantage of his youth and inexperience in this forty-one-second event? Did they disregard the facts and truth? Did he have a delusion that his six-foot-two-inch, 190-pound-framed life was threatened by an unarmed five-foot-four-inch, 129-pound black guy who was lying face down on the dirt, with his foot and gun pressed against his back, in full view of six civilian witnesses? Or was it an accident as Wayne Reid suggests? Could be. If *that* had been the defense strategy, with tears, there might not even have been a prosecution. Perhaps, his blue line pals obliterated and overrode the main line of common sense in the service of their professional egos.

Incredible to me. Incredible to the jury. A problem for the appellate court. I have a problem with this, too. You have read Scott Smith's testimony. In my opinion, here is the most shocking part:

Q. Did you believe he had obtained a weapon and was about to use it on you?

A. Absolutely.

Q. What did you do?

A. I fired my gun one time.

Shocking, because given other testimony heard in court, he could have added, "I killed an unarmed, young man in broad daylight on a main street with my foot on his back as he laid in a prone position with my experienced partner a few feet away and six civilian witnesses testifying to this."

At that moment during his testifying, I recalled the companion New York trial of four police officers who killed an unarmed, twenty-two-year-old guy named Amadou Diallo. The cops fired not one, but forty-one shots at the victim with nineteen of them striking him. During the trial, I had traded observations with the presiding New York judge, Justice Joseph C. Teresi. He told me that all four officers on trial broke down and cried when they testified. Their jury found them all not guilty because they admitted they made mistakes and showed sorrow in front of them. All four were acquitted. Watching a stoic Smith testify, I was thinking,

Cry, you son of a bitch, cry. Show some remorse. I waited—but no emotion whatsoever. I will never understand why not. No one ever will.

It is rare for a trial judge to criticize an appellate court decision that reverses him. But that court clearly earned it in this case. Recall that the sole reason for the reversal was my refusal to have three experts testify to an identical issue—training as to police use of force. (And recall also that Scott Smith had absolutely no training whatsoever as a plainclothes police officer.) To allow three experts to testify on precisely the same subject is unheard of in American Law. What if twelve witnesses were offered? Or ten or eight? Why were three testifying on the very same subject considered enough? According to the law, only one expert witness is required to testify—if the trial judge feels that would be sufficient. The law for both the trial judge and the appellate court is found in the Connecticut Code of Evidence.

Here is a peek at what it says about trial judges dealing with what the law calls "cumulative" evidence (witnesses testifying to the exact same subject). Section 4-3 of the Code states:

"Relevant evidence may be excluded if...waste of time or needless presentation of *cumulative evidence.*"

The Official Commentary to the section clearly states that decisions on the admission of cumulative evidence are "relegated to the [trial] court's discretion."

Section 4-3 makes this point twice referring to this issue as, "needless presentation of cumulative evidence." The code cites Connecticut Supreme Court decisions that support this law.

Police use of force is a *professional* standard, not a *legal* standard. Because of this, police have no exception to the statutory law of self-defense. It may be relevant on some issues, but not self-defense. For the appellate court to adapt it as such is not only a stretch of the law, but a stretch of the imagination and a negation of justice.

Although Connelly raised the issue of cumulative evidence half a dozen times in his oral argument to the appellate court, they never responded to those words.

The following observations are for lawyers, judges, and court observers. The law emanates from a Yale Law School researcher on this very case. The statute that led the appellate court astray is General Statute section 53a-22(c). It discusses the remarkable police officer standard in the use of deadly force, for which the appellate court wanted testimony by three different witnesses.

This statute was enacted in Connecticut to adopt the standard for the police use of force proffered by the Supreme Court of the United States in Tennessee v. Garner. According to the Garner standard, evidence of police department training does not determine the issue of reasonableness in police use of deadly force cases. In Garner, the court held that a police officer who shot and killed a fleeing burglar acted unreasonably, Garner, 471 U.S. at 22. The court reached that conclusion despite the fact that the officer was "*acting...pursuant to police department policy.*"

Hence, by arguing that section 53a-22(c) required the

trial court in Smith's case to admit evidence regarding police department training policies, the appellate court ignored section 53a-22(c)'s legislative history and the intent of Connecticut's legislature in enacting that statute.

The opinion in Part One of the appellate court decision would seem to clearly allow a jury verdict of guilty. Below are the exact words the appellate court used in reversing the jury's verdict because of my "errors." *You be the judge as to who committed the error.*

"Contrary to the claim made by the defendant, the evidence presented was sufficient to establish his guilt; construing the evidence in light most favorable to sustaining the verdict, the jury could reasonably have concluded that the cumulative force of the evidence established beyond a reasonable doubt the defendant's intent to cause the victim serious harm and that the State had disproved the elements of self-defense as set forth in the applicable statute (53a-22)."

Yet Part Two of the appellate court's decision says, "It's the law that trial judges must allow cumulative evidence in these circumstances."

That is not the law!

Regarding the error of the appellate court, here is what they said I did wrong.

You decide.

"The trial court's exclusion of the testimony of three expert witnesses relating to the defendant's training and to police training in general regarding the use of deadly force, denied the defendant his Constitutional Right to present a defense; the jury was entitled to hear the evidence to assist it in evaluating whether the defendant's belief that deadly force was necessary comported with the standard of a reasonable police officer, and, because this court could not conclude that the exclusion of that evidence was harmless beyond a reasonable doubt, the defendant was entitled to a new trial."

This may have been the first such decision in New England, if not America.

For guidance, let us look even further—at the Federal Rules of Evidence, Section 403, regarding cumulative evidence. How many witnesses can be put on the stand to testify about, say, how many ballistic experts it takes to tell a jury that this bullet came from this weapon, before belaboring the point? Where lies the threshold of sheer excess? The Federal Rules of Evidence leave that question to the trial court. Rule 403s, the Cumulative Evidence Clause, provides the trial judge with discretion to prohibit the admission of evidence for which the probative value of that evidence is substantially outweighed by one of several risks, including the risk of cumulation.

And guess what? The United States Supreme Court agrees!

This case stirred the emotions of the Reid family, the Smith family, the law enforcement community, civil rights supporters, and, frankly, myself. The conclusion by the Connecticut Appellate Court still causes me professional angst. It's made me somewhat doubtful that justice is always the final outcome in our wonderful judicial system.

And the result? This drama has no curtain call in the lives of the Reid and Smith families. Franklyn Reid is dead. Scott Smith committed suicide in 2013, and John Connelly died of cancer. At Connelly's funeral, the church was packed with police officers, prosecutors, judges, and justice-seeking people like myself.

ACT VI SCENE VIII

UNITY

While there have been increasing numbers of minority citizens killed by police, many of our dedicated police officers of all races are also killed. Neither situation is acceptable.

When a loved one's life is suddenly taken through violence, the shock is powerful. It feels like heaven and earth have opened a floodgate of emotions. Futures are destroyed, families torn apart. Such acts bring forth emotional suffering which leaves many to beseechingly ask, "Why did this happen to my loved one?"

When answers elude us, I believe some people who seek understanding (like myself), turn toward Divine solace. It can feel like a soothing retreat from everlasting pain to have faith that a loved one is in a better place, and one day there will be a great reunion.

We cannot change what's been done. We can only seek dignified answers to assist others and abolish future occurrences.

Everyone errs in judgment, though some decisions are so detrimental as to become catastrophic. When conflicts between blacks and whites become deadly, the race card is played. One may say this is a natural response. After all, investigations and police body cameras have helped identify the issues: the deaths of minorities by law enforcement from undue force, sometimes based on either unfounded fears for personal safety or brutality due to hate; *and* the senseless killing of police officers from those seeking retribution.

Personally, I believe our weaknesses and faults, including those which cause deep pain, can present learning opportunities. My hope is that they bring people together to seek lasting, positive resolutions.

Some police departments try tackling the situation directly with policy changes, while protests and the media keep attention on events when they take place. Yet, too often we find ourselves in tragic, repetitive cycles. How regrettable that this pattern results in missed initiatives for sustainable reforms. But that's who we are.

It's in our DNA to fight amongst each other, erect barriers of mistrust, and reinforce them with uncompromising stances. Humans create racism; we breathe life into it whether subtly or blatantly. It replicates like a virus from people to industries, often buried within one's mind like a cancerous cell hidden within the body. Racism is an authoritative structure which fosters the wielding of power over a group of people. And when has anyone volunteered to relinquish their power?

So, it looms over America as the ultimate "elephant in the room," with many hoping it will resolve itself while unaffected others don't mind its presence. But what does this passive point of view accomplish, except to allow the bringing forth of more division and anger? We continue to react emotionally and ignore the facts which cause the misunderstanding or conflict in the first place.

I believe we can move forward. How? Most importantly, we need to shift how we view violent actions from a racially-based framework to the simple perspective of *right versus wrong*. If one abolishes skin color references and reports solely on the actions of a person, then judging whether someone is guilty of wrongdoing becomes easier to assess.

I harbor no animosity or hatred toward Officer Smith. Perhaps the sentiment was reciprocal. The majority of people involved in the trial showed respect and acted peacefully, because both families exemplified civility. Given the circumstances, I hope that the way we conducted ourselves can inspire others to also act with restraint. By switching the focus to right versus wrong, rather than this race against that race, we can *all* embrace the opportunity to move down a path toward trust and change.

Here is a lesson in unified citizenship that our America needs to learn, understand, and remember:

Do not presume that every minority person is inherently dangerous to Americans. Do not make presumptions that all police officers are inherently dangerous to minority persons.

Many minorities have earned the Medal of Honor for their defense of America.

One minority member became president of the United States of America.

There are many honest and courageous law enforcement personnel who expose their lives when protecting us every day. I and my family sincerely salute and thank them.

In the greater scheme of life, we are all brothers and sisters—albeit dysfunctional families with issues that need to be resolved and can be. For a harmonious and safe society, we must work together, support each other, and seek common ground.

At the time of the incident, Scott Smith (like my brother) was twenty-seven years old. Perhaps their paths were fated to meet. How many life stories has destiny intertwined in communities across our beautiful country? How many are waiting to occur?

Perhaps *why this incident occurred* is to tell the story now—when our country is in great peril, divided, and at an impasse.

Let us renew a movement! Together, we can become a unified nation again. Together, we can reshape our future. Together, we can end racism. Together, we can shift from hate to caring about each other. Let our human spirit connect what is right and good in all of us.

Through unity, may we discover and revel in peace! Amen! And God Bless All!

IN MEMORY OF FRANKLYN REID, SCOTT SMITH, AND ATTORNEY JOHN CONNELLY

Franklyn Reid, 1988

Franklyn Reid, 1998

Officer Scott Smith after testifying in his own defense

Defense Attorney John J. Kelly

Pearlylyn and Dwight Reid

The scene along Route 202 after Franklyn was shot by Officer Smith

Waterbury State Attorney John Connelly

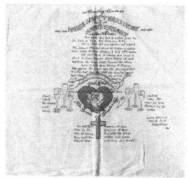

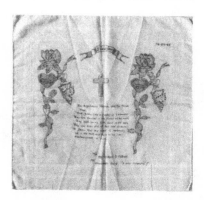

Franklyn picked up drawing while in prison. He used handkerchiefs to capture his artistic work which he in turn, mailed to his parents. The hearts represent the connection Mom and Dad have had since their marriage. He expressed his feelings by penning a poem, for their birthday and anniversary.

Scott Smith Direct Examination

Front row: Assistant State Attorney Robin Lipsky and John Connelly. Judge Gill (center stage). Scott Smith on the right testifying. Defense lawyer John Kelly (standing). The closest row is my mother Pearlylyn (braided hair), my Dad Dwight and myself.

ABOUT THE AUTHORS

WAYNE REID attended the University of Scranton and received a bachelor of science degree in accounting. After considering multiple career paths, ranging from professional wrestler to the military, he is currently pursuing a career in finance as an assistant controller for a global PR agency headquartered in New York City.

When not crunching numbers, Wayne enjoys challenging himself through physical training. He inspires office colleagues to join in by leading outdoor fitness training sessions each spring and organizing groups to attend vigorous obstacle course races. Wayne considers this a fun (and muddy) way to encourage team building among his coworkers.

Wayne wrote an essay for his firm's PN Perspectives: We Stand for Love campaign. He previewed his message of unity and felt encouraged by its overwhelmingly positive reception.

Connecticut Superior Court Judge CHARLES D. GILL is a tireless advocate for the rights of children. Married to Joan Gill and the father of three, he began his career as a neighborhood legal service lawyer, perhaps the first in the United States. A constant mentor to minorities, he has partnered with Big Brothers and Big Sisters and lends a helping hand to those in need. He has been honored by President George H. W. Bush in the Oval Office, President Bill Clinton in the Rose Garden, has testified in Congress, and was a consultant to the US Department of Justice.

Judge Gill has been invited to share his knowledge and perspective at speaking engagements in over forty states, Canada, Europe, Asia, and the United Nations General Assembly, where he received an award from the International Earth Day Committee.

Additionally, he has made guest appearances on NPR and numerous nationally syndicated television programs such as *20/20* and *Good Morning America*. A highlight of Judge Gill's life was his debate with Janet Reno, attorney general of the United States, on Ted Koppel's *Nightline*, regarding the fate of the Cuban boy, Elian Gonzalez.